"*The Propaganda of Freedom* makes a significant contribution to our understanding of the Cold War. The thesis that an ideology of 'freedom' made it impossible for leading American intellectuals to recognize the cultural achievements of Soviet artists during the Cold War is compelling and convincing—even for readers unversed in the cultural or musical history of the twentieth century. Moreover, it exposes one of the weaknesses of an omnipresent American world view: the fallible notion that, by virtue of its devotion to individual liberty, the United States surpasses the rest of the world in its ability to nurture artistic, scientific, and cultural achievement. In fact, all too often American foreign policy is based on the false premise that promoting 'individual freedom' must remain at the heart of the nation's efforts to exert influence abroad.

"The book raises important questions not only about the efficacy of U.S. foreign policy, but also about the relationship between culture and democracy, even about the nature of democracy itself—questions extremely pertinent in a world where populist political movements have called into question democratic norms that once seemed unassailable.

"Above all, it is the author's extrapolation of a 'fetishization of freedom' that makes this work so vital. Horowitz writes: 'That so many fine minds could have cheapened freedom by over-praising it, turning it into a reductionist propaganda mantra, is one measure of the intellectual cost of the Cold War.' I would argue that these same reductionist tendencies have played a significant part in the rise of volatile populist movements, as well as in the construction of the so-called war on terror that followed the 9-11 attacks. In this sense, the book serves as a warning that the American tendency towards political and cultural unilateralism is not only naïve, but dangerous."

—David Woolner, Resident Historian, the Roosevelt Institute;
author of *The Last One Hundred Days: FDR at War and at Peace*

"*The Propaganda of Freedom* is an impressive achievement, a wholly absorbing read, a valid indictment of Nicolas Nabokov and the whole Congress of Cultural Freedom project as supremely misconceived and clumsily executed—something of a mirror image, in fact, of postwar Stalinist Russia itself. In that sense they deserved each other. And there can be no doubt that the approach both countries came to embrace by the late 1950s, enshrined in the 1958 cultural diplomacy agreement, changed many more minds and attitudes over the decades that followed."

—John Beyrle, former United States Ambassador to Russia
(2008–2012)

"Readers of Joseph Horowitz's seminal *Understanding Toscanini* and *Wagner Nights* will know what to expect from *The Propaganda of Freedom*: a brilliant, combative work where the intensity of historical research is matched by the force of analysis. He has spotted what he calls an 'imposed propaganda of freedom' in John F. Kennedy's arts advocacy—an analysis that raises important questions for historians of the Kennedy Administration and the Cold War. Not the least of these is the relationship between the artist (embodied here by Shostakovich and Stravinsky) and the state in Cold War society. As one of the leading cultural historians and public intellectuals of the last four decades, whose world-class research and writing have had such a profound impact on the study of twentieth century American culture, Mr. Horowitz has written another exceptional revisionist work that completely upends our understanding of the cultural Cold War."

—Richard Aldous, author of *Schlesinger: The Imperial Historian* and
Reagan and Thatcher: The Difficult Relationship

THE PROPAGANDA OF FREEDOM

MUSIC IN AMERICAN LIFE

A list of books in the series appears at the end of this book.

THE PROPAGANDA
OF FREEDOM

JFK, Shostakovich, Stravinsky,
and the Cultural Cold War

JOSEPH HOROWITZ

UNIVERSITY OF
ILLINOIS PRESS
Urbana, Chicago, and Springfield

Appendix A, "Nicolas Nabokov, 'The Case of Dmitri
Shostakovitch'," copyright © 1943 Harper's Magazine. All
Rights Reserved. Reproduced from the March issue by special
permission.

Library of Congress Cataloging-in-Publication Data
Names: Horowitz, Joseph, 1948– author.
Title: The propaganda of freedom : JFK, Shostakovich, Stravinsky,
    and the cultural cold war / Joseph Horowitz.
Description: Urbana : University of Illinois Press, 2023. | Series:
    Music in American life | Includes bibliographical references
    and index.
Identifiers: LCCN 2023000825 (print) | LCCN 2023000826
    (ebook) | ISBN 9780252045271 (cloth) | ISBN 9780252054792
    (ebook)
Subjects: LCSH: Music—Political aspects—United States—
    History—20th century. | Music—Political aspects—Soviet
    Union—History—20th century. | Cold War—Music and the
    war. | Congress for Cultural Freedom. | Kennedy, John F. (John
    Fitzgerald), 1917–1963. | Shostakovich, Dmitriĭ Dmitrievich,
    1906–1975. | Stravinsky, Igor, 1882–1971. | Nabokov, Nicolas,
    1903–1978.
Classification: LCC ML3917.U6 H67 2023 (print) | LCC ML3917.U6
    (ebook) | DDC 780.973/0904—dc23/eng/20230110
LC record available at https://lccn.loc.gov/2023000825
LC ebook record available at https://lccn.loc.gov/2023000826

When I was in Mexico I was a little envious of the opportunity composers have to serve their country in a musical way. When one has done that, one can compose with real joy. Here in the U.S.A. we composers have no possibility of directing the musical affairs of the nation—on the contrary, I have the impression that more and more we are working in a vacuum.

—Aaron Copland (1933)

[In dictatorships,] music cannot develop freely; no really great work of music can be born from such systems.

—Nicolas Nabokov (1942)

The arts incarnate the creativity of a free society. . . . [Art] means the free and unconfined search for new ways of expressing the experience of the present and the vision of the future. When the creative impulse cannot flourish freely, . . . then society severs the root of art.

—President John F. Kennedy (1962)

People with a lot of power often don't understand. They think they are able to direct everything in their own way. But they can't stop the blossoming of thought.

—Mstislav Rostropovich (1981)

Necessity is the mother of invention.

—Plato, *The Republic* (ca. 375 BC)

CONTENTS

PREFACE

When I began writing books, there existed a sizable mainstream audience for explorations of classical music in the context of the American experience. The readers and reviewers of my *Understanding Toscanini: How He Became an American Culture-God and Helped Create a New Audience for Old Music* (1987) included both scholars and knowledgeable laymen. The hardcover was published by Knopf. The paperback editions were released by two university presses: Minnesota and California.

In the decades since, these readerships have diverged, as have trade and academic publishers. This schism is unfortunate for everyone: writers, readers, publishers. Scholarly books are today increasingly specialized. Books for "general readers" are increasingly general, with relatively little assumed knowledge in play. I aspire to continue to write for both readerships, to deploy a broad range of reference and subject matter without turning arcane. I am grateful to Laurie Matheson and the University of Illinois Press for publishing *The Propaganda of Freedom*.

My core topic, the cultural Cold War, has generated a sizable literature, both scholarly and not. The U.S. government's primary propaganda instrument was the Congress for Cultural Freedom, covertly funded by the Central Intelligence Agency (CIA). The best-known treatment of the CCF, Frances Stonor Saunders's invaluable *Who Paid the Piper? The CIA and the Cultural Cold War* (1999), fixates on (and deplores) the CIA relationship. Of a half-dozen books written in response, the most prominent is Hugh Wilford's *The Mighty Wurlitzer: How the CIA Played America* (2008). Of the many artists and intellectuals engaged in CCF activities, Nicolas Nabokov was the music specialist—and the subject of a long and detailed biography by Vincent Giroud (2015).

One thing all these books have in common is that the authors lack substantial familiarity with classical music. What therefore escapes their attention is that Nabokov's influential readings of Igor Stravinsky, whom he revered, and Dmitri Shostakovich, whom he reviled, cannot be taken seriously. His aversion to Shostakovich is so extreme that I have included in an appendix the entirety of his "The Case of Dmitri Shostakovitch" (1943), lest the reader suspect I am cherry-picking when quoting Nabokov's claims.

My critique of the CCF has little to do with its much-debated ties to the CIA. Rather, my topic is a fallacious "propaganda of freedom" that I discover traceable to the Russian exiles Nabokov and Stravinsky. I find that a fetishization of "freedom," construed as a panacea for governments, citizens, and artists, distorted American policy during the Cold War.

The CCF's counterempirical premise that the creative act is necessarily an "autonomous" initiative undertaken by "free artists" leads me far afield of the Cold War and into the realm of music history. Even more than the literature on the CIA, the vast literature on Stravinsky and Shostakovich is a minefield. The scope of my inquiry here is mainly confined to a single topic: the conditions for creativity established by the environment at hand.

Stravinsky's own view of the autonomous artist I simply extract from his own 1935 autobiography and the Norton Lectures he delivered at Harvard in 1939 and 1940. That these texts were mainly written by others matters not, because Stravinsky approved them. To illustrate that in fact even in California, remote from St. Petersburg or Paris, he was not an autonomous creator, I observe that the best-known product of his American exile, the Symphony in Three Movements, unquestionably draws inspiration from World War II newsreels. When I infer that Stravinsky in America was afflicted by a "freedom not to matter," that he suffered a creative decline, others may disagree. But I am far from the only person with these opinions.

Shostakovich claimed no creative autonomy. He believed that artists serve a great public. His music overtly responded to circumstance, to revolution, war, and Stalinist oppression. To what degree he may be regarded a dissident artist is a matter of furious debate. While I have no wish to engage in these "Shostakovich wars," I do not treat the debated author Solomon Volkov as a nonperson or his *Testimony: The Memoirs of Dmitri Shostakovich* (1979) as a nonbook. Many denounce *Testimony* as fraudulent. In my opinion, Volkov's book valuably imparts the personality and views of Dmitri Shostakovich as experienced by Solomon Volkov. The disputants in this controversy sometimes lose track of the fact that a human being has no fixed identity, that people change and are known to contradict themselves. Having written a somewhat similar book—*Conversations with Arrau* (1982)—I feel I know something about how such books are written and how they should be read. As was driven home to me by various readers, another interlocutor would have produced a different "Claudio Arrau." Where in *The Propaganda of Freedom* I have quoted Shostakovich as reported by Volkov, Shostakovich is expressing opinions or telling stories also reported by others. Mainly, however, I have quoted Volkov speaking for himself, as when he compares Shostakovich to the *yurodivy*—the trope of the "holy fool." That Shostakovich's music embeds encoded meanings, a central premise of *Testimony*, is undeniable. To what degree this made him a subversive artist is a question I do not need to address.

Finally, far afield from music and the Congress for Cultural Freedom, I deal with a topic little studied: President John F. Kennedy's advocacy of the arts. In fact, Kennedy's Cold War dogma that only "free artists" create consequential art is my point of departure—and, ultimately, a final point of return.

It is my good fortune that many events I describe fall within living memory—not least my own, of touring Soviet artists I vividly recall hearing in the 1960s. I was also able to confer with prominent Soviet-trained musicians, most notably the pianists Vladimir Feltsman, Alexei Lubimov, and the late Alexander Toradze (who was one of my closest friends). An important American pianist who enjoyed great success in the USSR, Byron Janis, shared some fresh stories with me. The diplomats with firsthand experience of the Cold War who generously imparted their knowledge and impressions included Leonard Baldyga, Ambassador John Beyrle, the late Ambassador Arthur Hartman, William Kiehl, and the late Hans Tuch. I bombarded with inquiries the historians Richard Aldous, Fredrik Logevall, Elizabeth Wilson, and David Woolner, all of whom read portions of my manuscript with scrupulous attention.

THE PROPAGANDA OF FREEDOM

FOREWORD

Why and What

This book was born in 2013 when I happened to attend an event, at the National Archives in Washington, DC, toasting the sophistication of the Kennedy White House. By way of recalling the first of a series of cultural evenings hosted by the president and the first lady, Mendelssohn's D-minor Piano Trio was performed—as it was by Pablo Casals, Mieczysław Horszowski, and Alexander Schneider on November 13, 1962, when Casals was the president's guest of honor.

I learned that President Kennedy, on this occasion, declared every artist of consequence a "free man." Other Kennedy cultural pronouncements, also cited, claimed "totalitarian" states incompatible with distinguished cultural achievement. The eloquence of Kennedy's oratory was hypnotic. No one in the room seemed to notice or care that the content of these speeches was counterempirical. Not only does history tell us that artists need not be "free" to create; it is in fact well known that adversity can spur and guide artistic production. This impression of Cold War cultural dogma lingered powerfully.

Some three years later, I had occasion to hear Danill Trifonov, then twenty-four years old, in recital at Carnegie Hall. Trifonov, who is Russian, is one of the most compelling concert pianists of his generation. He eschews glamour and personal eccentricity. He makes music. Trifonov's program comprised two well-known Schumann works, *Kinderszenen* and *Kreisleriana*; the Stravinsky showstopper Three Movements from *Petrushka*; and a novelty: five Preludes and Fugues from the set of twenty-four composed by Dmitri Shostakovich in

1950–51. The hall was packed and attentive. The evening's great ovation was not bestowed on the esteemed Schumann and Stravinsky compositions. Rather, it was ignited by Shostakovich's titanic D-minor Prelude and Fugue. I had myself played some of the Shostakovich Preludes and Fugues in my teens. I had long owned an Emil Gilels recording including the D-minor Prelude and Fugue. Yet my surprise was complete. Somehow, the magnitude of this surpassing musical accomplishment had previously escaped me.

The experience connected directly with Kennedy's speeches—because in 1951, two years before Stalin's death, Soviet culture was ostensibly enslaved to rigid totalitarian aesthetic dictates foreclosing the creative act. Yet—it now occurred to me—no "free" composer had during the Cold War decades produced solo piano music of such enduring importance.

I proceeded to contact the Kennedy Library in order to learn what I could about the origins of Kennedy's premise that only "free artists" produce great art. It proved surprisingly simple to connect the dots.

*   *   *

To many participants and observers, the Cold War seemed starkly binary. For the Russians, Communism was the universal panacea. For the Americans, "free societies"—elected governments, civil liberties—were in all places the best possible.

It logically followed that our cultural life thrived and theirs shriveled. Free artists were creative. Shackled artists were stunted.

The Soviets vigorously pursued cultural propaganda to woo artists and intellectuals in Western Europe and Latin America. They portrayed capitalists as boors. The United States retaliated with propaganda of its own, supervised by an agency secretly funded by the CIA: the Congress for Cultural Freedom. According to CCF dogma, the arts could flourish only when artists were free to say and think what they chose. That the falseness of this claim, contradicted by centuries of evidence, went unnoticed testifies to the strength of Cold War doctrine on both sides. It is a lesson in epistemology.

President Kennedy was himself an eloquent and implausible spokesman for artistic freedom. In fact, he further claimed that all "true artists," embodying freedom, were also "concerned for justice." No socialist realist manifesto would disagree with that. In fact, in retrospect Kennedy's claim sounds a little Soviet.

A crucial source of Kennedy's cultural dogma was a minor composer who served as secretary general for the CCF and consequently became the most influential American cultural Cold Warrior in the realm of music. This was Nicolas Nabokov—the central figure in my story to come. An exiled Russian aristocrat encumbered by memory and loss, he swiftly proved a predominant American authority on Soviet culture generally, and Soviet music specifically. As I will show, it was through Nabokov's intimate friendship with Arthur Schlesinger Jr. that his influence penetrated not only the CIA and the State Department, but the White House as well.

The book at hand looks back on this story, now more than a half century old, and discovers myriad surprises contradicting onetime cultural Cold War truths. In the process, I have occasion to ask three concentric questions. How effective was CCF dogma in furthering American interests? What conditions—personal, social, and political—actually foster creativity? What similarities and differences defined classical music in the Soviet Union and the United States during the Cold War years?

My answers focus on Nabokov's hero, Igor Stravinsky, and on Dmitri Shostakovich, for Nabokov a villain who, serving the Soviet state, betrayed venerable Russian traditions of arts and learning. The Cold War fate of Aaron Copland, an American composer influenced by Stravinsky and Shostakovich both, is also pertinent to my account.

In sum: My story samples the cultural Cold War as waged by the U.S. government and affirms that there were no cultural Cold War certainties. Rather, a web of paradox and contradiction ensnares all the participants. In particular, I will show that a faulty extrapolation—from the virtues of "free societies" to the virtuous prerogatives of "free artists"—distorted mutual understanding. And I will endeavor to surmise why this matters.

That the Cold War is now relatively distant confers perspective both on politics and on art. As I write these words, a reassessment of socialist realist painting and sculpture in the Soviet Union seems under way. And music historians, as I relate in my chapter 7, have newly explored how Soviet culture was governed—with surprising results. A general reassessment of modernism in the arts is an umbrella topic. Nabokov, Stravinsky, and Shostakovich are here highly pertinent.

*   *   *

I begin with "JFK, the Artist, and 'Free Societies': A Cold War Myth"—sampling President Kennedy's cultural pronouncements. My chapter 2—"Nicolas Nabokov and the Cultural Cold War"—introduces Nabokov via his 1943 assault on Shostakovich in *Harper's* magazine, and a fusillade condemning Soviet music in the inaugural 1953 issue of *Encounter* magazine, the CCF's English-language flagship publication. Arthur Schlesinger's *The Vital Center* (1949)—a manifesto for the non-Communist Left—is a crucial component.

Chapter 3—"Lines of Battle"—scrutinizes how American Cold War propaganda, conveyed by Nabokov in a variety of American periodicals, juxtaposed Stravinsky and Shostakovich as exemplars of good and bad. Nabokov's exegesis of Soviet cultural dictates is here critiqued. There was of course no "free society" equivalent of Stalin's insane prescriptions, purges, and murders: both art and artists suffered. But neither, in truth, were there always stark cultural polarities of sweetness and light versus servitude and darkness.

"CIA Battlegrounds: New York and Paris," my chapter 4, explores Nabokov's public activism, beginning with an infamous confrontation with Shostakovich at the 1949 Waldorf Astoria Peace Conference. "Cultural freedom" was already an anti-Communist mantra among intellectuals associated with the philosopher Sidney Hook. The Congress for Cultural Freedom was founded in 1950. Recalling all this, and also the CCF festivals and conferences Nabokov ambitiously conceived, I explore CIA efforts to propagate what would become Kennedy's faith that "the liberation of the human mind and spirit" finds "its greatest flowering in the free society."

Discarding Kennedy's aspirational myth of the "free artist," my chapters 5 and 6, inferring "Survival Strategies," extrapolates a psychological reading of how Stravinsky in Paris and Hollywood—however "free" in exile—denied his Russian lineage in order to initiate a new creative flow. Meanwhile, Shostakovich—however "enslaved"—sustained inspiration in the face of persecution by encoding extramusical meanings of a kind Stravinsky disallowed. I add that Nabokov, as well, necessarily conceived a strategy of survival because, as with Stravinsky, "freedom of expression" was accompanied by a vexing condition of rootlessness—a freedom not to matter. I here propose that a propaganda of freedom, influentially promulgated by Nabokov, amalgamated the "cultural freedom" polemics of Hook and Schlesinger with Stravinsky's insistence, in exile, on the autonomy of the creative act.

Chapter 7, "Cold War Music, East and West," is an overview in which resemblances are discovered. With the opening of Soviet archives, scholars have discerned that the Stalinist cultural bureaucracy was to a surprising degree bottom-up, with Shostakovich playing a leadership role. A bigger picture: In both Russia and the United States, composers became populists; in both Russia and the United States, a "new audience" was tutored in classical music. Composers were rebranded. The Russian effort, including factory ensembles, stressed Russian music. In the United States, "music appreciation" was a commercial enterprise favoring European composers.

"Enter Cultural Exchange," chapter 8, assays a post-Stalin tactic mistrusted by Nabokov. Though both the United States and Russia aimed to prove their artists "better," the unintended consequence of mutual cultural exposure, driven by the artists themselves, was to discover commonality. That this proved a better "propaganda" instrument than Nabokov's costly and tendentious CCF/CIA activities is a finding here supported by State Department testimony.

"Summing up," I return to John F. Kennedy's vision of a culturally enriched America. That Kennedy's eloquent aspirations for "a great democratic society" with "special responsibilities for the arts" were intertwined with Cold War diplomacy, I conclude, rendered them the more discardable once the Cold War ended. Commensurately, that the propaganda of freedom insisted that only "free societies" produce great art underestimated the resilience and universality of the creative act. My Afterword applies my story to the fate of the arts, and to issues of American national purpose, today.

No concept is more fundamental to the American experience than "freedom." Even in our fraught contemporary moment, it remains inspirationally pertinent—and also elusive, mutable, and fallible.

CHAPTER 1

JFK, THE ARTIST, AND "FREE SOCIETIES"

A Cold War Myth

On January 18, 1962, Igor Stravinsky was honored at a White House dinner on the occasion of his impending eightieth birthday. He was already in Washington to conduct his oratorio *Oedipus Rex*. Two days before, he had received a medal of achievement from Secretary of State Dean Rusk.

In a brief after-dinner speech, President Kennedy said: "We have been honored to have had two great artists here with us in the last months. As a student in Paris, my wife wrote an essay on Baudelaire, Oscar Wilde, and Diaghilev. I understand that you, Mr. Stravinsky, were a friend of Diaghilev. And I was told that rocks and tomatoes were thrown at you in your youth."

A Memorandum for the President earlier in the day had apprised him of Stravinsky's eminence and marital status, adding that "newspapers have reported that Stravinsky's favorite instrument is the piano and that he is an avid reader. . . . This will be his first party at the White House." In a dinner conversation with Stravinsky's wife, Vera, Kennedy learned, as well, about the riotous Paris premiere of *The Rite of Spring*—and laughed out loud. This anecdote became the "rocks and tomatoes." Kennedy's reference to another "great artist" was to Pablo Casals, who had performed at the White House the previous November 13.[1]

Recalling Kennedy's remarks sometime afterward with his amanuensis, Robert Craft, Stravinsky not very wittily quipped that he was afraid the president "was about to say his wife had made a study of homosexuality." He was miffed to have been preceded by Casals, who was known to think little of Stravinsky's music. Stravinsky, in turn, regarded Casals as a feeble eighty-five-year-old anachronism who played Bach "in the style of Brahms." At the White House, Stravinsky was seated opposite JFK and next to the glamorous first lady, who wore diamond pendant earrings and a long white-satin skirt for the occasion. Dinner consisted of filet of sole mousse and shoulder of lamb prepared with almonds and cold stuffed artichoke hearts—a sumptuous repast by White House standards. Vera Stravinsky afterward called it "a perfect dinner for concierges."[2]

The earlier evening with Casals had resulted in part from political sentiments expressed by the cellist himself. Casals lived in Puerto Rico in self-imposed exile from Francisco Franco's Spain. In a letter to "His Excellency John F. Kennedy," he called the presence of American military bases in Spain "a pact with one of the worst dictators of our times. It was a pact with a man who personifies despotism, slavery, and crime—an absurd position which denies the truly great cause to which the United States is dedicated and for which it is committed to fight." Casals reported "the resentment of the Spanish people against the United States" and warned that Spaniards might succumb to the specter of Communism "if they are not given any hope of an end to their miseries." The military bases, he continued, had been installed under Kennedy's predecessor, Dwight Eisenhower. But Kennedy, forty-three years old, was a fresh hope: "To the exiles and the pariahs now living in darkness, there is light in your words: 'I am fully conscious of the vital necessity of developing the significant potentialities of free governments in all continents.'"[3]

The twin visits of Casals and Stravinsky, however initiated, supported a learned White House tone reinforced by Special Assistant Arthur J. Schlesinger Jr., by Special Consultant on the Arts August Heckscher, and by the president's own Harvard breeding. Though Franklin D. Roosevelt had in fact invited Stravinsky to the White House, Stravinsky had been unable to attend. He was the first living composer ever honored by an American president.

Doubtless the Kennedys, and Mrs. Kennedy especially, were delighted to absorb the glow of accredited artistic genius. But diplomacy, too, was afoot. Introducing Casals at the White House concert, the president pointedly stated: "We believe that an artist, in order to be true to himself and his work, must be a free man."[4] He subsequently elaborated this theme in two major speeches and an article for *Look* magazine. His first premise was that great nations were known for fostering great civilizations. His second premise was that only "free societies" supported great creative achievement. Compared to the plain speech of Eisenhower and Harry Truman, the president's rhetoric soared on wings of aspirant song. But Kennedy's second claim was plainly counterfactual.

*   *   *

Our culture and art do not speak to America alone. To the extent that artists struggle to express beauty in form and color and sound, to the extent that they write about man's struggle with nature or society, or himself, to that extent they strike a responsive chord in all humanity. Today, Sophocles speaks to us from more than 2,000 years. And in our own time, even when political communications have been strained, the Russian people have bought more than 20,000 copies of the works of Jack London, more than 10 million books of Mark Twain, and hundreds and thousands of copies of Hemingway, Steinbeck, Whitman, and Poe; and our own people, through the works of Tolstoy and Dostoyevsky and Pasternak have gained an insight into the shared problems of the human heart. Thus today, as always, art knows no national boundaries. . . .

Aeschylus and Plato are remembered today long after the triumphs of imperial Athens are gone. Dante outlived the ambitions of thirteenth century Florence. Goethe stands serenely above the politics of Germany, and I am certain that after the dust of centuries has passed over our cities, we, too, will be remembered not for victories or defeats in battle or in politics, but for our contribution to the human spirit.

It was Pericles' proudest boast that politically Athens was the school of Hellas. If we can make our country one of the great schools of civilization, then on that achievement will surely rest our claim to the ultimate gratitude of mankind. Moreover, as a great democratic society, we have a special responsibility to the arts, for art is the great democrat calling forth creative genius from every sector of society, disregarding race or religion or wealth or color. The mere accumulation of wealth and power is available to the dictator and the democrat alike. What freedom alone can bring is the liberation of the human mind and spirit which finds its greatest flowering in the free society.

Thus, in our fulfillment of these responsibilities toward the arts lie our unique achievement as a free society.

Embellished with Whitman and Hemingway, with Tolstoy, Dostoyevsky, and Pasternak, with Aeschylus, Plato, and Pericles, with Dante and Goethe, this was John F. Kennedy's vote of support for the national cultural center chartered by Congress in 1958—from a speech delivered eleven days after the White House dinner for Igor Stravinsky. "Freedom alone," Kennedy maintained, supports the "greatest flowering" of "the human mind and spirit." A second version of the same conviction is embedded in an article, signed by the president, in *Look* magazine on December 18. Kennedy again envisioned a national cultural center "hospitable to the best coming from this country, an institution encouraging the development of the performing arts in all their diversity." His article continued:

"The life of the arts, far from being an interruption, a distraction, in the life of a nation, is very close to the center of a nation's purpose—and is a test of the quality of a nation's civilization. That is why we should be glad today that the interest of the American people in the arts seems at a new high." Kennedy cited statistics: "Books have become a billion-dollar business; more money is spent each year in going to concerts than to baseball games; our galleries and museums are crowded; community theaters and community symphony orchestras have spread across the land; there are an estimated 33 million Americans who play musical instruments." But the nub of his argument was an admiring portrait of the artist: courageously solitary, autonomous, transcending the quotidian, disdaining the political fray.

> Too often in the past, we have thought of the artist as an idler and dilettante and of the lover of arts as somehow sissy or effete. We have done both an injustice. The life of the artist is, in relation to his work, stern and lonely. He has labored hard, often amid deprivation, to perfect his skill. He has turned aside from quick success in order to strip his vision of everything secondary or cheapening. His working life is marked by intense application and intense discipline. As for the lover of arts, it is he who, by subjecting himself to the sometimes disturbing experience of art, sustains the artist—and seeks only the reward that his life will, in consequence, be the more fully lived.
>
> It is part, too, of a feeling that art is the great unifying and humanizing experience. We know that science, for example, is indispensable—but we also know that science, if divorced from a knowledge of man and of man's ways, can stunt a civilization. And so the educated man—and very often the man who has had the best scientific education—reaches out for the experience which the arts alone provide.

Referring implicitly to the Soviet Union and its Bolshoi Ballet, whose prima ballerinas Galina Ulanova and Maya Plisetskaya had conquered the West on tour in *Swan Lake* and *Sleeping Beauty*, Kennedy concluded:

> Above all, we are coming to understand that the arts incarnate the creativity of a free society. We know that a totalitarian society can promote the arts in its own way—that it can arrange for splendid productions of opera and ballet, as it can arrange for the restoration of ancient and historic buildings. But art means more than the resuscitation of the past: it means the free and unconfined search for new ways of expressing the experience of the present and the vision of the future. When the creative impulse cannot flourish freely, when it cannot freely select its methods and objects, when it is deprived of spontaneity, then society severs the root of art.

Though the Soviet Union could boast the prerevolutionary legacy of Tchaikovsky's ballets and Tolstoy's novels, it nonetheless severed "the root of art"—contemporary composers and writers were apparently out of luck.

Kennedy's crowning arts manifesto, delivered a mere twenty-six days before his untimely death, was an Amherst College oration dedicating the Robert Frost Library on October 26, 1963. Kennedy built a characteristically impressive frame: "The problems which this country now faces are staggering, both at home and abroad. A country which lived in isolation for 150 years and more is now suddenly the leader of the free world." Moving forward, it behooved the nation to honor its artists as other great nations had done before. The polished cadence of the president's oratory again invites an extract of considerable length.

A nation reveals itself not only by the men it produces but also by the men it honors, the men it remembers. The men who create power make an indispensable contribution to the nation's greatness, but the men who question power make a contribution just as indispensable, especially when that questioning is disinterested, for they determine whether we use power or power uses us. Our national strength matters, but the spirit which informs and controls our strength matters just as much.

When power leads man towards arrogance, poetry reminds him of his limitations. When power narrows the areas of man's concern, poetry reminds him of the richness and diversity of his existence. When power corrupts, poetry cleanses. For art establishes the basic human truth which must serve as the touchstone of our judgment.

The artist, forever faithful to his personal vision of reality, becomes the last champion of the individual mind and sensibility against an intrusive society and an officious state. The great artist is thus a solitary figure. He has, as Robert Frost said, a lover's quarrel with the world. In pursuing his perceptions of reality, he must often sail against the currents of his time. Yet in retrospect, we see how the artist's fidelity has strengthened the fiber of our national life.

If sometimes our great artists have been the most critical of our society, it is because their sensitivity and their concern for justice, which must motivate any true artist, makes him aware that our nation falls short of its highest potential. I see little of more importance to the future of our country and our civilization than full recognition of the place of the artist.

If art is to nourish the roots of our culture, society must set the artist free to follow his vision wherever it takes him.

A corollary of Kennedy's "free world" cultural doctrine was that propagandistic political art is not genuine art. The point was to counter Soviet cultural doctrine. Citing a famous Stalin metaphor, Kennedy continued: "We must never forget that art is not a form of propaganda; it is a form of truth. In free society art is not a weapon and it does not belong to the spheres of polemic and ideology. Artists are not 'engineers of the soul.' It may be different elsewhere." Kennedy here omitted from his scripted text: "In Soviet Russia, Chairman Khrushchev has informed us, 'It is the highest duty of the Soviet writer, artist and composer, of every creative worker, to be in the ranks of the builders of communism, to put his talents at the service of the great cause of our Party, to fight for the triumph of the ideas of Marxism-Leninism.'" And Kennedy concluded:

> But democratic society—in it, the highest duty of the writer, the composer, the artist is to remain true to himself and to let the chips fall where they may. In serving his vision of the truth, the artist best serves his nation. . . . I look forward to an America which will reward achievement in the arts as we reward achieve- ment in business or statecraft. I look forward to an America which will steadily raise the standards of artistic accomplishment and which will steadily enlarge cultural opportunities for all of our citizens. And I look forward to an America which commands respect throughout the world not only for its strength but for its civilization as well.[5]

When Kennedy grouped Boris Pasternak with Tolstoy and Dostoyevsky in his National Cultural Center speech, he undermined his insistence that only "free" artists are great artists. Pasternak acquired a special Western halo when his 1958 Nobel Prize became an embarrassment for the Russian government. He was already dead when Kennedy took office in January 1961. But in the short period of time between Pasternak's death, in May 1960, and the president's Amherst arts manifesto of 1963, a Soviet filmmaker, Andrei Tarkovsky, had in 1962 won the Golden Lion at the Venice Film Festival for *Ivan's Childhood*— disclosing to the world a cinematic genius of bewildering originality. A Soviet writer, Alexandr Solzhenitsyn, had in 1962 published *One Day in the Life of Ivan Demisovich*—inaugurating a career as a political novelist of the first rank. And a Soviet composer, Dmitri Shostakovich, had added to a singular catalog of symphonies and concertos one of his most acute musical tragedies: the auto- biographical String Quartet No. 8.

Kennedy, whose unresponsiveness to classical music was generally acknowl- edged,[6] may have known as little about Shostakovich as he apparently knew about Stravinsky: next to nothing. Perhaps he was vaguely aware of Shosta- kovich as a ruined talent: conventional wisdom during the Cold War decades. But is it possible that he refused to validate any twentieth-century political art? Sergei Eisenstein? Bertolt Brecht? Pablo Neruda? Diego Rivera? Did he truly believe dictatorial regimes were inimical to high cultural achievement? That an early period of Soviet rule coincided with vibrant, "revolutionary" artistic initiatives was doubtless less appreciated by Americans in 1963 than today. But as a Roman Catholic, Kennedy was well aware that Catholic Spain once dominated Europe, ironfisted, under Charles V and Philip II. These were decades of the Spanish Inquisition. They were also decades of the *siglo de oro*—the highwater mark for Spanish literature, music, and visual art. Kennedy was surely cognizant of Velázquez, El Greco, and Cervantes. Or did he frankly see himself as an ideologue, enwrapped by an East-West global conflict with the world's fate at stake?

It must be remembered that after World War II, Soviet influence suddenly began to swallow up Eastern Europe. In February 1946, an American diplomat in Moscow, George Kennan, sent the State Department the legendary "long telegram" in which he reported the Soviets resolutely committed to an epic confrontation. Speaking in Missouri, Winston Churchill coined the phrase "Iron Curtain" two weeks later. President Truman declared in March 1947 that "at the present moment in world history nearly every nation must choose between alternative ways of life," the choice being between freedom and oppression. Jill Lepore, in her recent history of the United States, opines that the newly proclaimed bipolar world resonated profoundly with a larger American trope, "reconfiguring . . . the struggle between 'freedom' and 'slavery' that had divided nineteenth-century America into 'free states' and 'slave states' and during which opponents of slavery had sought to 'contain' it by refusing to admit 'slave states' into the union. In the late 1940s, Americans began applying this psychologically embedded rhetoric internationally, pursuing a policy of containing communism while defending the 'free world.'"[7]

The term "cold war" was coined by Bernard Baruch in April 1947. Five months later, the National Security Act established the Central Intelligence Agency and the National Security Agency, and created the position of chairman of the Joint Chiefs of Staff. The War Department was enlarged and renamed the Department of Defense. Responding to continued Soviet aggression and espionage, the president poured military and financial aid into Western Europe. In February 1948, the Soviets staged a coup in Czechoslovakia. In April the United States implemented its Marshall Plan for the economic recovery of Western Europe. In June the Soviets blockaded Berlin, whose western sector was surrounded by Communist East Germany. In July Congress enacted a peacetime draft. In 1949 NATO was created as a bulwark against further Soviet expansion. Months later, the USSR tested its first atomic bomb and Chinese Communists won a civil war. Mao Zedong and Stalin clinched an alliance. Meanwhile, between 1949 and 1951, U.S. military spending tripled.

The Cold War next spread to Korea; in Asia, the Communists seemed to be winning. Russia and the United States also competed for influence in Latin America and Africa. In 1956 a failed invasion of Egypt by Western allies empowered Gamel Abdel Nasser to pursue authoritarian pan-Arab unity. Five years later, Berlin was split by a wall. A surfeit of nuclear weapons guaranteed mutual destruction should the Cold War ignite. The Cuban Missile Crisis of 1962 propelled both sides to the brink.

A concurrent propaganda war, mutually prosecuted both overtly and covertly, was self-evidently vital. For the Americans, the European and Latin American Left, split between Communist and non-Communist factions, was a paramount concern. Both France and Italy seemed potentially amenable to elected Communist governments. Intellectuals and artists needed to be persuaded that American-style democracy was best for them. But Jean-Paul Sartre and countless other leaders of European thought mistrusted American culture as debased and commodified. Meanwhile, there were more people in the Soviet bloc working on disinformation than serving in the armed forces and the defense industry combined. The American propaganda effort, by comparison, started late. Its strategies and ramifications would prove fascinating and controversial not merely for foreign policy, but for American national identity.

*   *   *

The day John Kennedy died, the White House was poised to name a new Council of the Arts under the leadership of a formidable Kennedy insider: Richard Goodwin.[8] Six months earlier, August Heckscher had accompanied his resignation as JFK's arts adviser with a thirty-six-page report, "The Arts and the National Government," critical of governmental neglect. The arts council, announced in June 1963 in tandem with the Heckscher report, had subsequently gone nowhere; in fact, both Heckscher and Arthur Schlesinger had expressed impatience that members and a leader be named.

Heckscher's parting recommendations emphasized the need for sophisticated oversight of the aesthetics of government buildings, ornaments, and publications. He called for a "substantial increase" in the "number and worth" of artworks acquired by the government via the National Gallery of Art, the Smithsonian Institutions, and the Library of Congress. He urged greater vigilance be exercised toward preserving historic buildings and cites. In the realm of cultural exchange, he regretted the "relatively small amount of money" being allocated, "despite the proven value" of government-sponsored tours of exhibits and performing artists. He called for "a system of awards in specific artistic fields," and for changes in the tax code affording relief for artists and enhanced incentives for charitable giving. He recommended that the office of special adviser on the arts be maintained, with "consideration to be given" that it become a full-time position. Finally, he endorsed a National Arts Foundation, already proposed to Congress, that would administer grants to cultural institutions and to the states in pursuit of "cultural diversity, innovation, and excellence"—a foretaste of the National Endowment for the Arts.

Additionally, Heckscher's report usefully summarized past governmental policy. He began by observing "a growing awareness that the United States will be judged—and its place in history ultimately assessed—not alone by its military of economic power, but by the quality of its civilization," words that would find their way into Kennedy's Amherst speech months later. "Government in the United States has not in the past showed consistent concern for the state of the arts," Heckscher continued. During "the formative period of the Republic," statesmen possessed appreciation of artistic ideals. "This awareness was dimmed during most of the period of westward expansion and industrial progress." Theodore Roosevelt brought artists, scholars, and poets to the White House. William Howard Taft established a Commission of Fine Arts. Franklin Roosevelt undertook "fertile experiments" in arts leadership. Harry Truman commissioned a report on "Art and Government." Dwight Eisenhower established a Commission on National Goals, including "cultural life." Concurrently, during the Cold War "the evident desirability of sending the best examples of America's artistic achievements abroad" had "led to our looking within, to asking whether we have in fact cultivated deeply enough the fields of creativity." Beginning with an inaugural ceremony privileging the arts, the Kennedy administration registered "mounting popular enthusiasm for the arts"—the so-called culture boom of the sixties—as well as "a growing concern on the part of the Government." Heckscher's own appointment, in March 1962, was unprecedented but part-time: he was to work approximately two days a week, and for approximately six months, with a single full-time assistant. As it happened, he stayed on longer than he anticipated or wished. The Goodwin appointment, aborted by the president's death, would have been a step forward from that.[9]

To what extent John Kennedy's arts advocacy was a Cold War tactic, to what extent a personal campaign for a more civilized America, is impossible to say. Unquestionably, it was both. That American attitudes toward the artist had often been unfriendly or uncomprehending was a legacy Kennedy's speeches, and incipient initiatives, acknowledged and sought to reform.

A much-noticed 1962 book by historian Richard Hofstadter—*Anti-intellectualism in American Life*—evinced the frustration and alienation of intellectuals during the Red Scare and the Eisenhower presidency. Hofstadter sketched an enduring New World stereotype of the effete intellectual: impractical, artificial, arrogant, seduced by European manners. A related American stereotype, he contended, holds the "genius" to be lazy, undisciplined, neurotic, imprudent, and awkward. Two years later, Edward Shils, a widely influential sociologist, regretted that in the United States "the political elite gives a preponderant impression of indifference toward works of superior culture." Another prominent observer, Christopher Lasch, in 1965 looked back at the 1950s and wrote: "The intellectual's cosmopolitanism [seemed] un-American, his sophistication snobbery, his accent affectation, his clothes and his manner the badge, obscurely, of sexual deviation." Though not himself an admirer of the Kennedy style, Lasch added that the allure of Kennedy's "Camelot"—of a suave intellectual surrounded by intellectuals—registered changing American perceptions.[10] That Kennedy and Arthur Schlesinger were Harvard alumni, that Press Secretary Pierre Salinger had once aspired to become a concert pianist, contributed to a high-toned aura seemingly more enticing than offensive.

At the same time, conventional wisdom about culture and the state retained a laissez-faire bias: artists and art institutions should either support themselves or—a practice long associated with Carnegies, Rockefellers, Mellons, and other great families—make ends meet with the help of philanthropists and institutions of philanthropy. The closest Washington had come to emulating European arts subsidies was when during the New Deal the Works Progress Administration (WPA) undertook to employ writers, composers, visual artists, and performers via Art, Music, and Theater Projects. The Music Project alone gave 225,000 free or popularly priced performances, attended by 150 million people, many of whom had been strangers to live concert music. Its educational centers rejected the commercialized "music appreciation" agenda otherwise pursued. More than the lives of the great composers and the canon of European masterpieces, the WPA curriculum included instrumental instruction and lessons in singing, theory, and composition. American music was stressed. Among the many orchestras started under WPA sponsorship, the Utah Symphony is today a prominent concert institution.[11]

Speaking in May 1939 at the Museum of Modern Art—an institution already covertly linked to the intelligence community—President Franklin D. Roosevelt said:

> The arts cannot thrive except where men are free to be themselves and to be in charge of the discipline of their own energies and ardors.... A world turned into a stereotype, a society converted into a regiment, a life translated into a routine, make it difficult for either art or artists to survive. Crush individuality in society

and you crush art as well. Nourish the conditions of a free life and you nourish arts, too. In encouraging the creation and enjoyment of beautiful things we are furthering democracy itself. That is why this museum is a citadel of civilization.

Such bipolar thinking pervaded the non-Communist Left; notably, Sidney Hook's Committee for Cultural Freedom, founded in 1939, linked free non-"totalitarian" societies with free thought and free creativity. Roosevelt's espousal of the arts, and his alignment of culture with democracy, in some respects echoed Hook, in some respects forecast the Congress for Cultural Freedom and Kennedy's Cold War culture campaign. Three months before the Hitler-Stalin pact of August 23, Roosevelt is, however, here condemning Nazi Germany[12] and Imperial Japan, not Soviet Russia. And during the New Deal, there was no culture ideology remotely as elaborate as the propaganda of freedom that Nicolas Nabokov would codify and Kennedy adopt. FDR embraced a notion of democratizing culture, popularizing great art for new audiences. He also embraced "spirituality" as a human necessity. The cultural Cold War, in comparison, would be elitist and secular. And the aesthetic predilection of the WPA, most notably in the influential government-funded murals of Thomas Hart Benton, was conservative, even socialist realist in complexion; cultural Cold Warriors to come, many of them CIA intellectuals, would espouse modernism.

Notwithstanding Roosevelt's enthusiasm, notwithstanding the conservative patriotic bent of WPA murals, ideological limits were imposed. The most famous outcome of the WPA Federal Theater Project was Marc Blitzstein's pro-labor musical play *The Cradle Will Rock* (1937), a send-up of corporate greed in "Steeltown USA." Other New Deal agencies—the Resettlement Administration and Farm Security Administration—produced two classic government-funded documentary films, *The Plow That Broke the Plains* (1936) and *The River* (1938), extolling the federal response to drought and to flooding, respectively. But the film initiative was terminated by Congress, which (correctly) perceived New Deal propaganda embedded in both movies, however artfully. And *The Cradle Will Rock* was denied a theater because it, too, strayed too far to the left. With the waning of the Great Depression, and the onset of World War II, American governments—national, state, and local—terminated arts funding. Meanwhile, the Soviet Union made cultural policy a state priority.

A little-known or -remembered landmark was an unsuccessful campaign to implement an "American BBC," climaxing in 1934 with congressional defeat of a proposal to set aside a fixed number of radio frequencies for nonprofit use. An alliance of university and radio leaders argued that a public radio system would ghettoize "education." "Controlled radio" was also denounced as a "threat to democracy." Crucially, David Sarnoff and William Paley, leading NBC and CBS, were visionaries for whom an educational mission incorporating culture was a genuine priority, whatever its commercial liabilities. Beginning in the thirties, a gamut of educational shows—ranging broadly from NBC's thirty-two-week lecture series "Aspects of the Depression" to friendly mentorship by such popular radio intellectuals as Clifton Fadiman, Alexander Woollcott, William Phelps, and Oscar Levant—purveyed higher learning. In the realm of classical music, a steady diet of live symphonic concerts reached millions of families every week. At CBS and Mutual Broadcasting, such studio conductors as Bernard Herrmann and Alfred Wallenstein raised a flag for American composers; Herrmann's guests included Béla Bartók, Paul Hindemith, Darius Milhaud, Igor Stravinsky, and Heitor Villa-Lobos. Abram Chasins's *Piano Pointers* on CBS and *Chasins' Music Series* on NBC were workshops for amateur pianists. When television entered the picture, CBS initiated Leonard Bernstein's *Omnibus* specials and *Young Peoples' Concerts*. NBC televised its *NBC Symphony*; more remarkably, Sarnoff created an *NBC Opera* offering innovative productions of opera in English, emphasizing American and twentieth-century works. But Paley retired in 1959, Sarnoff in 1970; their successors abandoned the high mission at hand. American public radio and television, ironically, offered nothing remotely as prominent or ambitious as the arts programming CBS and NBC had once championed.[13] If American classical music failed to sink deep roots, if (as my story will argue) its audiences proved less sophisticated and hungry than those in Europe and Russia, the minimal role of the state is far from irrelevant.

A second wave of federal support for the arts, during the Cold War, was less apparent than the WPA—not least because it was entirely directed abroad. The Congress for Cultural Freedom, founded in 1950 with covert CIA funding, was a cultural propaganda arm producing festivals in Europe and Asia. A veritable American Ministry of Culture, the CCF concealed its dependency on Washington in part because many legislators would doubtless have opposed spending money on progressive modern music and painting. Overlapping the CCF, and ultimately displacing it, was Soviet-American cultural diplomacy as practiced by the State Department beginning in 1959. One year before, Van Cliburn was hailed as the "American Sputnik" for beating the Russians at their own inaugural Tchaikovsky International Piano Competition. Though he endorsed "person to person" cultural diplomacy, President Eisenhower did not pretend to be any kind of connoisseur (he once thanked Leonard Bernstein for a White House concert of Mozart and Gershwin by saying: "I like that last piece you played. It's got a theme. I like music with a theme, not all them arias and barcarolles").[14] As we will see, Eisenhower was late to acknowledge Cliburn's victory. His secretary of state John Foster Dulles chose to ignore it altogether. By the time John Kennedy took office in 1961, however, Soviet-American cultural exchanges were mutually robust. The resulting story of Washington's Cold War arts advocacy, first via the CCF, later via cultural diplomacy, is a central thread in the chapters to come.

Unquestionably, Kennedy's passion for government engagement in cultural policy lent a new tone to the White House. Whatever might have been his private convictions, however much Cold War alarms may have complicated his thinking, his arts manifesto made a fresh case. At the same time, the anti-Soviet claims with which his arts orations bristled were not new. His was merely the most elegant, most public, most aspirant formulation of what had for some time been State Department and CCF arts propaganda doctrine. Its primary purveyor was someone, unlike JFK, who could claim intimate knowledge of the enemy.

CHAPTER 2

NICOLAS NABOKOV
AND THE CULTURAL COLD WAR

Stephen Johnson's pungent little book *How Shostakovich Changed My Mind* (2019) begins with an unforgettable story. In 2006 Johnson traveled to St. Petersburg to meet an aged clarinetist named Viktor Kozlov. Kozlov was a member of the Leningrad orchestra that somehow performed Dmitri Shostakovich's Symphony No. 7 on August 18, 1942. The city was under Nazi siege. Hundreds of thousands had died. The survivors were starving. Only fifteen members of the Leningrad Radio Orchestra remained alive. They were joined by dozens of additional instrumentalists, mainly from military bands, brought in under armed convoy. Special rations were procured. The players were so weak that the initial rehearsals lasted only fifteen to twenty minutes. The seventy-five-minute symphony, composed in wartime, mirrored the fraught moment. Kozlov remembered: "There was a lot of applause, people standing. One woman even gave the conductor flowers—imagine, there was *nothing* in the city! And yet this one woman found flowers somewhere. It was *wonderful*! The music touched people because it reflected the Siege. . . . People were thrilled and astounded that such music was played, even during the Siege of Leningrad!" Johnson next writes: "'When you hear this music today,' I asked hesitantly, 'does it still have the same effect?' Despite all I had heard, nothing prepared me for what happened next. It was as though a huge wave of emotion struck that apartment, and instantly both Kozlov and his wife were sobbing convulsively. He grasped my forearm tightly—I can feel it again as I'm writing—and just about managed to speak: 'It's not possible to say. It's not possible to say.'"

Two months after the Leningrad premiere, Shostakovich's *Leningrad* Symphony was performed by Arturo Toscanini and the New York Philharmonic. The most cited review of that performance was written by the composer/critic Virgil Thomson in the *New York Herald-Tribune*. It ended: "That [Shostakovich] has so deliberately diluted his matter, adapted it, by both excessive simplification and excessive repetition, to the comprehension of a child of eight, indicates that he is willing to write down to a real or fictitious psychology of mass consumption in a way that may eventually disqualify him from consideration as a serious composer."

Obviously, the wartime catharsis of the Leningrad performance did not grip Thomson at Carnegie Hall. He had experienced the *Leningrad* Symphony as music and nothing more. But he knew the backstory. Everyone did. The miraculous Leningrad premiere, the microfilm of the score airlifted to New York via Tehran, the *Time* magazine cover story showing Shostakovich in a fire-brigade helmet, the American premiere led by Toscanini and his NBC Symphony. However privately, Thomson had all this in mind when he opined that Shostakovich's symphony "seems to have been written for the slow-witted," that it disclosed "no real freedom of thought," that it was "as limited in spiritual scope as a film like *The Great Ziegfeld* or *Gone with the Wind*."[1]

This juxtaposition of Kozlov and Thomson barely samples the layered complexity of the Shostakovich phenomenon. A book could be written about the books written about Shostakovich. The pertinent controversy even has a name: "The Shostakovich Wars." And there was yet another Shostakovich war, postdating World War II, Kozlov, and Thomson. This was the propaganda war waged by the Soviet Union and the United States during the Cold War, in which Shostakovich was, as ever, a hero and villain, actor and pawn. In the United States, the public flash point was a "World Peace" conference at New York's Waldorf Astoria Hotel in March 1949. The conference was denounced in *Life* magazine as an elaborate instrument of Soviet propaganda—which it partly became. And the American participants—including such celebrities as Norman Mailer, Arthur Miller, Lillian Hellman, and Aaron Copland—were designated in *Life* as dupes or traitors. As for the seven-man Soviet delegation, its celebrity was Dmitri Shostakovich. Stalin had personally telephoned and instructed him to go. Shostakovich played the piano, answered questions, and listlessly read two speeches apparently prepared by others. At one point, he apologized for his formalist deviations, losing touch with "the people" and with "big themes." In response, a member of the audience demanded to know if Shostakovich stood by "bilious" Soviet denunciations of the Western composers Stravinsky, Schoenberg, and Hindemith. This provocation compelled a necessary and humiliating response: yes, he did. The questioner's name was Nicolas Nabokov.

The following year, a Congress for Cultural Freedom was organized to combat Soviet cultural propaganda, with Nabokov as secretary general. Covertly funded by the Central Intelligence Agency, the CCF aimed to woo the intellectual Left. To this end, it founded magazines in Western Europe and Latin America. It also organized conferences. As the CCF music expert, Nabokov wrote copiously for a variety of CCF and non-CCF publications. He also organized music festivals in Paris, Rome, Venice, and Tokyo. And he made his way to the Kennedy White House, which had cultural Cold War aspirations of its own.

*   *   *

Nicolas Nabokov was a Russian expatriate composer, a man of acknowledged learning and charm.[2] He was born in 1903 to a distinguished family of landed gentry (Vladimir Nabokov was his first cousin). He spoke German with his father, Russian with his mother, English and French with his governesses. With the eruption of revolution, the Nabokovs fled to the Crimea, where they owned land.

In 1921 Nicolas wound up in Berlin, where he studied composition. In Paris, where Nabokov attended the Sorbonne, Serge Diaghilev commissioned and premiered his *Ode* with choreography by Leonide Massine; this was in 1928, when Nabokov was all of twenty-five years old. He moved to the United States in 1933 at the invitation of the eccentric chemist/businessman/collector Albert C. Barnes, who engaged him to lecture on music for his Barnes Foundation. After that, Nabokov taught at Wells College, then St. John's of Annapolis, then the Peabody Conservatory. He became a U.S. citizen in 1939. During the last months of World War II, at the insistence of the poet W. H. Auden (who turned up in DC in a military uniform),[3] he signed onto the U.S. Strategic Bombing Survey in Berlin, charged with studying the effects of Allied bombing on civilian morale. He stayed on as a civilian cultural adviser in occupied Germany, where he had occasion to observe the machinations of Soviet cultural propaganda. He returned to America a member in good standing of the non-Communist Left with special authority on Soviet culture. He became the first chief of the Voice of America's Russian Broadcast Service. A post at the American Academy in Rome briefly preceded his appointment, in 1950, as secretary general of the Congress for Cultural Freedom—finally, a suitable job, which he assumed the following year. The CCF collapsed in 1967 when it was revealed to be a creation of the CIA. Nabokov taught some more. He frequently visited Jerusalem ("the only city I really love"). He died in 1978 at the age of seventy-four.

All of this submerged his continued vocation as a composer. His *Ode* for Diaghilev was followed six years later by *Union Pacific*, which he called "the first truly American ballet"; choreographed by Massine, it was premiered by Colonel Wassili de Basil's Ballets Russes. These proximate scores, arguably the two most noticed that Nabokov would ever produce, do not attempt to fulfill the modernist criterion of originality he otherwise cherished. The *Ode* is conservative Russian music. *Union Pacific* mildly orchestrates such tunes as "Oh! Susanna" and "Pop Goes the Weasel"; there is no attempt to disassemble vernacular materials in the modernist manner. Later on, two big Nabokov operas—*Rasputin's End* (to a libretto by Stephen Spender, 1958) and *Love's Labour's Lost* (to a libretto by W. H. Auden and Chester Kallmann, 1971)—were mounted with fanfare in Cologne and Brussels; *Love's Labour's Lost* enjoyed a subsequent run at Berlin's Deutsche Oper before disappearing. More noticed was *Don Quixote* (1966), for which George Balanchine famously returned to the stage to dance the title role opposite his muse Suzanne Farrell. Nabokov's score, which took some hard hits from music critics, is frankly eclectic (the introduction is twelve-tone). It remained in the City Ballet repertoire for another thirteen years. Nabokov's eventual catalog shows five more ballets, incidental and film music, twenty orchestral scores (including three symphonies and a piano concerto), chamber music, and vocal music in five languages—some of it prominently premiered, none of it now heard. Late in life, he said, "I'm an old-fashioned Russian composer, a Russian lyricist with an addiction to melody." He called the idiom of *Love's Labour's Lost* "tonal, non-experimental, and consistently melodic," detached "from any school or aesthetic ideology." The conductor/composer Igor Markevitch placed Nabokov's music in a line with Prokofiev and middle-period Stravinsky.[4]

Nabokov's initial American teaching posts did not remotely suit him. Tall, handsome, restless, gregarious, he was an expansive multilingual bon vivant stuck in the hinterlands. It was through Auden, then Charles Bohlen and George Kennan—preeminent State Department Cold Warriors—that Nabokov discovered a plausible cosmopolitan milieu: international diplomacy and espionage. He plied his charm and influence among a range of acquaintances so large and varied as to constitute a personal achievement far more formidable than composing ballets.

From an early age, he had enjoyed striking access to the famous and influential personalities of his time. In Berlin, still a teenager, he fell in with the louche entourage of Count Harry Kessler. He discovered himself drinking with Isadora Duncan and Sergey Esenin. He met Rainer Maria Rilke. However briefly, he studied composition with Ferruccio Busoni, through whom he encountered Kurt Weill and who knows how many other young musicians of consequence. Via his uncle, who had founded a Russian émigré daily, he kept company with

Konstantin Stanislavsky, Olga Knipper-Chekhova, and other visiting members of the Moscow Art Theater. Stanislavsky came to tea with Alexander Moissi, a famed member of Max Reinhardt's troupe. With his uncle, he heard the Philharmonic under Arthur Nikisch and, after Nikisch's death, Wilhelm Furtwängler.

And this was nothing compared to Paris, where Nabokov partnered both Diaghilev's entourage, not excluding George Balanchine, Jean Cocteau, Serge Prokofiev, and Pavel Tchelitchev. Upon arriving in New York, he wound up living with Henri Cartier-Bresson. In DC in 1945, working for the War Division, he bonded with Isaiah Berlin. The Congress of Cultural Freedom brought into play Benedetto Croce, John Dewey, Karl Jaspers, Bertrand Russell—all honorary chairmen. During subsequent decades, a de facto New World cultural ambassador, Nabokov crossed paths with Willy Brandt, André Malraux, Jawaharlal Nehru, and Robert Oppenheimer. His ultimate range of musical acquaintances was equally copious: How many other composers could claim to have known both George Gershwin and Pierre Boulez?

Cosmopolitan breadth and rootless wanderings are twin motifs of the Nabokov journey. If the CCF furnished a degree of anchorage, the same was true of Nabokov's signature musical ally: Igor Stravinsky, king of cutting-edge neoclassicism. Beginning in 1944, Nabokov produced articles and books celebrating Stravinsky as the "discoverer" of new domains of rhythm, instrumentation, and harmony. Stravinsky's concert and stage works, perpetually evolving, signified "a necessary and sound development" in the dynamic evolution of twentieth-century modernism, "overleaping" the twelve-tone rigors of Arnold Schoenberg and his acolytes.[5] Stravinsky in turn acclaimed Nabokov the "cultural generalissimo" of the non-Communist West. He was also called, by an émigré acquaintance of mine, a "consummate opportunist." This description was knowing, not pejorative. Nabokov created a singular persona as a Cold War cultural ideologue. And this act of self-invention was by no means cynical. Rather, it was born in exigency: a life experience encumbered by continuous change and displacement (Nabokov titled his 1975 memoir *Bagazh*—baggage). The end result, intellectually, was a signature cultural/historical credo: that only in freedom could creativity flourish. The central example was Stravinsky, who had escaped pitiless Soviet shackles that ensnared his antipode Shostakovich. And the keynote of authentic creativity, without which art lacked a validating originality, was innovation.

Between 1941 and 1957, Nabokov wrote for a dozen variegated American periodicals, including the *Atlantic Monthly*, *Encounter*, *Harper's*, *High Fidelity*, *Musical America*, *Partisan Review*, *Politics*, the *Reporter*, and the *Saturday Review*.[6] Every one of the resulting two dozen articles directly or indirectly addressed the fate of twentieth-century music in the democratic West versus Soviet Russia, the prime exemplars being Stravinsky and Shostakovich. Concomitantly, he curated cultural festivals for the CCF, of which the first, biggest, and most noticed was "L'oeuvre du vingtieme siècle" (titled in English "Masterpieces of the Twentieth Century") in Paris in 1952.

All of this has been touched upon in the two best-known studies of the CCF: *The Cultural Cold War: The CIA and The World of Arts and Letters* (1999) by Frances Stonor Saunders and *The Mighty Wurlitzer: How the CIA Played America* (2008) by Hugh Wilford. There is also a painstaking 550-page biography, *Nicolas Nabokov: A Life in Freedom and Music* (2015), by Vincent Giroud. An inescapable focus has been the covert CIA role in American cultural propaganda—and whether Nabokov knew about it. Though it seems that he became increasingly aware of a CIA link around 1960, he never acknowledged full understanding prior to a series of *New York Times* articles that in 1966 clinched prior disclosures. (I deal with this question in detail in a note.)[7] His final word, in *Bagazh*, was that the secrecy apparatus was in any event pointless and self-defeating: "Was it really impossible to find open channels of subsidizing the CCF . . . ? Could it not have been done imaginatively, courageously, through the establishment of a worldwide fund made up of those famous 'counterpart funds' that in the late 1940s were spread all around the world? A kind of Marshall Plan in the domain of the intellect and the arts?"[8]

While this much-rehearsed debacle can now be put to rest, none of the pertinent commentators, to date, was sufficiently knowledgeable about music to glimpse a second finding hiding in plain sight: Nabokov's readings of Soviet music were wildly inaccurate, and his concurrent doctrinal pronouncements formidably implausible. What is more, these mistakes of reportage and judgment are in retrospect explicable—and the explanations are fascinating and instructive. And so my critique of the CCF does not focus on covert CIA funding or manipulation. Rather, I discover the entire exercise distorted by a fallacious propaganda of freedom traceable to the Russian exiles Stravinsky and Nabokov.

*   *   *

The locus classicus for Nabokov's Shostakovich critique is "The Case of Dmitri Shostakovitch [*sic*]," published March 1943 in *Harper's*—that is, in the wake of more than three dozen highly publicized and acclaimed American performances of Shostakovich's Seventh Symphony. (See Appendix 1 for the complete text.) Characteristic of all Nabokov's journalism is its flat perspective, redundant content, generalized opinion, and aggressive tone. In short, "The Case of Dmitri Shostakovitch" is a species of ideological propaganda. Like most good propaganda, it wears a disguise: that of "a thorough and objective investigation."

The music of Shostakovitch should be carefully scrutinized, brought into proper focus and related to the general artistic production of our time so that we may determine to what extent it deserves this tremendous success, and to what extent the success is the result of a propitious political constellation. As yet there have been only scattered evaluations of Shostakovitch . . . Except for a few articles in musical magazines—mostly international—nothing more complete has been attempted.

What is the objective content of Shostakovich's music? It is "orthodox," "well-behaved," "not new or imaginative," "neither daring nor particularly new," "old-fashioned," "provincial." Nabokov proposes a metaphor: "It is as difficult to describe the music of Shostakovitch as to describe the form and color of an oyster . . . it is shapeless in style and form and impersonal in color." He concedes only "two positive qualities." The first is "great versatility and efficiency in Conservatory training, which enables him to solve technical problems of a broad variety in a highly skillful manner." The second "is the inherent optimism of his music," which "takes a redundant, blatant, and unconvincing form." "It drives the young composer to naïve and dated formulae such as an excessive and very conventional use of major triads, tunes and cadences in major keys." It "becomes dreary and monotonous."

The closest Nabokov comes to sustained consideration of a single composition are three long paragraphs on the Symphony No. 1, well known in the West, which Shostakovich composed (amazingly) in 1925 at the age of nineteen. Reading the score, Nabokov discovered "something old about the music, something essentially conservative and unexperimental. I could not feel any definite personality in it, nor did I see very much authentic invention. . . . [I]n the long run [it is] extremely dull." Things got even worse after that: "his music ceases to be an artistic language in which the adventurous human mind discovers new laws and new problems which it endeavors to solve in a new way."

The most revealing sentence in this nine-thousand-word treatment is an aside: "In Russian terms the Shostakovitch family typified that admirable element in Russian society—the intelligentsia—which comprised in its ranks all that was vital, imaginative, and creative in the nation." The second most revealing sentence, critiquing Shostakovich's earliest piano pieces, reads: "They lacked completely the audacious experimental spirit which was sweeping through the music of central and western Europe in the nineteen-twenties." What fascinates here is that the twenties were also famously audacious and experimental in Russia—but not for Nabokov. The cheekiness of Shostakovich's First Symphony, the bold polyvalence of his tragicomic score for the classic Soviet silent film The New Babylon (1929), do not register in Nabokov's account because for Nabokov the Revolution evicted and betrayed the intellectual class to which he belonged. Hence, the root problem with Shostakovich: he is a child of the Revolution; he maintains a political agenda. The First Symphony, to Nabokov's ears, already embodies "a new era" in art. "This synthetic and retrospective score, although foreign and unacceptable to me, was perhaps the true expression of a new period in which the aim was to establish easily comprehensible, utilitarian, and at the same time contemporaneous art." It augured a Russian music "subordinated to such principles as absolute and immediate comprehensibility to large masses of people and fulfillment of an educational mission, political and social." In sum, "there are many composers who both write better and have more to say than Shostakovich. American and alien composers in this country have composed music . . . which says infinitely more than his celebrated Seventh Symphony." Nabokov's list of composers better than Shostakovich includes Walter Piston, Aaron Copland, William Schuman, and (his friend) Vittorio Rieti.

The big picture into which all this fits finds fuller expression in Nabokov's contribution to the premiere issue of the Congress for Cultural Freedom's *Encounter* magazine, published in October 1953: "No Cantatas for Stalin?" Stalin has died, yet Russia's composers have not contributed suitable funeral music. Why is that? Because as socialist realists, they exclusively compose music of "joy and praise." Only infrequently does the Soviet composer use minor triads to describe "the 'abject sadness' of pre-revolutionary life." In the "immense refrigerator" of Stalin's Russia, all "novel tendencies"—"signs of life"—were frozen to death. Only in freedom can artists explore the complexity and originality that are hallmarks of genuine creativity. In sum: "It is difficult to detect any significant difference between one piece and another. Nor is there any relief from the dominant tone of 'uplift.' The musical products of different parts of the Socialist Fatherland all sound as though they had been turned out by Ford or General Motors."

This breathtaking overview, based upon "close inspection"—for Nabokov is "reading musical scores from the U.S.S.R."—appeared some ten months after the Leningrad premiere of Shostakovich's set of Twenty-Four Preludes and Fugues for solo piano, culminating in a titanic D-minor Prelude and Fugue that stands up to Bach. His Eighth Symphony of 1943, cataclysmic World War II music surpassing the simpler, more sanguine message of the Seventh, was by no means unknown in the United States. His Tenth Symphony, whose premiere was two months away, would respond to Stalin's death not with obligatory sorrow, but a fiercely defiant celebration. It hardly bears saying that these were works that could only have been composed by Shostakovich. The music of Prokofiev and Khachaturian, also familiar to American listeners, could only have been composed by Prokofiev and Khachaturian.

The personal aggrievement firing Nabokov's displeasure peaks in the final sentences of "The Case of Dmitri Shostakovitch."

> I sincerely hope that Shostakovitch has the power to . . . emerge a truly significant composer. But it is a gross misunderstanding of "collectivist" art to accept the popularity of his music now as evidence that he has found a universal formula. Soon his eclipse may come as swiftly as his leap to fame; this would be just as unfair and would indicate the same disbalance we see at present. Shostakovitch is a young man; he should develop as a solid and respectable musician of the great new Russia. He does not now merit the injudicious acclaim he is receiving here; neither will he deserve the inevitable repudiation which will come in its wake. Both extremes are shameful evidence that contemporary music is judged indiscriminately and contemporary composers are used irresponsibly.

Whence this patronizing sermon? Nabokov in 1943 was also "a young man"—at forty, less than three years Shostakovich's senior. Nabokov was an obscure composer, Shostakovich a famous one. Neither did Nabokov's music embody the originality and complexity he could not find in Soviet compositions. The high persona he here inhabits is that of Igor Stravinsky, the sixty-one-year-old modernist lodestar, honored by Nabokov as a symbol of perpetual, cutting-edge renewal. As we will discover, this implicit embodiment was hardly lost on Stravinsky himself.

*   *   *

It was Nicolas Nabokov's longtime association with Arthur J. Schlesinger Jr. that brought him into direct contact with the Kennedys. Schlesinger's topic was twentieth-century liberalism—it history, theory, and practice. Though he made his name as a historian with the Pulitzer Prize–winning *The Age of* [Andrew] *Jackson* (1945), his third book, *The Vital Center: The Politics of Freedom* (1949), plunged directly into the history of the moment: it influentially proposed a recipe for the non-Communist Left. Schlesinger's chapter "The Communist Challenge to America" launched a warning shot that steered clear of McCarthyite red-baiting a year away. The Soviet campaign against the United States, Schlesinger wrote, had two aspects: "the pressures exerted in the traditional manner of power politics; and the pressures exerted through the network of Communist parties." The first was easy to handle because overt. The second was harder because hidden: Communists "in our midst," while small in number, were tireless ideologues. They might be unemployed and homeless; they might be residual intellectual enemies of fascism; they might be double agents in the U.S. security services. They included foolish knaves and courageous fighters. Notwithstanding the powerful resistance of Walter Reuther's United Auto Workers, they had infiltrated the national leadership of many labor unions. They had activated Henry Wallace's third-party presidential campaign of 1948. But the greater threat they posed was "dividing and neutralizing" the political Left.

Schlesinger's chapter also briefly assayed popular culture. He regretted "the cult of 'proletarian literature'" fostered by the American Writers' Congress of 1935. He derided "bush-league" cultural ideologues like Mike Gold, whose slashing literary critiques enlivened the *New Masses* and the *Daily Worker*. He fingered "certain types of 'fake folk art'"—like Earl Robinson's *Ballad for Americans*, popularized by Paul Robeson. He named Dalton Trumbo and other "fellow-traveling, ex-proletarian writers [who] go to Hollywood and become film hacks." The result was "a dangerous inroad upon the moral fabric of American culture," an "influence toward lowering and softening artistic standards in a pseudo-democratic direction."

Citing "a renewed sense of the meaning of freedom," Schlesinger's joined company with such seminal postwar studies as Friedrich Hayek's *The Road to Serfdom* (1945) and George Orwell's *Nineteen Eighty-Four* (1949). His book would also resonate with Hannah Arendt's *The Origins of Totalitarianism* (1951) for limning an oppressed mind-set inimical to the creative act.

But Schlesinger waded out of his cultural depth in his chapter "The Case of Russia." Here, the referenced authority is not Hayek or Orwell or Arthur Koestler, but Nicolas Nabokov. Vigorously addressing issues of artistic freedom, Schlesinger broached the contested merits of Stravinsky and Shostakovich:

> The recent Soviet campaign against cultural freedom and diversity becomes all too comprehensible. . . . The totalitarian man requires apathy and unquestioning obedience. He fears creative independence and spontaneity. He mistrusts complexity as a device for slipping something over on the regime; he mistrusts incomprehensibility as a shield which might protect activities the bureaucracy cannot control. . . .
>
> The paintings of Picasso, the music of Stravinsky are strangely disturbing. They reflect and incite anxieties which are incompatible with the monolithic character of "the Soviet person." Their intricacy and ambiguity, moreover, make them hard for officialdom to control; they thus tend to create intellectual enclaves within the totalitarian whole. Nicolas Nabokov quotes a character in a famous anti-tsarist satire: "What I don't understand is undoubtedly dangerous to the security of the state."

The reference to Stravinsky's "strangely disturbing" music does not inspire confidence—in 1949 Stravinsky had for some decades pursued Apollonian equipoise, not Dionysian upheaval. A footnote cites Nabokov's "brilliant" article "The Music Purge" in the spring 1949 issue of *Politics*. Nabokov asks why the Soviets have cracked down on Shostakovich. His answer is that the Soviets realize that "creative individualism" may lead to "political individualism." (I suggest another answer—that Shostakovich's music in fact conveyed moral and political content—in my chapter 5.) No less than with Nabokov, Schlesinger's notion of a "free left," unencumbered by party loyalty, yields a false cognate: the "free artist," creatively fulfilled because unencumbered by the state. In short: a heady dose of Nicolas Nabokov here flavors *The Vital Center*.[9] Even years later, in an essay titled "The Future of Liberalism," Schlesinger notably prioritized culture in calling for a "new liberalism" attentive to (among other things) "the *quality* of civilization to which our nation aspires."[10] Nabokov doubtless concurred with this emphasis.

The conjunction of views was no coincidence: Schlesinger and Nabokov were long aligned, socially, politically, and professionally. During World War II, Nabokov contacted the Office of War Information and the Office of Strategic Services (OSS, precursor to the CIA), hoping to be sent to Europe as a government employee. This preceded his 1945 assignment with the U.S. Strategic Bombing Survey in Germany. Schlesinger was an OSS intelligence analyst from 1943 to 1945. Nabokov and Schlesinger met, and bonded, in 1947, at a dinner party in Georgetown (DC's prime residential neighborhood for diplomats, journalists, and politicians). Their circle subsequently included the short-lived "Europe-America Groups" launched by the writer Mary McCarthy; Dwight Macdonald (the editor of *Politics*), the writers Elizabeth Hardwick and Alfred Kazin, the artist Saul Steinberg, and the actor Montgomery Clift were also on board. Nabokov had already emerged as the reigning authority on Soviet music within the non-Communist Left; though his views at first seemed extreme to some, Russian ideologues unwittingly strengthened his hand with decrees in 1946 and 1948 censuring prominent writers and composers. In 1949 Schlesinger was part of the dissident clique that challenged the Waldorf Astoria Peace Conference—the occasion for Nabokov's confrontation with Shostakovich. The same year, both took part in a Berlin Congress for Cultural Freedom—like the Waldorf dissidents, covertly funded by the CIA; Arthur Koestler—the West's most charismatic repentant Communist—was the star speaker. When the Congress for Cultural Freedom was launched in 1950, Nabokov was a leader, Schlesinger a participant and advocate. In 1970 Schlesinger was a witness at the last of Nabokov's five marriages. And it was Schlesinger who secured Nabokov a job as a visiting professor at the City University of New York, post-CCF, in 1968.

As a public intellectual and political attaché, Schlesinger served six Democratic presidents and presidential candidates between 1952 and 1980. His most prominent governmental role was as John F. Kennedy's special assistant, rendering advice, writing speeches, and ultimately chronicling the Kennedy presidency in *A Thousand Days* (1966)—for which he won a second Pulitzer Prize. Ten of its one thousand pages deal with "Kennedy and the arts." Schlesinger begins by citing William Faulkner's pre-Kennedy opinion, in 1958, that "the artist has no more actual place in the American culture of today than he has in the American economy of today, no place at all in the warp and woof, the thews and sinews, the mosaic of the American dream." He ends with Lewis Mumford, in 1964, calling Kennedy "the first American President to give art, literature and music a place of dignity and honor in our national life." As observed by Schlesinger, the Kennedys "were wholly unaffected in their attitude toward the arts—cultural refinements were simply a part of their daily lives." The president "responded most deeply and spontaneously" to literature. He acquired "a growing interest in architecture and . . . some knowledge of painting." "Serious music, it must be said, left him cold." Schlesinger himself, though keenly interested in theater and film, likewise took no particular interest in classical music.[11] Though his parents were concertgoers, Kennedy, as president, would exercise to the accompaniment of favorite country-and-western and show tunes; he acquired a particular affinity for the title song from the Lerner and Loewe musical *Camelot*. He was also known to listen to the Lerner/Loewe *Brigadoon* (and Alan Jay Lerner was a former Choate and Harvard chum).[12]

Other observers of the Kennedy White House, no less than Schlesinger outsiders to the arts, knocked his assessment down a notch. Richard Rovere, whose political journalism was a liberal staple, applauded Kennedy's emphasis on "the whole quality and tone of American life," but conceded that the president himself "did not respond much to painting or music, or even to literature"; rather, he dutifully "looked at paintings he didn't enjoy, and listened to music he didn't much care for, because people who he thought were excellent people had told him they were excellent things." A caustic observer of the same phenomenon was Christopher Lasch, for whom "the cult of the New Frontier" was laced with jargon and cant ("freedom," "the free world") and polished by a style of casual authority.

> The cult of the Kennedys showed that culture had become practically synonymous with chic. . . . Looking at the Kennedy administration from a distance, one could not avoid the suspicion that what liberals called his style consisted largely of a Harvard education, a certain amount of conscientious concertgoing, and a feeling, never very precise, that the arts ought somehow to be officially encouraged. The desperate gratitude with which intellectuals welcomed even these few crumbs from the presidential table was disheartening.[13]

At the Kennedy inauguration, Robert Frost read a poem. The audience included W. H. Auden, Paul Tillich, Jacques Maritain, Robert Lowell, John Hersey, John Steinbeck, and Allen Tate. (There was also a gaudy preinauguration party hosted by Frank Sinatra.) The Casals and Stravinsky dinners we have already glimpsed were the first in a series of White House "cultural evenings."

It was thanks to Schlesinger that Nabokov was first received at the White House in 1961 during a visit to fund-raise for CCF programs; the first lady gave him a tour. Nabokov had already, on February 23, 1961, written to Mrs. Kennedy to say: "In the eyes of intellectuals and artists in the U.S. and abroad, Washington has been for a long time the center of political power and not the symbol or the home of artists and intellectuals. In other words, in America and all over the world there was a feeling of alienation of the cultural community from Washington and from the White House." Nabokov went on to propose that the president acknowledge outstanding intellectual or artistic achievement, sending a message that "the White House is a cultural center concerned with the life of the mind and the arts, and that in fact it is their home where they are appreciated, invited and honoured."[14] Subsequently, at Schlesinger's suggestion, Nabokov compiled for Mrs. Kennedy a list of cultural personalities worthy of White House notice. A year later, with Schlesinger's support, Nabokov helped to plan Stravinsky's eightieth birthday dinner.

No less than to the Russia hands Bohlen and Kennan, the White House doubtless deferred to Nabokov's expert understanding of Soviet musical life. And Schlesinger connected the dots. Of the three Kennedy pronouncements on culture earlier cited, the author or authors of the first two—the National Cultural Center speech and the article for *Look*—cannot be traced. But it was Schlesinger—after Kennedy rejected a draft by Theodore Sorensen as "thin and stale"[15]—who drafted Kennedy's main address on the artist in free societies: his Amherst speech of October 26, 1963, delivered with little revision. The Kennedy Archives show that the sole significant addition to Schlesinger's text, by the president himself, is the phrase "their concern for justice, which must motivate any true artist." This bizarre alteration encapsulates the anomaly at hand: Kennedy, Schlesinger, and Nabokov all conflated the necessary prerogatives of the democratic citizen with the sources and purposes of artistic creation. Not every great poet, painter, and composer is impelled to create by "concern for justice."

Igor Stravinsky being a case in point. Having moved to Los Angeles in 1940 for the climate, and to be left alone while Europe imploded, he told Nabokov: "As far as I am concerned, they can have their generalissimos and Fuhrers. Leave me Mr. Truman and I'm quite satisfied."[16] Still, Stravinsky was an incidental

American. Behind the scenes, getting him to the White House in 1962—an event we can now reprise with fresh understanding—was not simple. As we have observed, Stravinsky was annoyed that Casals had preceded him. He had already accepted a similar invitation, honoring his eightieth birthday, from the Union of Soviet Composers—a circumstance that, according to Stravinsky's secretary Lillian Libman, was not irrelevant to the presidential invitation. Stravinsky, his wife, Nabokov, and Stravinsky's assistant Robert Craft all quipped naughtily about their White House welcome. Apart from Nabokov, the event was "more a Kennedy-circle dinner, with political pay-offs, than an I.S. dinner," Craft recorded. He also testified that before dinner the president mainly attended to Lee Radziwell's glamorous friend Helen Chavchavadze, that the president proved intellectually impressive, and that Nabokov made "droll and unprintable comments" about portraits of William Howard Taft and Warren Harding. At the same time, Craft thought the president intellectually impressive. Nabokov himself wrote to Michael Josselson of the Congress for Cultural Freedom that the guest list had been "handled God knows by whom and completely absurdly." He found the Kennedys a little gauche and likened the first lady's idea of hostessing to a mixture of Dior, Chanel, Saint Laurent, and Broadway. In the green room, he observed Kennedy asking Stravinsky what he thought of the leading Soviet composers. Stravinsky, Nabokov later recalled, "turned to the president, in his most courtly manner, and replied: 'Mr. President, I have left Russia since 1914 and have so far not been in the Soviet Union. I have not studied or heard many of the works of these composers. I have therefore no valid opinion.' And the president looked at me over Stravinsky's shoulder and smiled approvingly." Nabokov doubtless appreciated this acknowledgment.

Photographs show Stravinsky bowing courteously to the Kennedys wearing his warmest grin. Two hours later, he left the dinner early, inebriated from a surfeit of double martinis. Jack and Jacqueline graciously attended to the Stravinskys until their chauffeur arrived. The next morning, the first lady phoned to check on Stravinsky's condition. She also sent red roses. He sent her yellow ones. To Craft, Stravinsky called the Kennedys "nice kids." In a world terrorized by what their Russia had become, both Nabokov and Stravinsky were grateful Americans. They were also, both of them, strangers in a strange land.[17]

CHAPTER 3

LINES OF BATTLE

The Case for Stravinsky; The Case against Shostakovich

Arthur Schlesinger wrote of his first encounter with Nicolas Nabokov: "The sad, dark room was suddenly bathed in light and exhilaration. [Nabokov] over-flowed with vitality, was a notable raconteur in half a dozen languages, was also a notable mimic, and had, what was rare in an artist, a penetrating and ironical political intelligence." Years later, he added: "Nicolas always had the same en-livening effect on me as at that first meeting—light and laughter in a dark age."[1]

Isaiah Berlin, whom Nabokov considered possibly his closest friend, re-called: "I found him to be one of the most civilized men I ever met, a perfect representative of the pre-Russian Revolution intelligentsia. He had mastered vast amounts of knowledge, had wide horizons and a wonderful imagination; he was also one of the warmest and most sympathetic of men, very generous, and with a very fine character. His charm was extraordinary." Berlin also called Nabokov "large hearted, affectionate, honourable, gifted with sharp moral and political insight and a well developed sense of the ridiculous, an irrepressible source of torrential wit and fancy."[2]

George Kennan eulogized Nabokov as

an intensely gregarious man, delighting, basking even, in the company of a host of friends and acquaintances, knowing everyone worth knowing, speaking all the languages, familiar with every great city of the West . . . the epitome of the cultured cosmopolitan of our age; at home everywhere, and at home nowhere, unless it be in the companionship and affections of his friends. . . . He enjoyed people immensely. He lived by their warmth; he reflected it. He had an unerring eye for their failings: their pretentions, their ridiculousness. He was a superb mimic. . . . Yet the criticism implied in his mimicry was seldom, if ever, cruel. It was his way of understanding others. He took life as he found it, not caring to inquire into its philosophic implications; and he loved every bit of it . . . and above all the amusing spectacle of the impact of colorful individuals upon one another.[3]

He called Berlin "Carissimo," the poet Stephen Spender "Milyii Stiva," Edward d'Arms of the Rockefeller Foundation "Chat."[4] He was the life of every party. His conversational aplomb is preserved in Tony Palmer's exceptional 2008 Stravinsky documentary, in which Nabokov elegantly frames Stravinsky's "inherent quality of irony" with reference to his duality: "Stravinsky on one side was a hedonist, enjoying all the pleasure of life—loving to eat, good wine, and for a very long time pretty girls. On the other side, he was a rigorously ritualistic and religious person—like ancient people are." Nabokov is also delectably observed in Richard Leacock's *A Stravinsky Portrait* (1965), sipping Scotch with Stravinsky in five languages. In the company of genius, the rumpled, wavy-haired Nabokov persona remains ripely self-possessed, whimsically casual yet not without undertones of gravitas.

This ingratiating force of personality was spontaneous and oral, never adequately conveyed at the writer's desk. Even when not laden with ideology, Nabokov's prose rarely takes sustained flight. His tenderest writing, and his best story, are reserved for the legendary dancer Vaslav Nijinsky, whom he once kidnapped alongside Serge Diaghilev. At Diaghilev's insistence, Nijinsky was removed from the mental institution that was his home and dragged to a performance by Diaghilev's latest discovery: Serge Lifar. Nabokov's ten-page tale—"The Spectre of Nijinsky"—ends:

> It was past midnight when the limousine stopped at the sanatorium gate, and the ceremony of extracting Nijinsky from his seat began again. He looked paler than before, and because his body had become as limp as an oyster, it took some time to put him on his feet. Finally, a mere shadow of a prisoner between two jailers, he walked past me toward the gate. I watched him from the car, saw him stop, turn around, and although the car's motor was on I heard him say in a gentle, halting, and somewhat tearful voice, "Skajte yemou chto Lifar horosho prygayet." (Tell him that Lifar jumps well.)[5]

Stravinsky's was the personality Nabokov most assayed in print, notably in two chapters of *Old Friends and New Music* (1951) describing a five-day 1947

Christmas visit to the Stravinskys' exquisitely ordered, eagerly welcoming Los Angeles home. These glimpses of the famous composer, while pointedly intimate, never attain the empathy of the Nijinsky anecdote, nor the acuity of the Stravinsky observations—one side a hedonist, the other ritualistic and religious—Nabokov so seamlessly extemporized on film. The most tellingly detailed portraits of Stravinsky in America—that of his secretary Lillian Libman in *And Music at the Close: Stravinsky's Last Years* (1972) and Paul Horgan's *Encounters with Stravinsky* (1972)—combine deep affection with supreme respect; they take for granted Stravinsky's importance on the world stage. Nabokov, by comparison, feels compelled to protect and defend the Stravinsky reputation: a tendentious chill interrupts anecdotes of delicious camaraderie.

Stravinsky's "leadership of modern Western music" is "incontestable." He was "the unquestionable leader of modern music in Paris and the West throughout the early thirties." Whereas Arnold Schoenberg, the other "founding father" of twentieth-century music, is merely "a dogmatician, a theorist," Stravinsky is "an artisan, a craftsman." Because Schoenberg's twelve-tone method so radically charted new terrain, Nabokov resorts to hyperbole, positioning Stravinsky as the bolder, more original musical thinker. "Stravinsky's devices are always the same: a remarkable economy of means coupled with an infallible sense of proportion, time, and form." "Stravinsky is, I believe, unquestionably the greatest living investigator of instruments as 'individuals,' perhaps even the greatest since the middle of the eighteenth century." "The primary importance the art of orchestration holds in contemporary music is largely due to the influence of Stravinsky. If we consider that at least two thirds of the quality of an instrumental piece is in its adequate orchestration, we must give credit to Stravinsky's approach to and his discoveries in the instrumental field." "In these last twenty-five or thirty years, the orchestral texture of his music has acquired a degree of transparency, lucidity and crystalline fragility unequalled by any of his contemporaries." "It was Stravinsky's art, I believe, which showed the musicians of my generation new horizons in the domain of rhythm, new possibilities in the use of musical instruments, and a new concept of harmony, fuller, broader, and nobler than the sterile harmonic concepts of the late nineteenth century. Yet to me the most important discoveries of Stravinsky lie in his artful perception and measurement of the flow of time by means of the most complex and beautiful rhythmic patterns and designs." Seven years later, assessing "Stravinsky: Fifteen and Three Score" for *High Fidelity* magazine, Nabokov coupled Stravinsky with Picasso for their supreme "imprint on our time"—and continued that Stravinsky surpassed Picasso because his output was not uneven.[6]

And there is the inevitable Nabokov leitmotif: that Stravinsky is a "discoverer" validates his greatness. He can be original because he is "free." Stravinsky himself, Nabokov wrote, is "fearful and contemptuous of conditions in which the creative work of the artist is subject to supervision or dictation (and possibly extinction) by the authorities of the state." In fact, of all the Stravinsky observations and opinions documented by Nabokov, the most surprising—and unflattering—is an endorsement of Nabokov's Shostakovich metaphor: upon reading "The Case of Shostakovitch," Stravinsky sent Nabokov "a warm congratulatory letter" for comparing Shostakovich's music to the flabby anatomy and impersonal color of an oyster. For Nabokov, Shostakovich was ideologically anathema. Stravinsky's objections to Shostakovich were in part aesthetic. He was also doubtless aware that, at the Waldorf in 1949, Shostakovich said Stravinsky had "betrayed his native land and severed himself from his people by joining the camp of reactionary modern musicians."[7] But in Nabokov's telling, there was another basic ingredient: a fundamental disdain for what Russia had become.[8]

It is pertinent that the compositional personality about whom Nabokov most wrote, after Stravinsky, was Serge Prokofiev, whom he knew in Paris in the late twenties and early thirties. Among Soviet composers, Prokofiev became for Nabokov the exception that proves the rule. His cosmopolitan aplomb is his saving grace. Educated in czarist Russia, he left as soon as the Revolution broke out. His overcoat is "flashy herringbone tweed complemented by a flat tweed cap and cream-colored gloves." He is a gastronome. He plays chess at the highest level. His mother "belonged to the intelligentsia." His wife is half-Spanish. A member of the elite Diaghilev circle, he is widely traveled, having reputedly undertaken "extensive and lucrative concert tours to North and South America and all over Western and Central Europe."[9]

Otherwise, however, Nabokov's Prokofiev inhabited a thicket of contradictions arising from two inescapable complications. Post-Paris, Soviet hostility to free artists notwithstanding, he and his family chose to permanently resettle in Moscow in 1936. And the music Prokofiev subsequently composed was by no means inconsequential. A standard reading of this odyssey would be that he experimented with modernism in the West, ultimately producing a Fifth Piano Concerto (1932) dispensing with the familiar forms and thematic recurrences that anchored his previous compositions in this form. It and other "expressionist" pieces proved an apparent cul-de-sac. By his own testimony, Prokofiev needed to replenish his Russian roots. A popular alternative reading is that, jealous of Stravinsky, he sought a musical culture in which he could be king. Nabokov's explanation of Prokofiev's volte face is twofold:

He was . . . sympathetic to the Soviet regime and . . . had rejected the ideological position of an émigré. His music was performed all over the [USSR], and his operas and ballets were produced with great success by the best theaters of the two Russian capitals, Moscow and Leningrad. . . . What sort of longing made him turn his back on his established position as a famous composer of the Western world? . . . First, the Soviet Union of that period was not quite the same thing as the Soviet Union of today. Second, the feelings of a forward-looking and revolutionary-minded Russian intellectual toward his fatherland and its government were quite different then from what they are now and were on the whole rather mixed.[10]

Assessing the outcome of Prokofiev's decision, Nabokov is trapped between respect for his friend and the tenacity of his own anti-Soviet ideological convictions. He writes that Prokofiev's music "almost never changes . . . unresponsive to the moment, . . . as naïve as . . . Schubert, Chopin, even Mozart." Yet the Soviet pressure cooker imposed an "at times excessive simplification." This new simplicity was "not of the highest order"—as in *Peter and the Wolf* and the Second Violin Concerto, parts of which were "in essence trivial and terribly old-fashioned." Nabokov was disappointed and threatened by the success of *Romeo and Juliet*, which would swiftly occupy an exalted niche alongside the full-length ballets of Tchaikovsky. It was "banal," "full of trivial and obvious themes, conventional harmonies, and a general artificial simplicity." In a 1944 letter to Stravinsky, whose relations with Prokofiev were never warm, he confided that Prokofiev had succumbed to "bourgeois infantilism." Three years later, however, Nabokov—contradicting his insistence that Soviet composers could not compose—extolled the Symphony No. 5 as "probably one of [Prokofiev's] best compositions, extremely thoughtful, full of imagination and thoroughly impregnated with a sincere and delightful lyricism."[11] As of 1951—seven years after the Fifth was premiered, and some two years before Prokofiev's death—Nabokov summarized: "Whether Prokofiev can achieve full redemption and regain his position of as the dean of Soviet composers is doubtful. For in the eyes of those who rule the destinies of the Russian people he is the symbol of Russia's former close association with the modern Western world with its great emancipatory tradition and its spirit of intellectual and artistic freedom. This the tyrants of the Kremlin cannot endure. It endangers the very foundations of their obsolete and reactionary state."[12]

Shostakovich, who did not wear herringbone coats, was a nervous wreck in public. His gaming passion was watching soccer, not playing chess. Though like Prokofiev he was an accomplished pianist, he never toured widely outside the Soviet orbit. His distaste for the West, especially the United States, was notorious.

So far as Nabokov was concerned, Shostakovich was essentially provincial: a manacled artist whose submissiveness to totalitarian dictates precluded any possibility of originality or innovation. Scouring more than a dozen articles about Soviet culture that Nabokov produced between 1941 and 1953, I find a single positive assessment of a Shostakovich composition: in the *Atlantic Monthly* of January 1942, he called Shostakovich's Piano Quintet "an attractive piece, every bar of which rings absolutely true." (Notwithstanding Nabokov's finding that Soviet composers were never contrapuntists, its second movement is a twelve-minute fugue.) Only one Shostakovich work is explored in any detail. This is the Symphony No. 9, reviewed by Nabokov in June 1947 in *Notes*—the journal of the Music Librarians' Association. *Notes* reviews were (and are) scholarly descriptions for a scholarly readership. But Nabokov, ever the polemicist, cast Shostakovich's Fifth in the shadow of Prokofiev's Ninth, wielded as a whip.

> Despite certain "genetic" similarities . . . the two symphonies have little in common. They differ in content, intention, and intrinsic value. While Shostakovich's Symphony No. 9 is mostly unimaginative, light-weight, and unforgivably superficial . . . a futile and silly piece.
>
> When you glance at the score, you are struck first of all by a lack of melodic inventiveness. Most of the themes are derivative and synthetic, some of them cheap and even vulgar. You are astonished by the attempts of the composer to use full and out-worn circus march tricks in order to convince you (or himself) that this is a gay piece, and last, you are appalled at the complete lack of harmonic and contrapuntal artisanship.

Conductors and audiences of today may well find Shostakovich's Ninth delectably droll, and Prokofiev's Fifth overwrought, but never mind.

The finishing touch on the "Shostakovich case" was inflicted via an enemy tool: class analysis. In the BBC music periodical *The Listener* (October 11, 1953), Nabokov again assayed "Changing Styles in Soviet Music." "One all important phenomenon took place towards the second half of the nineteenth century which profoundly altered the evolution of Russian music. This was the rise of various heterogeneous groups and classes in Russian society, which filled the vacuum between the intelligentsia and the peasants, and whose birth and whose tastes gave birth to a middle brow culture. What were these new elements? . . . Mainly the Russian lower middle class; and the industrial proletariat, the small but vocal working class of large cities."

The Russian factory song of the nineteenth century, Nabokov wrote, had been corrupted by Western songs—banal tunes imported by revolutionary leaders "who did not care for good music." Meanwhile, peasants were losing touch with their modal, "profoundly religious" folk music, supplanted by optimistic songs of the postrevolutionary era. Furthermore, the growing "lower middle classes" were enamored of "Russian sentimental romances." As a result, "petite bourgeois musical habits" proliferated. Though the workers and lower middle classes had little in common, socially and economically, it was "important to state that both groups had one common denominator, which I would like to call cliché-ism; that is, the ready acceptance of all worn-out formulas of western low-brow musical production." And, absent the influence of the expelled intelligentsia, this was the very musical aesthetic of the new party and army bureaucracy, prejudiced "against any form of artistic experimentation." Soviet composers, in turn, capitulated to the insularity of "the new uneducated middle strata of Soviet society."[13] (Nabokov's article for *The Listener* was based on a radio talk for the BBC—a script toned down by a BBC editor. An excised sentence: "The indigenous Melpomene of the Socialist motherland has apparently been quite an erratic lady for in these last 20 years she has undergone treatment varying from the tender and lavish caresses due a beloved concubine, to something resembling police action against a dissolute trollop.")[14]

Whatever the truth of this analysis—a topic to which I will return—it sheds further light on Nabokov's mind-set. His friend Dwight Macdonald would influentially coin the term "midcult" to describe a cultural stratum, propagated by the "new middle classes," that "pretends to respect the standards of high culture while in fact it waters them down and vulgarizes them" for mass consumption. Macdonald also likened Stalinist cinema to Hollywood—a spurious "people's art." Nabokov, too, saw something "watered down" happening in Soviet Russia, but with a different keynote: betrayal. That is why he could use an adverb like "unforgivably" in condemning the "superficiality" of Shostakovich's Ninth: Shostakovich was a cancer symbolizing the provincialism of the new Russia.

Concomitantly, Stravinsky, representing the intelligentsia in exile, was the living iconic embodiment of what Russian culture had been. When in 1948 *Partisan Review* published a polemic by the Schoenberg acolyte René Leibowitz, Nabokov responded with a *Partisan Review* article of his own: "Under the cloak of impartiality [Leibowitz] attempts to prove the greatness of Schoenberg by smearing Stravinsky without either an understanding of the ideas underlying Stravinsky's music or a thorough analysis and comparison of both composers' recent works." It was Stravinsky, not Schoenberg, who was "working in a completely new direction."[15] This was six years before Stravinsky adopted Schoenberg's new direction in place of his own.

As ever, Nabokov's high-pitched tone was revealingly fraught.

*   *   *

Nabokov's articles on Russian music deal with the notorious Soviet cultural bureaucracy in addition to the composers it afflicted. A composer himself, he is quick to acknowledge and appreciate that, in Russia, composers are paid, published, and performed. But his emphasis is of course on what they cannot do.

With its myriad rewards and punishments for writers and composers, the Soviet system could be lethal. Isaac Babel was arrested before dawn on May 15, 1939, at the writers' commune in Peredelkino. Two NKVD officers seized pages of unfinished stories and novels. Babel was driven to Moscow and deposited at the Lubyanka prison. His books were withdrawn from libraries. His name, once eminent, was erased. The charges against him cited conversations in which he condemned Stalin's purges. His three-day interrogation likely included torture. He confessed to spying and to participating in a Trotskyite conspiracy. He denounced his own work. He later uselessly retracted his confessions. He was shot on January 27, 1940. That Babel was Jewish was not irrelevant. The same fate awaited the famous Jewish actor Solomon Mikhoels in 1948.

Stalin did not execute any famous composers. But Shostakovich at times feared for his life. Reportedly, he kept packed bags under his bed in anticipation of an unannounced nighttime visit. And his opera *Lady Macbeth of the Mtsensk District* was the object of one of the most chilling cultural edicts: the January 28, 1936, *Pravda* editorial "Muddle Instead of Music." Though *Lady Macbeth* had premiered two years before, and was widely acclaimed (not merely in Russia) an extraordinary addition to the Russian operatic canon, Stalin had only belatedly attended a performance—and was disgusted by what he saw and heard. Based on a tale by Nikolai Leskov about a bored, abused wife turned murderess, Shostakovich's opera relished the degradation of the participants. It also evoked sexual intercourse with lascivious trombone slides. The *Pravda* editorial read in part:

> From the first moment, the listener is shocked by a deliberately dissonant, confused stream of sound. Fragments of melody, embryonic phrases appear—only to disappear again in the din, the grinding, and the screaming.... Here we have "leftist" confusion instead of natural, human music.... The danger of this trend to Soviet music is clear.... Petty-bourgeois innovations lead to a break with real art, real science, and real literature ... All this is coarse, primitive, and vulgar. The music quacks, grunts, and growls, and suffocates itself in order to express the amatory scenes as naturalistically as possible....
>
> *Lady Macbeth* enjoys great success with audiences abroad. Is it not because the opera is absolutely unpolitical and confusing that they praise it? Is it not explained by the fact that it tickles the perverted tastes of the bourgeoisie with its fidgety, screaming, neurotic music?

With his First Symphony and *The New Babylon*, Shostakovich had seized the brashness of the Soviet twenties. Some twenties composers—notably Alexander Mosolov, Nikolai Roslavets, and Sergei Protopopov—were marginalized and forgotten. But in *Lady Macbeth*, Shostakovich was still at it. Meanwhile, a new aesthetic doctrine, socialist realism, had been administered. "Depicting reality in its revolutionary development" was—as a 1934 set of Composers' Union guidelines put it—"directed towards . . . all that is heroic, bright, and beautiful." The antithesis, dubbed "formalism," was art for art's sake: decadent, bourgeois, Western. *Lady Macbeth* had blatantly crossed a line. (It is little known that in the United States, as well, a line seemed crossed: the opera was censored to accommodate conservative critics like Ruth Knowles of the Clean Amusement Association of America.)[16]

The consequences could be dire. Stalin's "Moscow Trials"—three show trials lasting from 1936 to 1938—charged that leading party members were conspiring with Western powers to assassinate Stalin, undermine the Soviet state, and restore capitalism. Confessions were extracted. Many were executed. The larger context was the "Great Purge," which resulted in as many as one million deaths. Whether observers of Stalin's ruthlessness, Russian or Western, already gleaned his murderous paranoia or not, the risks of opposing Soviet authority were overwhelming. This was when Shostakovich—willingly or not—placed his sprawling Fourth Symphony in a drawer and his Fifth (1937) was proclaimed a "creative reply to just criticism."

World War II blurred Soviet aesthetic dogmas; the times were tragic. But all hope that the German defeat could further liberate creative expression was dashed by Stalin's rabid new cultural ideologue, Andrei Zhdanov. The writer Ilya Ehrenburg's reaction was typical: "I had believed that, after the Soviet peoples' victory, the 1930's could not repeat themselves, yet everything reminded me of the way things had gone in those days: writers, film director, and composers were called together, 'abettors' were singled out, and every day new names swelled the list of those censured."[17]

Beginning in August 1946, Zhdanov issued a series of edicts. The first, governing writers, set the tone:

> Works which cultivated a non-Soviet spirit of servility before the contemporary bourgeois culture of the West have appeared . . . Contributions saturated with gloom, pessimism, and disillusionment with life had been published . . . The editors . . . have forgotten the thesis of Leninism that our journals—whether scientific of literary—cannot be non-political . . . They are a mighty instrument of the Soviet state . . . Any preaching of "art for art's sake" . . . is harmful to the interests of the Soviet people and the Soviet state.[18]

Zhdanov pronouncements on film and theater followed the same year. In January 1948, he met with members of the Composers' Union. The exchange was fractious. In a final summary, Zhdanov condemned formalism as "radically wrong," "anti-People," "false," and "ugly" versus the "beautiful, natural, human intonations" of healthy Soviet music. "Music that is unintelligible to the people is unwanted by the people. Let the composers not blame the people, let them blame themselves." The ensuing resolution, dated February 10, fingered Shostakovich, Prokofiev, Aram Khachaturian, Vissarion Shebalin, Gavril Popov, Nikolai Miaskovsky, "and others." In effect, it threatened loss of employment, cancellation of performances, delays in publication and production—or worse. Though Zhdanov died suddenly in August, his pounding fist was felt until the death of Stalin five years later: a witch-hunt climate of paranoia and recrimination throttled musical expression.[19] Vocal genres and Soviet themes were stressed. Shostakovich and Prokofiev both were awarded Stalin Prizes—for the Stalinist patriotic cantatas *Song of the Forests* (1949) and *On Guard for Peace* (1950), respectively.

All of this was duly reported by Nabokov for American readers. "The Music Purge," for *Politics* (spring 1948), reproduced the entirety of Zhdanov's 1948 resolution. "Russian Music after the Purge," for *Partisan Review* (August 1949), reported that Shostakovich and Miaskovsky had lost their teaching positions and that Shostakovich had engineered a "comeback" with two film scores: *The Young Guard* (1948) and *Michurin* (1949). Excerpts from the latter "will disappoint the congenial American Shostakovitch lover—they are timid to a degree which makes them pitifully empty (it seems that poor Shostakovitch is afraid of using *any* kind of dissonance, even the most conventional ones)." "Music in the Soviet Union," for *Musical America* (February 1951), summarized a post-1948 wasteland:

> Most . . . works reflect a complete rejection of any kind of experimentation, even of the tamest variety. All forms of musical experimentalism are branded as formalist. . . . Complete unanimity on such questions as content, form, etc., has now been so solidly established that soon the glorious moment will come when one will not be able to tell which work is by Shostakovich and which by Kabalevsky. . . . The type of melodies used in this so-called new music . . . remind one of the most trivial and dull pseudo-folk-songs of the turn of the nineteenth century. Translated into American terms they represent a cross between the barber-shop quartet and the college song. The style of this music is . . . practically devoid of counterpoint.

And Nabokov produced an "*index prohibitorum*" showing what compositions could and could not be performed. For Shostakovich, the "accepted" works included the First, Fifth, and Seventh Symphonies; "rejected" were the Fourth and Ninth Symphonies and *Lady Macbeth*; the Eighth Symphony was acceptable but "rarely performed." A related Nabokov discourse—reflecting modernist discomfort with unadulterated vernacular sources—criticized "sentimental" appropriations. "Folklore is good in its place, but at the present time progressive contemporary composers well realize how unendurable is music based almost entirely on folk themes. . . . It is difficult to find fresh folk sources."

Vincent Giroud, in his Nabokov biography of 2015, observes: "Nabokov had established himself as an authoritative voice on the question of the state of Soviet music. Easily dismissed by some people as excessive and biased when he first expressed them in 1941, . . . those views seemed to be vindicated in the climate of the Cold War, especially after Stalin and Zhdanov . . . launched an unprecedented attack on the arts."[20] How credible is Nabokov's assessment of the Zhdanov legacy today? The years 1946 to 1953 truly marked a ruthless crackdown. Yet, notwithstanding Nabokov's "General Motors" metaphor, and despite *Song of the Forests*, there was never a Shostakovich assembly line. Nor was he ever a featureless "oyster." Boris Schwarz, in the first significant Western history of *Musical Life in the Soviet Russia* (1972), finds versatility a Shostakovich keynote. A people's composer, a Soviet composer, a victim of edicts, a searcher for fresh expressive currents, he is as elusive as the provenance of his public pronouncements. "I consider that every artist who isolates himself from the world is doomed," Shostakovich told the *New York Times* in 1931.

I find it incredible that an artist should want to shut himself away from the people who, in the end, form his audience. I think an artist should serve the greatest possible number of people. I always try to make myself understood as widely as possible, and, if I don't succeed, I consider it my own fault. . . .

There can be no music without ideology. . . . We, as revolutionaries, have a different conception of music. Lenin himself said that "music is a means of unifying broad masses of people. It is not a leader of masses, perhaps, but certainly an organizing force! For music has the power of stirring specific emotions. . . . Music is no longer an end in itself, but a vital weapon in the struggle.[21]

What, then, to make of Shostakovich's much-criticized self-criticism? The Fourth Symphony, which occupied Shostakovich both before and after the *Pravda* attack, makes no concessions to "broad masses of people." Its themes do not repeat. Its forms are inscrutable. The premiere, scheduled for December 1936, was canceled after ten rehearsals. An announcement explained that the symphony "in no way corresponds to [Shostakovich's] current creative convictions and represents for him a long-outdated creative phase." A year earlier, Shostakovich was quoted saying, "I am not afraid of difficulties. It is perhaps easier, and certainly safer, to follow a beaten path, but it is also dull, uninteresting and futile."[22] The Fifth Symphony, with memorable themes and standard forms, triumphed in 1937. In 1961 the Fourth was finally heard. Today, both symphonies are frequently performed—and the Fourth remains challenging.

If nothing like the Fourth Symphony was produced by Shostakovich during the five frigid years between Zhdanov's resolution and Stalin's death, his monumental cycle of Twenty-Four Preludes and Fugues (1950–51), however "conservative," is neither political nor (as his critics—including on this occasion Kabalevsky and Khrennikov—observed)[23] socialist realist. His First Violin Concerto (1947–48) wound up in a drawer, as did the Fourth String Quartet (1949); both were premiered after Stalin's death. Another, deeper, drawer contained *Anti-formalist Rayok*, a subversive cantata wickedly ridiculing the party's 1948 music resolution. Shostakovich's subsequent output ranged from the cartoon capers of the Second Piano Concerto (1957) to the morbid Fourteenth Symphony (1969) and a valedictory Viola Sonata (1975). With the end of Soviet rule, newly accessed Soviet music archives added another layer of Shostakovich complexity: his dedicated and influential role in the adjudication of lucrative Stalin Music Prizes. It turns out that, to a surprising degree, authority within the cultural bureaucracy was as much exercised from the bottom up as from the top down. In the United States, autonomous composers were satellites occupying the outskirts of the nation's cultural life. If Shostakovich was more confined, he could also be more empowered. These perspectives on totalitarian culture were unglimpsed by the Cold Warriors Kennedy, Schlesinger, and Nabokov.

In sum, Nicolas Nabokov's writings portrayed Dmitri Shostakovich as a Soviet musical ideologue of modest creative capacity. Not only did Nabokov underestimate and misrepresent Shostakovich's compositional output; he did not remotely glean the tightrope act that sets Shostakovich apart from all previous composers of comparable stature. In his 1931 *New York Times* interview, Shostakovich predicted: "Soviet music will probably develop along different lines than any the world has ever known."[24] From an early age, he was a world-class Russian composer invested in a lineage beginning with Bach and Beethoven. At the same time, he was an artistic patriot committed to serving a mass audience. And he necessarily navigated a doctrinal labyrinth that in various ways facilitated or obscured his goals.

Chapters 5 and 6 will explore the unusual "survival strategies" Shostakovich devised and the state responsibilities, also unusual, he resented or enjoyed. But first, to complete our overview of Nabokov's anti-Soviet activities, we must assay his considerable presence on the public stage.

CHAPTER 4

CIA CULTURAL BATTLEGROUNDS

New York and Paris

RED VISITORS CAUSE RUMPUS

In New York City last weekend a strange furor surrounded the Waldorf-Astoria Hotel. Inside was gathered an oddly assorted group of thinkers from all over the world. Outside milled a loud and angry group of pickets, proclaiming that the proceedings were strictly pro-Communist propaganda. Between the picketing and the chance to see some real live visitors from behind the Iron Curtain things were really in an uproar.

The lead story in *Life* magazine, on April 4, 1949, festooned with photos, reported the gaudiest political pageant in anyone's memory: a "Cultural and Scientific Conference for World Peace." According to *Life*, "It was an outgrowth of the cultural conference of 1948 in Wroclaw, Poland—at which the US writer and artist were described as producing 'disgusting filth' marred by the dollar sign." The New York conference, coinciding with the final weeks of the Berlin airlift, was hosted by the National Council of Arts, Sciences, and Professions, a group "dominated by intellectuals who fellow-travel the Communist line." The foreign guests included a contingent of Russians, among whom Dmitri Shostakovich was the "star of the show."

There was no doubt that [the conference] had been engineered by Americans who knew exactly what they were doing—i.e., providing a sounding board for Communist propaganda. Every time the Russian delegation stood up it got a tremendous ovation. But among the speakers were many gentle souls, a little bewildered by the world outside their laboratories or textbooks, who were sincerely looking for world peace and who embarrassed the fellow travelers mightily by putting at least half the blame for the Cold War on the Russians.

Fifty head shots of "DUPES AND FELLOW TRAVELERS" came next.

> These are the prominent people who wittingly or not, associated themselves with a Communist-front organization and thereby lent it glamor, prestige and the respectability of American liberalism. . . . [They ranged] from hard-working fellow travelers to soft-headed do-gooders who have persistently lent their names to organizations labeled by the US Attorney General or other government agencies as subversive. . . . Some of them were receptive to shrewd Communist persuasiveness. Some in high positions stubbornly ignored their critics in the honest belief that there would eventually be a meeting of minds. Still others cynically pursued a personal ambition thinking that the Communists could help them along in their careers. Not a few became so notorious that they were accused of being actual members of the party. Some of those pictured here publicly and sincerely repudiate Communism but this does not alter the fact that they are of great use to the Communist cause.

Those pictured included the composer Aaron "Copeland," the composer/conductor Leonard Bernstein, and the African American conductor Dean Dixon (who subsequently secured a career in Central Europe when American orchestras proved unwelcoming). Outside music, the dupes and travelers included Charlie Chaplin, Albert Einstein, Lillian Hellman, Langston Hughes, Norman Mailer, Thomas Mann, Arthur Miller, and Adam Clayton Powell. Shostakovich was pictured lighting a cigarette with closed eyes and taut features. Another photograph showed a picket brandishing a sign reading: "SHOSTAKOVICH! JUMP THRU THE WINDOW!"—in reference (a caption explained) to Oksana Kasenkina, who leaped to freedom from a Russian Consulate window in 1948.

   This lavish magazine spectacle was itself a specimen of the Cold War propaganda manufactured by *Life*'s monarchic publisher/editor, Henry Luce. (The same issue included an editorial deploring the American decision "to write off China as a total loss," rather than "strengthening our fringe positions of the coast of Asia, as General Douglas MacArthur so strongly recommended to Washington three months ago.") Equally typical of Cold War dogma is that the justice of Luce's claims and judgments remains elusive—they can neither be written off nor wholly substantiated. "International peace conferences," in 1949, were a Soviet propaganda ruse portraying the United States, with its atomic bomb and North Atlantic Treaty Organization, as a warmonger. At the

1948 World Congress of Intellectuals in Defense of Peace, in Wrocław, Poland, a closing resolution claimed that the governments of England and the United States were planning a world coup. The Russians in attendance included the novelist Alexander Fadeyev, who called American writers "jackals" and "hyenas," and claimed the United States was planning an atomic attack on the Soviet Union; he would lead the Russian delegation to New York in 1949. The Soviet Cominform—an alliance of European Communist parties supervised by Moscow—played an active role. The same was true of a subsequent peace conference in Paris in April 1949.

Was the Waldorf Astoria peace conference a kindred event? The organizers were Americans, led by the Harvard astronomer Harlow Shapley. Shapley traveled on the Left. He had attended the Wrocław conference. But he insisted that his National Council of Arts, Sciences, and Professions was independent even of the U.S. Progressive Party. He told Secretary of State Dean Acheson, "Our conference is not related in any way whatever to conferences that have been held elsewhere or that are being planned." In another letter, he conceded that "those who seek malice" could allege "pro-Soviet sympathies." And he maintained that the Soviet delegation was selected by the Soviets themselves, not his National Council. When he learned who was coming, he understood the stakes. "[This] suddenly gives our Conference a high significance," he wrote to a British scientific colleague. "I cannot believe that Fadeev [sic] will mess things up the way he did in Poland. Of course, much of our press, and some of our Government, will look on this whole matter as peace 'offensive,' or some political trick. But the hell with them!"[1] It is widely reported that Stalin himself phoned Shostakovich and instructed him to go to New York—and that Shostakovich had the nerve to point out that his music was banned in the Soviet Union. Stalin rescinded the ban, and Shostakovich joined Fadeyev and six other delegates on the flight to America. Given his controversial American fame, Shostakovich's presence at the Waldorf was bound to matter greatly. It bears stressing that Shapley could neither anticipate nor control what happened next—and neither could anyone else.

The conference lasted three days. At the opening dinner, in a packed grand ballroom, the speakers included Norman Cousins of the *Saturday Review of Literature*. He had been invited by Shapley to offer an "opposing perspective." Shapley presumably expected Cousins to reiterate his opposition to the atomic bomb. Instead, he told the assemblage that the government of the United States did not seek war. Democracies, he added, "protect the individual against the right of the state to draw the blueprints for its painters and writers and composers." This provoked boos and hisses. Lillian Hellmann—a celebrated playwright loudly on the Left—remarked: "I would recommend, Mr. Cousins, that when you talk about your hosts at dinner, wait until you have gone home to do it."[2]

But Shostakovich was already the center of attention. A blue-ribbon selection of American-based musicians had cabled him beforehand to "welcome you as one of the outstanding composers of the world" and express hope that "your visit will serve to symbolize the bond which music can create among all peoples." (Stravinsky, who conspicuously refused to sign, stated: "All my ethic and aesthetic convictions oppose such gesture.")[3] Shostakovich told the opening night delegates, "We are united. . . . in the noble task of defending the peace." The panel topics the next day included education, religion, ethics, and economics. Dwight Macdonald confronted Fadeyev by asking about the fate of certain Russian writers—were they alive or dead? "Alive," Fadeyev snapped. Robert Lowell adopted a different tone: "My heart goes out to Mr. Shostakovich. I would like to ask him how many writers and musicians have benefited by the criticism of his government?" Speaking quickly, Shostakovich replied (through an interpreter): "Our musical criticism is a reflection of the life and movement of our music. It brings us much good, since it helps bring my music forward." He was generally perceived as a man in distress.

The music panel the next day was the most noticed and discussed. Olin Downes, the *New York Times'* chief music critic, was moderator. Speaking to Shostakovich directly, he said many Americans found the Seventh and Eighth Symphonies expressions of the battle of "our two nations" against Hitler—and also that he personally considered both works "too long."

Aaron Copland delivered an address titled "The Effect of the Cold War on the Artist in the United States." Copland had paid his dues as a fellow traveler. He began by declaring: "Nobody told me what to say." He nonetheless believed that American foreign policy could lead to a third world war. He repudiated American attitudes that transformed "the very word 'peace' into a dirty word" and argued that American hostility had prompted the Soviet Union to officially adopt "a disapproving attitude toward much contemporary art, and especially in the field of music." He urged Americans to reject a binary mind-set postulating "two diametrically opposed systems of thought." He believed the impact of the Cold War stunted creativity by provoking "fear and anxiety," "ill-will and dread"; artistic achievement demanded "real faith." Calling upon the United States and Soviet Union to pursue friendly cultural relations, Copland welcomed Shostakovich's visit as a positive step.

Shostakovich's own music panel speech totaled more than five thousand words. Its fiery rhetoric was delivered by an interpreter while the putative author sat silent and inscrutable, his features twitching, his fingers twisting the tip of a cigarette. Countering "lies" spread by "enemies of democracy," Shostakovich proposed a picture of Soviet dedication to ideals of "peace, progress, and democracy." Meanwhile, the United States had perfected "weapons for mass destruction" and built military bases "thousands of miles from their frontiers." As for Soviet composers, they pursued a "harmonious, truthful, and optimistic concept of the world." Though his own efforts had sometimes strayed from "intimate contact with the life of my people," his ongoing "search for a great theme" would, he pledged, be newly pursued. Prokofiev, too, would benefit from constructive direction. But Stravinsky, abroad, was a lost cause. Captive to "reactionary modern musicians," he had "betrayed his native land." Detached from a popular base and high political ideals, his music was "morally barren."

That evening, at Madison Square Garden, Shostakovich performed for eighteen thousand people—the only live music of the conference. Four spotlights illuminated an elevated grand piano in the center of the sports arena. Shostakovich chose to play a piano transcription of the five-minute Scherzo from his most popular symphony: the Fifth. The ambience was reverent. A standing ovation sealed the occasion—and clinched Shostakovich's participation as the weekend's central event.[4]

During the following two weeks, the Soviet visitors were to undertake a national "peace" tour. But the State Department decided that it was time for them to leave. Among the canceled visits was one to Yale University—whose president, Charles Seymour, found "no educational value in opening the university halls to such a meeting."[5] Shostakovich and his colleagues headed home April 3—one week after the Waldorf conference ended. What Shostakovich actually thought of what he said in New York, or was said for him, remained and remains unknowable. (The text of his music panel speech has been traced to two articles in *Soviet Music* and a speech by Tikhon Khrennikov.)[6] But his response to this first visit to the United States (there would be two more) was reasonably unambiguous. He found America crude. An object of controversy from the moment he landed, he had been greeted by shouting reporters calling out "Shosty!" Outside the sanctum of his hotel, he was thronged by aroused anti-Soviet demonstrators. He found Carnegie Hall, where he attended a program of Russian and American music, big and unbeautiful—and Manhattan the same. "People dash about as if in a state of frenzy," he told a Soviet reporter afterward. "Everybody is rushing somewhere." Shopping for recordings and cigarettes, he was shocked to discover classics of world literature repackaged as "thin booklets in which, of all the amazing wealth of ideas and sentiments, only the love scenes are left in." *Anna Karenina* had been "reduced to thirty-two pages and supplied with a colorful pornographic cover."[7]

If Shostakovich also retained favorable impressions of the United States, he would hardly have dared to share them. Two decades later, he reportedly told Solomon Volkov: "The typical Western journalist is an uneducated, obnoxious, and profoundly cynical person. He needs to make money and he doesn't give a damn about the rest. Every one of these pushy guys wants me to answer his stupid questions 'daringly' and these gentlemen take offense when they don't hear what they want." He also said:

> I still recall with horror my first trip to the U.S.A. I wouldn't have gone at all if it hadn't been for intense pressure from administrative figures of all ranks and colors, from Stalin down. People sometimes say that it must have been an interesting trip, look at the way I'm smiling in the photographs. That was the smile of a condemned man. I felt like a dead man. I answered all the idiotic questions in a daze, and thought, When I get back it's over for me. Stalin liked leading Americans by the nose that way. He would show them a man—here he is, alive and well—and then kill him. It cost me a lot, that trip, I had to answer stupid questions and keep from saying too much. They made a sensation out of that too. And all I thought about was: How much longer do I have to live?[8]

*   *   *

The foregoing account tells half the story of the Cultural and Scientific Conference for World Peace. The other half, equally tendentious, was a counterconference. This anti-Communist uprising, both spontaneous and planned, had a chief engineer: Sidney Hook, professor of philosophy at New York University. A squat forty-seven-year-old Jewish agnostic with spectacles and a black mustache, Hook is pertinent to our story for two reasons. The first is that, like Nicolas Nabokov, he was a prime participant in the Congress for Cultural Freedom. The second is that he was in every way Nabokov's adversarial antipode: not an aristocratic cosmopolite, but an erudite street fighter as likely to cite Aquinas or Kant as Engels or Trotsky; not an exile, but the certified product of a polyglot Brooklyn slum; not a lifelong enemy of Lenin and Stalin, but a reformed Marxist, trained in New York City, Berlin, and Moscow, who intimately knew the American Communist Party and its acolytes.

Hook had already formed a Committee for Cultural Freedom in collaboration with his mentor, John Dewey. This was in 1939, in response to Stalin's sudden pact with Hitler. He raged against the leftist Popular Front, whose organizations in his opinion "dominated the cultural, literary, and in part the academic landscape" in the United States. A manifesto, issued May 15, 1939, read in part:

> The tide of totalitarianism is rising throughout the world. It is washing away cultural and creative freedom along with other expressions of independent human

reason. Never before in modern times has the integrity of the writer, the artist, the scientist and the scholar been threatened so seriously. . . . Art, science and education—all have been forcibly turned into lackeys for a supreme state, a deified leader and an official pseudo-philosophy. . . . The results have been sterility, an enslaved intellectual life, a tragic caricature of culture.[9]

Curiously, the 151 signatories included a single musician: New York University music professor Felix Robert Mendelssohn. Few creative artists signed, and none were big names. Hook's refusal to call Nazi Germany a greater evil than Communist Russia was (as ever) a red cape. Dwight Macdonald responded with a counterorganization, the League for Cultural Freedom and Socialism, that decreed "the liberation of culture . . . inseparable from the liberation of the working classes and of all humanity."[10] In point of fact, Hook's early postulation of a doctrine of "cultural freedom" was already empirically unsupportable: whatever one may make of the arts of the Third Reich (including the films of Leni Riefenstahl), Lenin's Soviet Union, while totalitarian, cannot plausibly be characterized as culturally "sterile" or a "tragic caricature of culture." (I deal with music under Lenin in chapter 7.)

Ten years later, at the Waldorf, Hook created yet another anti-Communist organ, Americans for Intellectual Freedom, and set up headquarters in the tenth-floor bridal suite. Its rotating occupants, plotting tactics and assigning duties, comprised a battalion of prominent anti-Stalin intellectuals, including Nicolas Nabokov, already the author of nine magazine articles scorching Soviet culture; Schlesinger, who as usual found Hook's anti-Communism disagreeably obsessive; and David Dubinsky, president of the Ladies' Garment Workers Union, who—interestingly—paid the bills in coordination with the CIA's Frank Wisner. The floor was strewn with telephone cords. The air was dense with cigarette smoke. One of the bathrooms was preempted by a mimeograph machine spewing press releases, some of which, according to William Phillips of *Partisan Review*, deployed "questionable tactics, such as intercepting mail and messages and issuing misleading statements in the name of the conference."[11]

Hook's counterconference amassed more than two hundred distinguished supporters, including such international luminaries as Igor Stravinsky, Benedetto Croce, T. S. Eliot, André Malraux, Bertrand Russell, and Albert Schweitzer (who at the same time lent his name to Harlow Shapley's event). Hook compared Soviet Communism to Hitler's fascism. He called the Waldorf conference a "fraud," a "sounding board for Communist propaganda." He insisted that he had been denied permission to speak by Shapley—and to press that claim, he forced entry into Shapley's hotel room, bringing along a reporter from the *Herald-Tribune* (he did not trust the *Times*). Shapley managed to coax Hook into the corridor, then locked him out—a conference vignette that made page 1 of the *Herald-Tribune* and was considered "hilarious" by *Life*.[12] Meanwhile, the counterdemonstrators on the street—variously chanting, singing, and praying—numbered as many as two thousand, including contingents from the American Legion, the Jewish War Veterans, the People's Committee for the Freedom of Religion, and Gold Star Mothers. The signage included GO BACK TO RUSSIA WHERE YOU BELONG and YOU CAN'T HAVE CULTURE WITHOUT FREEDOM.

Thirty-eight years later, at the age of eighty-four, Hook published a six-hundred-page autobiography, *Out of Step: An Unquiet Life in the 20th Century*. It is a basic-training manual for those who would equate Cold War anti-Communism with McCarthyism. Documenting a political underworld of ideology and deceit, Hook cites tactics and names names. Secret former members of the Communist Party, Hook wrote, "remained blackmailable; they could be relied upon in a pinch to spike an embarrassing revelation . . . or play up a story discrediting critics of Communists, out of fear of being exposed." He fingered, among other examples, the education editor of the *New York Times*.[13] At the same time, Hook was a lifelong socialist, and his story equally illuminates a variety of chronic leftist grievances with U.S. government policies: the Palmer "red raids" after World War I, the Great Depression as a casualty of capitalist economics, ongoing State Department restrictions on visas and cultural exchange, and the perennial injustice of Jim Crow.

Out of Step dedicates an entire chapter to the 1949 Waldorf Astoria peace conference, and a full paragraph to belittling Nicolas Nabokov's "misleading" account of the same event in *Bagazh*—which reads in part: "Many of us objected to the way Sidney Hook ordered, or at least tried to order, some of us around, telling us what to do where and at what time. But the ultimate PR and press success of our sabotage operation was largely due to his efficient handling of our inchoate and heterogeneous, but intellectually enlightened group of protestors."[14] As he would on subsequent occasions, Hook found Nabokov's participation irrelevant and self-serving.

Because he "scrupulously refrained from attending any of the sessions at the Waldorf," Hook neither witnessed nor reported Nabokov's much-noticed debut on the public stage—his interrogation of Shostakovich in response to the latter's ideologically inflamed mega-address. Speaking in Russian and English, Nabokov stated that a recent *Pravda* article denounced Hindemith, Schoenberg, and Stravinsky as "obscurantists," "decadent bourgeois formalists," and "lackeys of imperialism" whose music deserved to be banned in Soviet Russia. "Does Mr. Shostakovich personally agree with this official view as printed in *Pravda*?" Shostakovich replied that he agreed with *Pravda* about Hindemith and Stravinsky." And Schoenberg, too? asked Nabokov. Schoenberg, too, said Shostakovich. Nabokov was ferociously booed. Arthur Miller, who was on the dais, later wrote that the "memory of Shostakovich . . . still haunts my mind. God knows what he was thinking—what urge to cry out and what self-control to suppress his outcry lest he lend comfort to America and her new belligerence toward his country, the very one that was making his life a hell."[15]

As Nabokov surely anticipated, Shostakovich was no stranger to public self-control—his response was precisely the helpless acknowledgment of Soviet regimentation that Nabokov sought to provoke. Should Nabokov have done it? Opinions differ.[16] But what enabled him to humiliate a foreign colleague is easily understood: Nabokov so underestimated and depersonalized Shostakovich that he had rendered himself immune to heartlessness. In various writings and speeches during or recalling the events in New York, Nabokov more regarded Shostakovich as an invulnerable symbol than a human artist. He likened him to "dirty laundry . . . thrown in a clothes hamper, then suddenly picked up, washed, ironed out, and sent to America." He said, "We do not point at him an accusing finger. We know that he is not free to choose freedom and we understand that." He characterized Shostakovich's Waldorf speech as "part of a punishment, part of a ritual redemption he had to go through before he could be pardoned again. He was to tell, in person, . . . that he . . . is not a free man, but an obedient tool of his government." As in his writings, Nabokov's rare expressions of empathy for Shostakovich were patronizing: "No one . . . could help but feel compassion for the young and timid artist, and feel an overpowering wish to take him by the arm and lead him out of the clatter . . . into a quiet place, far and safe from the realities of the political world."[17]

Judging from the ovations Shostakovich received, and from his general treatment in the American press, Miller's haunted reaction to Shostakovich's contorted public persona was far more prevalent than Nabokov's clinical dissections. Sympathy for Shostakovich at the Waldorf was not a pro-Soviet phenomenon; it was a spontaneous response to the unknown man, newly glimpsed, behind the well-known symphonies. It could not have been planned or predicted, whether by Nabokov or Shapley or Hook.

One prevalent view was a pure manifestation of American Cold War "cultural freedom" dogma—that Shostakovich would be best off defecting to the United States. This was the gist of the placards urging that he jump out a window. The same advice was more humanely rendered by the eminent educational theorist George Counts, who appealed to Shostakovich to "seek sanctuary in a land that has so often opened its doors to the persecuted." Richard McCann, president of the New York musicians' union, opined that in America Shostakovich's "genius would flower" as it never had abroad.[18] That a composer whose artistic lifeblood was wholly Russian, who took his cues from a vast populace with whom he identified from birth, whose vigorous participation in the musical life of a nation, however vexed by the next Zhdanov or Khrennikov, was a necessary part of his calling should detach himself from every artistic mooring was a logical consequence of the "free artist" doctrine preached by Nabokov. It exposes the naïveté of free-world cultural propaganda as irrefutably as the Berlin Wall would crush the myth of a Soviet "German Democratic Republic."

*   *   *

Whatever one makes of the chaos of impressions inflicted by the Waldorf Astoria peace conference, they coherently dramatized the ideological moment. They also dramatized a need for American counterpropaganda, covert or overt. In fact, the CIA was already there. So, more predictably, was the Federal Bureau of Investigation.

Along the conference's anti-anti-Communist political spectrum of true believers, fellow travelers, and "dupes," one extreme was embodied by Clifford Odets, who denounced suggestions that Soviet Russia threatened world peace as "one of the greatest frauds ever perpetrated on the American people."[19] An illuminating middle ground was occupied by another prominent playwright: Arthur Miller, who years later recorded impressions additional to his haunted memory of the tense Shostakovich "stiffly erect as a doll." There was "simply no question," Miller wrote in 1987, "that without Soviet resistance Nazism would have conquered all of Europe as well as Britain. . . . Thus, the sharp post-war turn against the Soviets and in favor of a German unpurged of Nazis not only seemed ignoble, but threatened another war that might indeed destroy Russia but bring down our own democracy as well."[20]

Such gradations of opinion, however fascinating to historians, were less consequential to J. Edgar Hoover's Federal Bureau of Investigation. Miller's FBI file dated back to the 1930s. Other files were newly opened—including one for the twenty-six-year-old Norman Mailer, whose conference address, attacking both sides, was so intense that he broke into a sweat. To what extent the FBI may have played a role in impeding the professional activities of those it surveilled would become a topic of strident speculation. The CIA's presence, however, remained unknown.

In addition to its bridal suite office at the Waldorf, Sidney Hook's American Intellectuals for Freedom had commandeered the aptly named "Freedom House" not far away. The small hall was packed for a Sunday-night counter-conference meeting at which Nabokov was one of the speakers. The audience so overflowed into the street that an entire block was roped off, with loud-speakers set up on the Freedom House balcony. Afterward, Nabokov noticed a familiar face in the back row. "It was an acquaintance of mine from Berlin who, like me, had worked for OMGUS [the American military government in occupied Germany]. He congratulated me warmly. 'This is a splendid affair you and your friends have organized,' he said. 'We should have something like this in Berlin.'"[21] The acquaintance, conspicuously unnamed in this passage from Nabokov's autobiography, was Michael Josselson, whose employer in a matter of months would become the Central Intelligence Agency. Within three years, he would emerge as the undisputed administrative head of the Congress for Cultural Freedom.

Born in Estonia in 1908, Josselson spoke four languages without an accent. He and his parents fled Estonia in 1917 and resettled in Germany. In Berlin he acquired a German cultural base during a period of dynamic artistic ferment. He called the Philharmonic's Arthur Nikisch "the dean and forerunner of all the great German conductors." He knew Berlin's vibrant Russian expatriate community. He enrolled at the University of Berlin to pursue a history degree but ran out of money. At the age of twenty, he took a job with Gimbel's, the American department store—which was also a major sponsor of fine art. By 1937 he was in Paris, in charge of all Gimbel's European purchases. He next fled France (he was Jewish), immigrated to the United States, and in 1942 became an American citizen. A year later, he was stationed abroad in the army (and would never again reside in the United States). At OMGUS Nicolas Nabokov and Melvin Lasky—later perhaps his closest CCF associates—became friends and colleagues. It was in collaboration with Nabokov, at OMGUS, that Jossel-son facilitated the denazification of the conductor Wilhelm Furtwängler—an episode that revealed in them both a flexibility of purpose and cultural un-derstanding not always compatible with ideological combat. Others at OM-GUS, American born, lobbied for harsher treatment of the eminent German conductor, who while staying on at the helm of the Berlin Philharmonic had never joined the Nazi Party. The Soviets' "almost fanatical worship of art and artists, paired with the belief that artistic activity in itself was good and nec-essary for the people in times of uncertainty and suffering" was observed by OMGUS bureaucrats with passivity. Bonded by their love of music, Josselson and Nabokov would enjoy ample opportunity to reshape American cultural policy abroad. It bears adding that neither of them embraced American culture as they did their European intellectual roots; Josselson was later observed by a CIA colleague "fighting against his need to like America and his instinctive dislike of much of what he saw."[22]

The "something like this in Berlin" that Josselson had anticipated in New York materialized in 1950. So effective had been Sidney Hook's raucous counterconference in 1949 that afterward the Cominform was perceived to reemphasize its focus on Western European artists and intellectuals susceptible to Stalinism. The next "peace conference," in Paris in April 1949, featured Paul Robeson singing "Old Man River." Picasso's *Dove of Peace* was appropriated as an insignia. Charlie Chaplin sent a message of support. Again, a counterconference was produced with CIA patronage—but seemed ineffective in the face of French opinion. "The French public, by and large, is shockingly ignorant of American life and culture," reported Hook, who was there. "Its picture of America is a composite of impressions derived from reading the novels of social protest and revolt (Steinbeck's *Grapes of Wrath* is taken as a faithful and *representative* account), the novels of American degeneracy (Faulkner) and inanity (Sinclair Lewis), from seeing American movies, and from exposure to an incessant Communist barrage which seeps into the non-Communist press."[23] Four months later, the Soviet Union successfully tested an atomic bomb.

This was the backdrop against which Josselson and other major players on the non-Communist Left conceived a Berlin gathering to formulate a definitive propaganda remedy. Their Berlin Congress for Cultural Freedom, quietly guided and supported by the CIA, opened on June 26. Nabokov, Schlesinger, and Hook were among the two hundred delegates. An aggressive tone was conspicuously set by Arthur Koestler, whose *Darkness at Noon* (1940) was a canonic text. The consensus backed Schlesinger's measured tone as a sounder tactic of persuasion. But it was Koestler who composed the fourteen-point Freedom Manifesto adopted by the conference and addressed to "all men who are determined to regain those liberties which they have lost and to preserve and extend those which they enjoy." It stated: "We hold it to be self-evident that intellectual freedom is one of the inalienable rights of man. . . . Such freedom is defined first and foremost by his right to hold and express his own opinions, and particularly opinions which differ from those of his rulers."[24] Koestler's text was notably silent about "free artists"—to become Nabokov's special doctrinal realm. Wisner, at the CIA, offered "heartiest congratulations." General John Magruder, of the Defense Department, hailed "a subtle covert operation carried out on the highest intellectual level."

Wisner proceeded to consolidate the Congress for Cultural Freedom, based in Paris, as a permanent covert propaganda instrument. There would be an executive director, editorial director, research director, Paris Bureau director, and Berlin Bureau director, and—to direct "cultural relations"—a secretary general. Koestler favored a fellow disillusioned ex-Communist, Louis Fischer; their predilection was to launch mass rallies and other frontal assaults on the enemy. Schlesinger and Josselson were among those preferring a "soft sell" approach. They lobbied hard for Nabokov's candidacy for secretary general, as did Chip Bohlen and George Kennan. According to Sidney Hook, who was himself elected to the CCF executive committee:

> After several weeks of correspondence . . . in which among others Arthur Schlesinger took a lively role, Nicolas Nabokov was selected. Sol Levitas, the editor of *The New Leader*, was the only one who expressed strong doubts about the choice. In Nabokov's favor were his European origins and experience as a Russian exile, his linguistic abilities, his status as an intellectual and musical composer in his own right, and his claim, somewhat exaggerated, to be acquainted with almost everybody worth knowing in the literary and cultural world of Europe. It turned out to be a perfect job for Nabokov.

Hook's sentence continued with a caveat not included by Vincent Giroud in his Nabokov biography: " . . . but unfortunately in my view, not for the Congress."[25]

Nabokov had become the impresario of the cultural Cold War—a big job that liberated him from Sarah Lawrence and the Peabody Conservatory. He relocated to Paris in April 1951 and commenced a torrent of activity: lectures and meetings in Brussels, Bordeaux, Oxford, Berlin, Frankfurt, Strasbourg, and Rome. A CCF coup, stage-managed by Nabokov, was the defection from Communist Poland of Czesław Miłosz, who would win the Nobel Prize for literature in 1980. And Nabokov in 1951 helped to launch a Paris-based CCF journal, *Preuves* (Proof), poised to compete with Jean-Paul Sartre, Simone de Beauvoir, and other Left Bank intellectuals for whom the United States was a capitalist cultural wasteland.

Meanwhile, Nabokov's articles on Soviet music, always propagandistic in tone, continued apace. His *Saturday Review* piece "Festivals and the Twelve-Tone Row" (January 13, 1951) included observations lifted from the CCF playbook:

> Europeans, chiefly continental Europeans, are as everybody knows extremely proud of their great cultural tradition and today cannot envisage the possibility of losing leadership in this realm. Uneasiness on this score is one of the sources of irritation with America and of their sometimes ironic, despondent, self-conscious, and even violently inimical attitude towards America. It is also one of the reasons why it is so difficult for Americans to find a modus operandi with European intellectuals and establish an active, working partnership. . . .
>
> A number of European musicians have suggested to me that Stravinsky's, Bartók's, or even Schoenberg's music deteriorated after these composers settled in the United States. "Their music has lost some of its meaning, and has become popularized in spirit." What they really imply is that music in the American cul-

tural environment "inevitably" deteriorates; artists are bound, they suggest, to succumb to "mass-production culture" and to cater to "The Tin-Pan Alley taste of the average American." . . .

Whether the characteristic one-sidedness of these Nabokov claims served or weakened their purpose is, as ever, a ponderable question. There can be little debate that Stravinsky, Bartók, and Schoenberg produced their most important music before emigrating to the United States. The reasons, however adduced, have nothing to do with "Tin-Pan Alley taste." Nabokov continues:

> Part of the trouble, lies, of course, in the fact that most Europeans still know very little about America and American culture. . . . Their incomplete or incorrect image has been formed by biased reports, by irresponsible journalism, and last but not least, by anti-American Communist propaganda.
>
> In music, for example, they are unaware of the tremendous change that has occurred in American culture. While in the Twenties American music or, perhaps more correctly, music written in America was ten years behind European music, both ideologically and technically, today the music written in America is completely in step with European developments. In certain respects composers in the United States are in advance of European composers.

However it was processed in 1951, such reasoning cannot be taken seriously today. If after World War I Europeans took a relatively dim view of American composers, it was not because of Communist mind control; the United States self-evidently lacked homegrown composers comparable in stature to Stravinsky, Bartók, and Schoenberg. And the modernist notion of being "behind" or "advanced" is simplistic and arbitrary. Ives and Gershwin were twentieth-century American composers of world stature; both fell outside Nabokov's modernist purview.

It is instructive that when Nabokov's "Music in the Soviet Union"—the *Musical America* lecture (February 1951) climaxing with an *index prohibitorum*—was reprinted in *Revue international de musique*, it provoked a furious rebuttal. The editor, the Sorbonne musicologist Jacques Chailley, announced that "out of a concern for objective information," Nabokov's article had been shared with the Communist "Association des musiciens progressistes" with an invitation to respond. And it is unsurprising that the resulting diatribe, by Jean Prodromides, was even more extreme and less nuanced than Nabokov's screed. That said, Prodromides's claim that Stravinsky, once a "great" Russian composer, had succumbed to a rootless modernism cannot be dismissed as hot air. Prodromides also wrote, prophetically: "Calumniating a people and its artists . . . seems to us extremely grave at a time when misunderstandings between various nations can only increase current tensions. Conversely, the better one knows the culture of a people . . . can only reinforce the possibilities of rapprochement and mutual understating."[26]

When Stravinsky's opera *The Rake's Progress*—the biggest undertaking of his American years—premiered in September 1951, Nabokov wrote a review for *Preuves* hailing "an indisputable masterpiece, whose Mozartian dimensions and lucid beauty have no equal in the lyric theater of the first half of this turbulent century." It bears mentioning that, whether writing for American, French, or British readers, Nabokov was never identified as a member of the Congress for Cultural Freedom secretariat. The CCF was not an underground organization. But from the first, it was viewed with suspicion. And this was especially so in Paris, "the world capital," Nabokov quipped, "of the fellow-travelers."[27]

And so it went—and grew. Funding was often channeled through a dummy front organization: the Farfield Foundation, ostensibly led by Julius "Junkie" Fleischman, heir to a Cincinnati gin fortune and a patron of the arts. The congress would ultimately be active in thirty-five countries and publish more than twenty magazines. All this, in turn, was part of a vast tentacled network of covert operations, an invisible consortium inspired by CIA director Allen Dulles, for whom success depended on appearing "independent from government" and seeming "to represent the spontaneous convictions of freedom loving individuals."[28] Frank Wisner, as the agency's chief of political warfare, liked the analogy of a "Mighty Wurlitzer" organ, capable of playing any propaganda tune he desired. Hugh Wilford bravely extrapolated this overview in his landmark 2008 study:

> For roughly twenty years, ending with the disclosures of 1967, there were three broad phases of front operation mounted by the CIA. . . . First, there were organizations intended to provide a cover for emigres and refugees from the communist-bloc countries, who were viewed as a potential secret army capable of infiltrating and undermining the Soviet empire from within. . . . Then, in rapid succession, came a series of operations [like the CCF] designed to shore up civil society in western Europe against communist destabilization. . . . Finally, as the Cold War began to spread into new theaters in the so-called Third World . . . , the CIA secretly sponsored a host of new programs, often ostensibly concerned with development or modernization.[29]

The fundamental modus vivendi of infiltration was to create mainly unwitting CIA actors, whose anti-Communist zeal furthered American interests without knowledge of CIA oversight and funding. The degree to which such unwitting actors (including Nabokov, if his word can be trusted) were guided remains a perennial topic of dispute. That unintended consequences were part of the bargain cannot be denied; in effect, operatives were permitted to improvise. The coalition included innumerable philanthropic foundations and business corporations. A 1965 study by the CIA itself references funding "a seemingly limitless range of covert action programs affecting youth groups, labor unions, universities, publishing houses, and other private institutions." Of the participating foundations, more than 170 wittingly facilitated CIA funding "passes."[30]

What it all cost can only be guessed. Saunders writes of "tens of millions of dollars" poured into "the Congress for Cultural Freedom and related projects." This included not only government funds made available to the CIA, but agency-linked private funding sources, prominently (but quietly) including the Ford and Rockefeller Foundations. Saunders quotes the CIA's Gilbert Greenway: "We couldn't spend it all. I remember once meeting with Wisner and the comptroller. My God, I said, how can we spend that? There were no limits, and nobody had to account for it. It was amazing." A telling anecdote: C. D. Jackson, who influentially advised the agency on cultural matters, extolled sending the Metropolitan Opera to Europe: "I believe that the Met would wow them. . . . [T]his impact would be absolutely terrific in the capitals of Western Europe, including Berlin." The CIA duly amassed $750,000, mostly from its own funds, to send the Met to Paris in 1966.[31] The visit proved notoriously ill-planned and acidly received. In this instance, Jackson and others at the CIA failed to understand that the Met had less to offer Europeans than performing institutions with a distinctive American stamp, like Leonard Bernstein's New York Philharmonic or George Balanchine's New York City Ballet.

Within the vast CIA Wurlitzer, the CCF functioned as a cultural/intellectual hub. A fortress of learned resistance to Communism, it proved both sophisticated and naive. "Our constant efforts should be directed towards proving to European intellectuals that the Congress for Cultural Freedom is not an American secret service Agency," wrote Nabokov in 1951.[32] In fact, its ties to the U.S. government were at all times widely suspected. Nabokov's particular role was multifarious. Among the most publicly prominent CCF activities were conferences and festivals that he organized. "Science and Freedom," in Hamburg in 1953, and "The Future of Freedom," in Milan in 1955, were esteemed even by Sidney Hook: "At these meetings there was a proper fusion of cultural and political positions in that the focal opposition between the free and totalitarian minds was central to the discussion."[33] Nabokov's impresario feats included the creation of a chamber orchestra, the Philharmonia Hungarica, composed of musicians who had fled the Soviet takeover of Hungary—a group provincial in comparison to Rudolf Barshai's much-traveled Moscow Chamber Orchestra, but of international prominence nonetheless. More enduring were the careers of the African American opera stars Leontyne Price and Shirley Verrett, both vigorously promoted by Nabokov—whose mandate called for counteracting Communist accusations of American racism. Price was virtually unknown as a recitalist (but had taken part in Virgil Thomson's *Four Saints in Three Acts* and Gershwin's *Porgy and Bess*) when she was cast by Nabokov to sing Henri Sauguet's *La voyante* and Samuel Barber's *Hermit Songs*, as well as taking part in *Four Saints* and the third act of Lou Harrison's chamber opera *Rapunzel*.

All four assignments were for Nabokov's single most conspicuous undertaking, the monthlong 1952 Paris festival "L'oeuvre du vingtieme siècle," called in the United States "Masterpieces of the Twentieth Century." As it directly implemented the Cold War premise that only "free societies" and "free artists" foster great art, this most ambitious, most contested manifestation of Nabokov's tenure, then and now an acknowledged milestone in the early history of the CCF, rewards close attention.

* * *

To what extent the Paris festival was a considered act of cultural propaganda, and to what extent an impetuous opportunity, lavishly bankrolled, to celebrate the arts is an appropriate question. Its purpose was framed by Nabokov as follows: "No ideological polemic about the validity and meaning of free culture can equal the products of this culture itself. Let the great works of our century speak for themselves. They alone can stimulate our faith in a free civilization and provide us with a living positive example of what the imagination of free men was able to achieve in the first half of our century." That is: only artworks fostered by "free societies" qualified for designation as "great works." While this characteristic assertion recapitulates the ideological thrust of magazine pieces Nabokov had been writing for ten years, its source—a four-page "introduction" to the festival, published in the April issue of *La revue musicale*—furnishes a kind of Rosetta stone denied his American readers. Nabokov's argument here, amplified in various unpublished writings, specifically (and only) applies to the opening modernist decades of the twentieth century, in which he perceives a "great Renaissance of Western music" enfolding "all of Europe" and transcending "nationalistic chauvinism or parochialism." The antithesis of Soviet totalitarian "provincialism," it embodies a "united front," a free, unrestrained exchange of musical influence. Experimental, innovative, open, it was "distanced from politics." Its signature achievement was the cosmopolitanism of Stravinsky. True, Stravinsky's neoclassicism had its critics and enemies. But an "assimilation of dissonance" was universally discovered and explored. Stravinsky, at the apex, specialized in new ways of using rhythm.

Nabokov buttresses this sanguine perspective by applauding the advent of radio and recordings as well as increased international travel. "Everywhere we find exchange and mutual influence. The hobbling spirit which had, more than once, led musicians towards the national, or even the nationalist, in the nineteenth century has, like it or not, given way to universalism." Scanning the festival repertoire, he observes "freedom to experiment, freedom to express oneself, freedom to choose one's own *maitres* and make one's own decisions, to choose irony or naivete, the esoteric or the familiar." And he adds, incredibly: "In the coming festival . . . there is scarcely a piece that does not owe its character, its soul even, to the fact of being the music of men who know the value of freedom."[34]

A second Rosetta stone of sorts is an eleven-page planning document, "not for publication," dated July 20, 1951.[35] Here, Nabokov attempts to frame the "general purpose" of his Paris festival. He begins with a series of scattered assertions. The "first half of this century" produced "an abundant crop of masterpieces whose essential characteristic was their great variety both in form and in content." This gambit ventures timidly toward a resounding assertion, that the pertinent artists "have as never before been painstakingly seeking and in many instances establishing a just relation between the artist and society"—but this hardly fits many a modernist. Next: "For the first time in history mass audiences have been attracted to the concert hall and to the picture gallery." "Counties which previously had only sporadically participated in the growth of Western art have . . . developed an intense artistic life of their own." Could this be Spain? Great Britain? The United States? "The art of the 20th century grew out of the stimulus of the modern metropolis, and thus gained a spirit of internationalism and became truly cosmopolitan." "At the same time, this century has witnessed a violent reaction against and the persecution of the free creative spirit of man." It is all a futile attempt, ex post facto, to construct intellectual scaffolding around an idée fixe hammered home, sans scaffolding, in the eventual program book: "The finest achievements of western civilization . . .—all the abundant riches which the mind of free man has created in the first half of our century—will be combined in a demonstration of the importance of freedom to creative thinking." The festival "will stand as an affirmation of our faith in our culture and as a manifestation of our undying belief that such cultural achievements are possible only in a climate of intellectual freedom."[36]

However parsed, Nabokov's lofty exegesis of "modernist decades" fails coherently to support the grandiose historic scope of the Nabokov/Schlesinger/

Kennedy doctrine that only free societies foster great art. It assumes what it seeks to prove. It was bound to antagonize and confound those for whom it was intended. And it did.

Certainly, the contents of Nabokov's Paris festival, however they were framed and interpreted, were individually impressive.[37] Aside from the Edinburgh Festival (beginning in 1947), the scope and caliber of international musical talent Nabokov managed to assemble in a single world capital, all at once, had no precedent.[38] He brought the Vienna State Opera performing Alban Berg's *Wozzeck* conducted by Karl Böhm and the Royal Opera of Covent Garden performing Benjamin Britten's *Billy Budd* conducted by the composer. Charles Munch and Pierre Monteux led the Boston Symphony. Bruno Walter led the Paris Opera Orchestra (with Kathleen Ferrier in Gustav Mahler's *Song of the Earth*), Ernest Ansermet his Suisse Romande Orchestra, Hans Rosbaud the French Radio/Television Orchestra, Ferenc Fricsay his RIAS Orchestra of West Berlin, and Igor Markevitch the Santa Cecilia Orchestra (with Arturo Benedetti Michelangeli as piano soloist).

Of the ensembles Nabokov showcased, George Balanchine's New York City Ballet was allotted six programs. By far the composer most feted was Stravinsky: twelve performances in all, including four works conducted by the composer: *Oedipus Rex* (with Jean Cocteau as narrator), *Capriccio* for piano and orchestra, the Symphony in C, and the Symphony in Three Movements.

Also included were the literary and visual arts. Of three "literary conferences," "Diversity and Universality" extolled "free inquiry and free expression . . . only our creative liberty tends to the universal."[39] Here, William Faulkner was the prize attraction—for propaganda purposes, an anomaly (he objected to being housed in the same hotel as the black cast of *Four Saints*).[40] The CCF art exhibit was entrusted to James Johnson Sweeney, former curator of the Museum of Modern Art. It, too, was anomalous, the favored painter being Pablo Picasso, who happened to be a Communist. Even more strangely, America's abstract expressionists were out of the picture. Yet, as countless books and articles have subsequently argued, the CIA was a pronounced behind-the-scenes proponent of a new American generation of nonrepresentational, nonpolitical painters whose ethos of aggressive nonconformity rebuked socialist realism as straitjacket kitsch—a campaign worth a brief detour.

Exhibit A was Jackson Pollack, born on a sheep ranch in Cody, Wyoming, who painted by dripping and flinging his pigments onto huge canvases lying flat on the floor—an artistic spectacle of freedom incarnate. That he was also moody and alcoholic, that he eschewed formal Old World studies abroad, supported his pedigree. The critic Clement Greenberg, himself an apostolic force, declared that thanks to Pollack and kindred talents "the main premises of Western Art have at last migrated to the United States, along with the center of gravity of industrial production and political power"—the aspirational prophecy John Kennedy would adduce a decade later. President Eisenhower also anticipated the absolutist Cold War "cultural freedom" dogma that would deny the possibility of Soviet art; in a 1954 address endorsing the Museum of Modern Art (MoMA), he said: "As long as artists are at liberty to feel with high personal intensity, as long of our artists are free to create with sincerity and conviction, there will be healthy controversy and progress in art. . . . How different it is in tyranny." Eisenhower's advisers included Nelson Rockefeller, whose long association with MoMA as both president and chairman dated back to 1939. Rockefeller was equally enmeshed in the intelligence community—and the same was true John Hay Whitney, like Rockefeller an influential advocate for the new American painters, and even Henry Luce, whose mass-circulation magazines extolled Pollack (including a generous spread in the August 1949 *Life* magazine).[41] These services proved vital, because many in Congress detested abstract expressionism as a leftist aberration: Pollack had apprenticed with the Mexican muralist David Alfaro Siqueiros, a known Stalinist (and coconspirator in the murder of Leon Trotsky in 1940). This was an instance in which the CCF, which disdained and feared McCarthyism, necessarily relied on secret support.

Yet the absence of abstract expressionism among the "masterpieces of the twentieth century" at the 1952 Paris festival is ultimately unsurprising: Pollack would have been out of place among the composers chosen by Nicolas Nabokov. Nabokov's frequent sympathies were that of a Francophile modernist. A certain inflexibility of taste is only natural in a composer—but can crimp a propagandist charged with subtly influencing public opinion. Though Nabokov eventually signed onto the CCF campaign for the likes of Pollack, Franz Kline, Mark Rothko, and Willem de Kooning, it bears stressing that his wide circle of acquaintances—the seedbed of his activism—did not include any of these famous painters. Nor did it include their closest musical associates—composers like Ralph Shapey and Morton Feldman. Though generalizations about iconoclasts are reckless, certainly the American expressionists to some degree align with German expressionism: the realm of the Stravinsky antipode Arnold Schoenberg, who resided in Los Angeles until his death in 1951.

Beyond doubt, introducing Paris to such landmark Balanchine ballets as *Orpheus* and *The Four Temperaments*, both less than a decade old; featuring Balanchine's colleague Jerome Robbins in his most notable Stravinsky ballet, *The Cage*; presenting the Paris premiere of Poulenc's *Stabat Mater*; presenting Ferenc Fricsay in all an all-Bartók program, including the Second Piano Concerto performed by Géza Anda—these were major cultural contributions. At the same time, it is possible to extrapolate no fewer than four categories of relative exclusion subtracting from the survey of twentieth-century masterpieces Nabokov assembled for European tastemakers he sought to sway.

First, and most obviously, the premise that only "free societies" deserved representation nixed the USSR. The Paris festival's only Soviet score, on thirty-four programs crammed into thirty-three days, was a suite from the work that notoriously provoked Stalin's censure: Shostakovich's *Lady Macbeth*. Nabokov had hoped to present the entire opera but could not acquire performance materials; locating a set of orchestral excerpts proved difficult enough. (Nabokov typically wrote scathingly about *Lady Macbeth*—except when he presented it as a victim of Soviet cultural repression, and thus "a work of real merit.")[42] Three Prokofiev works performed in Paris—the *Classical* Symphony, *The Prodigal Son,* and the *Scythian* Suite—were composed outside the Soviet Union.

The second category of relative exclusion comprised Schoenberg, Alban Berg, and Anton Webern, leaders of a "Second Viennese School" that as of 1952 was (more than Stravinsky) a predominant influence on international contemporary music. Here Nabokov's presentation of Berg's *Wozzeck* was the exception that proved the rule. Anton Webern, whose posthumous influence was at a peak, was represented by Five Movements for string quartet. (A Webern choral piece, impossible to trace, was also performed on a chamber concert program.)

Of Schoenberg, the festival only included *Erwartung* and the Second String Quartet, with the former juxtaposed with Stravinsky's *Oedipus Rex*—a bracing coupling of works mutually disesteemed by their composers. For Berg, *Wozzeck* was it. Nabokov attempted to argue for a transnational modernist consensus, a transcendent freedom product, "not going on in a spirit of nationalistic chauvinism or parochialism, but rather in a spirit of universal international collaboration." In fact, feverish Germanic modernism, overthrowing tonality and good manners, contradicted the French variety in method and aesthetics—and polemicists on both sides flung the mud with abandon.

Third: Nabokov repudiated the Romantic holdouts who seven decades later more than hold their own. His festival repertoire included nothing of Rachmaninoff, whose late Rhapsody on a Theme of Paganini and *Symphonic Dances* are both potently expressive and compositionally shrewd. It omitted such heroic twentieth-century symphonists, sharing lineage with Shostakovich, as Sibelius, Elgar, and Nielsen.

Finally, the fourth category of exclusion comprised American composers who no less than Jackson Pollack embodied the self-invented New World maverick, a list including Charles Ives, Carl Ruggles, John Cage, and Henry Cowell. There was also Roy Harris, born on an Oklahoma farm and once touted as the "great white hope" of American music. Nabokov, however, naturally more aligned with Aaron Copland, a Francophile modernist for whom Stravinsky mattered most. But Ives is the composer who could most credibly have showcased American originality. Only "Hawthorne" from his *Concord* Piano Sonata—the pinnacle of the American keyboard repertoire—was heard. While it may be true that in 1952 Ives's international stature had not yet been clinched, this was equally an argument for his inclusion. Nicolas Slonimsky had notably introduced Paris to Ives's *Three Places in New England* in 1931; it was "absolutely extraordinary," Slonimsky later recalled, that "so many important composers and critics of the time were in the audience. Their first experience of Ives left them impressed: Ives' music was not just interesting because it was composed by an American, it also fascinated them because the music really described America." (Slonimsky contributed a program essay, "On American Music," for the Paris festival.)[43]

Among the lesser composers chosen by Nabokov in 1952 were Frenchmen and Italians of the Stravinsky generation. Was the music of Georges Auric, Alfredo Casella, and Henri Sauguet as arousing as the *Ode to Napoleon* and *A Survivor from Warsaw*—furious wartime scores Schoenberg composed in California in response to Pearl Harbor and the Holocaust? As humanistically compelling as Shostakovich's Eighth Symphony? If the French critical response to "Masterpieces of the Twentieth Century" did not ask such questions, there were questions enough.

*   *   *

One keynote inferable from the mountain of notices in the French press was that "L'oeuvre du vingtieme siècle" seemed an act of personal presumption on behalf of American interests. If French snobbery was a contributing factor, this judgment was nonetheless plausible.

Eagerly following his own impassioned predilections, Nabokov had failed to gauge the non-Communist and Communist Left he wished to court. So far as the European avant-garde was concerned, the contemporary moment was politically charged and radically dissident. The impulse to break with art for art's sake was tidal, and so was the impulse to shatter tonality. The neoclassical Stravinsky—Nabokov's main event—seemed to many passé. With the single exception of Luigi Dallapiccola's *Canti di prigionia*, the Paris festival eschewed political art; absent were such significant twentieth-century musical activists as Berlin's Kurt Weill, Mexico's Silvestre Revueltas, and Britain's Michael Tippett. (A Tippett choral piece, impossible to trace, was performed on a chamber music program.) A smattering of contemporary nontonal repertoire included

a single work by the Parisian enfant terrible Pierre Boulez—programmed, as
were Ives and Webern, on a chamber music series curated not by Nabokov but
by the French musicologist/conductor Fred Goldbeck.

What became Boulez's signature diatribe—"Schoenberg Is Dead"[44]—was
published the same month as the festival. With impeccable logic, it argued that
Schoenberg's implementation of twelve-tone technique, jettisoning tonality,
indefensibly retained such tonal practices as favoring "tonic" and "dominant"
pitch relationships. The tone of Boulez's prose may be gleaned from a passage
reconsidering the meaning of artistic freedom: "It is not leering demonism but
the merest common sense which makes me say that, since the discoveries of
the Viennese School, all non-serial composers are *useless*. . . . It will hardly do
to answer in the name of so-called liberty, for this liberty has the strong flavor
of ancient servitude"—meaning "servitude" toward "the vocabulary of classi-
cism." Boulez called Nabokov a "mercenary lackey." So fractured was the French
cultural landscape that Serge Nigg, one of Boulez's prominent conservatory-
trained contemporaries, had turned into a Communist social realist. The Communist press accused Nabokov of facilitating "the ideological occupation of our
country by the United States"; promulgating "the formalist Stravinsky," Nabokov
had deliberately chosen works by Shostakovich and Prokofiev "that have been
criticized by the Soviet people and self-criticized by their authors." Sartre's *Les
temps modernes* perceived an embodiment of "Western neo-capitalist society
and its military policies."[45] For virtually any writer on the Left, the connection
between Nabokov, the Congress for Cultural Freedom (headquartered in Paris),
and the anti-Communist organ *Preuves* was evidence enough of what the festival
was about.

The mainstream press was of course far more appreciative. Echoes of Diaghilev's French triumphs—*Le sacre du printemps* conducted by Pierre Monteux,
who had led the tumultuous premiere for the Ballet Russes in 1913; the poetic
precision of Balanchine, once Diaghilev's discovery—were loudly applauded.
Wozzeck was the operatic sensation, far eclipsing Britten's *Billy Budd* and Thomson's *Four Saints for Three Acts*. Janet Flanner, whose *New Yorker* columns defined
cosmopolitan American reportage from Paris, wrote that "Masterpieces of the
Twentieth Century" "spilled such gallons of captious French newspaper ink,
wasted such tempests of argumentative Franco-American breath, and afforded,
on the whole, so much pleasure to the eye and ear that it can be called, in admiration, an extremely popular fiasco."[46]

More recent, retrospective verdicts remain mixed. A degree of musical sophistication helps to sort it all out. If Nabokov's 1952 summary of "twentieth-
century masterworks" is to be regarded as an attempt at prophecy, he failed: the
vision of Igor Stravinsky, majestically renewable, towering over a consolidated

Western cultural landscape is today a mirage. Rather, the fractured musical narrative of which Stravinsky was part dissipated without assignment of a victor. If, alternatively, Nabokov's festival is to be judged as propaganda, a positive verdict is at least as questionable. Days after it ended, Sidney Hook, writing to Nabokov from America, shared his "impression . . . that the festival was a success, that it was the only kind of thing that was possible in France at least, and indeed it was the only event that didn't turn out to be a psychological defeat for the cause of freedom."[47] Nabokov wrote back: "Yes, I think, despite what it may have looked like to people reading the French press, the festival was a psychological success in the complex and depressingly morbid intellectual climate of France. Of course, in any other country we would have had both more sympathy and more support."[48] But in his 1987 autobiography, alongside his verdict that Nabokov had enjoyed "a perfect job for [himself] . . . but unfortunately, in my view, not for the Congress," Hook delivered a crushing final assessment:

> Although there were efforts at desperate rationalization to show that all of these activities had something to do with the defense of the free world, actually [the festival] did more to further Nabokov's career and reputation than to further cultural freedom. . . . There is something awesome in the enumeration of the personages, organizations, and events and at the same time something much more depressing in the light of the cost and the realization that it had not the slightest perceptible effect in altering the climate of political opinion in Europe, especially in France. . . . It was an extravaganza that provided junket tours for hundreds, and left the congress saddled with a bureaucracy whose subsequent care and feeding was a burden on its resources. . . . Soon thereafter, the . . . French Parliament rejected the European Community Defense Treaty, which necessitated a rethinking of the plans for the defense of Europe.

Hook, in 1987, was also the rare observer to puncture the Nabokov doctrine that only "free artists" produce lasting art: "The whole premise of the undertaking was oversimplified, if not false. Since art has flourished even under political tyrannies, there was nothing the festival presented that could not have been offered to the world under the aegis of an enlightened despotism."[49] (Possibly unknown to Hook or Nabokov, in 1952, was the notably cosmopolitan and progressive cast of musical life in Leningrad and Moscow under Anatoly Lunacharsky. See my pages 121–22.) Melvin Lasky, who among other things was the CCF/CIA man in Berlin, opined in 1997: "I thought [the festival] was trivial. It's unimportant. . . . To spend such large sums on this kind of spectacular hype—it didn't make sense."[50]

What, finally, is one to make of the mixed messages and obscure meanings Nabokov projected onto his 1952 festival? The key remains his stated rationale, however implausible: to demonstrate that the first half of the twentieth century marked a musical summit transcending nationalism and politics in a lofty clime of freedom. Never mind that this claim is counterfactual; it fitted Nabokov's own circumstances and needs. He perceived himself as "a citizen of the Republic of Art, in short, a man who loves complete creative freedom, who has a horror of all frontiers, geographical and spiritual barriers and who will accept only the dictates of his own conscience, both artistically and intellectual." His whole life had "above all" been "a continuous vagrancy—a constant parting and searching for a new haven." He belonged to "that vast heterogeneous multitude of men and women set into motion by various forms of intolerance and oppression: The Refugees. As such, my vagrancies started in 1920 and . . . there seems no end to them." The "wave of life" had carried him "from exile to exile, from pre-and-post and post-and-pre wars and revolutions, through many lands and environments. And yet, as I think of it now, I loved it all." "We all believed, in our enthusiasm and in the free autonomy of the Republic of Music, that we had the power to preserve musical freedom."[51]

Investing his itinerancy with a romantic glow, Nabokov acquired a calling to save culture by fighting Communism. And that is the personal mission that his 1952 Paris festival attempted to abet. It is a truism that successful propaganda be credible and clever. The proof that Nabokov's freedom propaganda, so copiously articulated on this occasion, was neither may be found among the hot embers of the firestorm it predictably ignited. His CIA funders cannot be considered guiltless, nor does the CIA's reputation for intellectual sophistication escape embarrassment.

There exists a further, final, context for assessing the Paris festival. However confused its public purposes, however vague its public outcomes, it looms large in the narrative of Cold War propaganda; concomitantly, its impact within the concealed realm of the Congress for Cultural Freedom proved decisive. As we have seen, both FDR and President Eisenhower made speeches at the Museum of Modern Art aligning personal freedom with artistic achievement. The theme of unfettered thought and creativity was a ubiquitous response to the confinements of fascism and Communism; it did not take a Nabokov or Schlesinger to invent it. Abroad, for instance, André Gide claimed that "a writer's value is intimately linked . . . to the force of his spirit of opposition. . . . in all the countries of the world, a great writer has always been, more or less, a revolutionary, a fighter"[52]—a premise Schlesinger would reiterate in drafting President Kennedy's 1963 Amherst speech.

But Nabokov's freedom propaganda, as expounded in the run-up to "L'oeuvre du vingtieme siècle," was something more. No less than his Soviet counterparts, he created an embattled teleological narrative based in history; in effect, he became a kind of dialectician of freedom. In the process, he not only con-solidated his nascent role within the CCF; in the wake of the Paris festival, the Congress's fractious leadership consolidated in the person of Nabokov's spon-sor and ally Michael Josselson, formally named CCF administrative secretary in September 1952. Arthur Koestler, Sidney Hook, and other hard-liners had been decisively swept to the side. The CCF would not militantly challenge So-viet power. It would not attempt to liberate Eastern Europe. Its mandate would be fundamentally cultural. And Josselson, less an ideologue than a superior manager, would be its administrative leader, equally trusted by Nabokov in Paris and by his CIA superiors—Allen Dulles, Thomas Braden, and Cord Meyer, among others—in Washington. Thus empowered, the propaganda of freedom would eventually gird John F. Kennedy's aspirational vision of a great American civilization, a free society populated by free artists capable of forging a native cultural inheritance comparable to that of older, more venerable nations abroad.

Not so long after the Paris festival, the serial orthodoxy promulgated by Schoenberg and rigorously expanded by Boulez acquired an absolute impri-matur. With Schoenberg deceased, even Stravinsky capitulated: beginning in 1954 he composed nothing but twelve-tone music. Composers who resisted truly seemed—as Boulez had so famously put it—"useless." Cleavage with So-viet practice (there were no serialists in Russia) was therefore complete. Like abstract expressionism in visual art, the twelve-tone method became a signature of Western "freedom," bravely breaking with hoary tradition.

Nabokov, too, succumbed. Though he never acquired enthusiasm for non-tonal composition, as an American propagandist he had to march in step. The next CCF festival, in Rome in 1954, was "La Musica nel XX Secolo"—translated by Nabokov as "Music in Our Time." It notably (but not predominantly) em-braced the avant-garde: the serialists Anton Webern, Luigi Nono, and Luigi Dallapiccola were all featured. A single Stravinsky concert, with the Italian Radio Orchestra, was this time an anomaly. The European premiere of Elliott Carter's First String Quartet—densely argued nontonal music that eschewed twelve-tone organization—made so great an impression that Nabokov effec-tively launched Carter's international career as the American high-modernist composer of choice. Carter was very much part of Nabokov's circle. By his own reckoning, however, Nabokov experienced "gradual disenchantment" with his CCF responsibilities beginning in 1958[53]—the year of the CCF's "Tradition and Change in Music" festival in Venice. By this time composers in the West were immersed in musical idioms of consequence mainly to themselves. Dissidents were shunned and scorned. Figurative painters suffered the same fate. In retro-spect, the Soviet case for "formalist decadence" in music was at least as credible as were Boulez's sermons on "liberty." As for abstract expressionism—Jason

Epstein, long a bulwark of Manhattan's intellectual life, recalled in 1994: "It was like the emperor's new clothes. You parade it down the street and you say, 'This is great art,' and the people along the parade route will agree with you."[54]

Nabokov called "the strangest of all my festivals" the fourth and last: the prescient "East-West Music Encounter" in Tokyo in 1961. The proceedings began with a Gagaku Ensemble juxtaposed with a brass choir playing Gabrieli. Classical Indian music, the Royal Dancers of Thailand, Kathakali dancers from Kerala, the Royal Ballet, and the New York Philharmonic were all seen and heard. The composers on site included Luciano Berio, Elliott Carter, Henry Cowell, Luigi Dallapiccola, Lou Harrison, and Iannis Xenakis. (I deal with Nabokov's poor opinion of East/West cultural fusion in a note.)[55] Japanese Communists instinctively denounced the festival as Cold War propaganda—an accurate assessment.[56]

In 1960 Dmitri Shostakovich composed one of his most personal, most tormented compositions—the String Quartet No. 8. Its shattering impact on its first Soviet hearers was immediate and undeniable. It was music as remote from socialist realism—and from Nabokov's papier-mâché Shostakovich caricature—as were Stravinsky's ascetic chamber and choral works from the same period. Ostensible East/West polarities would ultimately crumble toward a recognition of common purpose. It would be driven by new proximity and—at long last—mutual knowledge.

* * *

In their invaluable studies of the Congress for Cultural Freedom, Frances Stonor Saunders and (in response to Saunders) Hugh Wilford render verdicts keying on the controversy over CIA sponsorship. Did covert government support undermine the integrity of Nabokov's operation? And did CIA insiders exert hidden control over content? Wilford writes: "The implied claim in the British title of Saunders's book, *Who Paid the Piper?*—that America's Cold War spy establishment called the tune of western intellectual life—is problematic." Addressing the rejection by *Encounter* in 1958 of a Dwight Macdonald article, "America! America!," skewering American culture—a clear case of censorship (in which Nabokov participated, as detailed in a note)[57]—Wilford comments: "True, this properly notorious incident shows that the editorial freedom supposedly enjoyed by the CCF's magazine was in fact mythical. Yet at the same time Macdonald's protests, and the negative publicity for the CCF that resulted, demonstrated that the Agency was by no means in control of Cold War intellectual discourse."[58] Saunders, for her part, acknowledges instances in which secrecy was unavoidable. She, for instance, cites former CIA officer Thomas

Braden's 1994 testimony that congressional opposition made it "very difficult" to implement "some of the things that we wanted to do—send art abroad, send symphonies abroad, publish magazines abroad, whatever. That's one of the reasons why it had to be done covertly: it had to be covert because it would have been turned down if it had been put to a voice in a democracy. In order to encourage openness we had to be secret." Saunders comments: "Here again was that sublime paradox of American strategy in the cultural Cold War: in order to promote an acceptance of art produced in . . . democracy, the democratic process itself had to be circumvented."[59]

The thrust of her book is to challenge this strategy, not defend it—and the resulting fusillade scores many points. An especially shrewd argument cited by Saunders[60] was made by Jason Epstein:

> What most irritated us was that the government seemed to be running an underground gravy train whose first-class compartments were not always occupied by first-class passengers: the CIA and the Ford Foundation, among other agencies, had set up and were financing an apparatus of intellectuals selected for their correct cold-war positions, as an alternative to what one might call a free intellectual market where ideology was presumed to count for less than individual talent and achievement and where doubts about established orthodoxies were taken to be the beginning of all inquiry.

That *Encounter* killed Macdonald's "America! America!" is apposite here, because he was as a result kicked off the CCF gravy train for writers and editors. If Nabokov ran a composers' gravy train, the first-class compartments were mainly occupied by Igor Stravinsky over and again, subsidized by American taxpayers. A compelling case could be made for such alternative passengers as George Gershwin, Charles Ives, Duke Ellington, or Lou Harrison: supreme products of a homegrown American musical culture, among whom Ives and Harrison were insufficiently known or appreciated abroad. But the entire exercise was mainly invisible, not least in America itself.

Another cost of "underground" machinations, generally exposed by Saunders's entire account, was a hubris bred by privilege, insularity, and the relative absence of checks and balances. Michael Josselson's wife, Diana, also his CIA partner, once reminisced:

> The atmosphere of the Congress [for Cultural Freedom] in its heyday was as I imagine the first hundred days of the Kennedy administration were. It was electric. You felt you were in touch with everything going on everywhere. . . . Michael would know everything. It was dazzling how in the morning he could be talking about playwrights in Bolivia, and then about writers in Asia in the afternoon,

and then he and Nicolas would be on the phone in the evening talking in four different languages. I remember sitting with Stravinsky at a café in Paris, and his wife telling me how to make blinis. It was an extraordinary time for us . . . it was like the French Revolution or the Oxford Movement. That's what it felt like.[61]

Whether or not hubris-inflected, Nabokov's freedom propaganda spiraled out of control—and so did his 1952 Paris festival, the premises of which were never sufficiently clarified or vetted. Afterward, some insiders boasted that the Boston Symphony had proved a supreme propaganda asset (a fulsome claim).[62] They might also have pondered whether everything else Nabokov had procured and paid for in 1952 was necessary or even desirable.

Nabokov's post-1966 commentaries do not address any such questions. Rather, as we have seen, he mainly insisted he was neither aware of nor impacted by the Congress's CIA entanglements—and that the same excellent work could and should have been accomplished with overt government subsidies, as was the Marshall Plan. Applying a wider lens to Nabokov's work, a pertinent alternative frame of reference is the practice of cultural exchange, which seesawed into an ascendant policy position as CCF activity declined. Whatever the intentions of the resulting cultural crossings, their ultimate affect was quite different from that of CCF gatherings of prior years—not bristling polemics, but soothing discoveries.

It bears stressing that Nicolas Nabokov disliked both the Rachmaninoff Third Concerto, whose sublime melancholia Van Cliburn purveyed to astounded Russian jurors and audiences in 1958, and the Shostakovich Fifth Symphony, in 1959 propelled by Leonard Bernstein and his New York Philharmonic with a Yankee enthusiasm foreign to earnest Soviet uplift. As we will discover, Nabokov also strenuously attempted to prevent Stravinsky from accepting Moscow's invitation to "come home." That he should have resisted cultural exchange was perhaps unsurprising. Firsthand knowledge could only undermine his binary view. It was bound to humanize his opponents, and make tangible the magnitude of a Soviet musical achievement he denied (but could not possibly have failed to suspect), whatever hardships it might impose on the lives of its participants.

An exploration of cultural exchange is therefore a necessary pendant to any account of the festival activities undertaken by the Congress for Cultural Freedom—and the reader is referred to my chapter 8. But first: a closer look at the two composers most directly at hand. Not only were Stravinsky and Shostakovich thrust into complex diplomatic roles they did not seek; they jointly furnish an irresistible opportunity to test the Nabokov doctrine that free artists and free societies embody conditions necessary to the creative act.

CHAPTER 5

SURVIVAL STRATEGIES

Stravinsky and Shostakovich

In private correspondence in 1943, Aaron Copland surmised in Igor Stravinsky a "psychology of exile" characterized (as in Henry James) by "exquisite perfection" and a "lack of immediacy of contact with the world around him." Copland added: "I don't think he's in a very good period. He copies himself unashamedly, and therefore one rarely comes upon a really fresh page—for him, I mean."[1]

Copland first encountered Stravinsky in Paris in the twenties. Stravinsky was already in exile from Russia. But, incredibly, there existed in Paris a community of Russian artists, headed by Serge Diaghilev, as formidable as any in Russia itself. Now Stravinsky was in Hollywood. Los Angeles had its own world-class collection of exiles—but Stravinsky had few intimate West Coast friends or associates. He lived comfortably at 1260 North Wetherly Drive with his Russian wife and, eventually, his American amanuensis, Robert Craft—who spoke no Russian. The conductor of the Los Angeles Philharmonic through 1939 had been Otto Klemperer—a German who remained closely associated with Stravinsky's rival Arnold Schoenberg. The Philharmonic's new conductor, Alfred Wallenstein, would ignore Schoenberg and Stravinsky both. As for the local specialty, Stravinsky had been ceremoniously engaged to score Darryl Zanuck's *The Song of Bernadette*—only to see his music dropped in favor of a replacement score by Alfred Newman. Copland himself was attempting to break in as a West Coast film composer—an effort he would abandon in disappointment. He knew a thing or two about Hollywood.

Stravinsky had one important American collaborator—a legacy of Diaghilev. This was of course George Balanchine, headquartered in New York City. Balanchine was the exception that proved the rule: the three best-known instrumental works Stravinsky would compose in the America—Symphony in Three Movements, *Orpheus*, and *Agon*—would chiefly become known as Balanchine ballets.

Compared to St. Petersburg or Paris, Los Angeles was frictionless: it left Stravinsky alone. His autonomous condition fulfilled a notion of unfettered "freedom" inculcated by John Stuart Mill and other Anglo-American thinkers. But in the Germanic philosophic tradition of which Karl Marx happened to be part, "freedom" is more a condition of metaphysical understanding. It is a freedom experienced in organic relationship to a collectivity—such as the state. It is interactive and dynamic: "dialectical." Concomitantly, friction is a dialectical catalyst for learning and creativity. The Frankfurt School notion of "negative culture," which would shortly exert ferocious influence in the United States, is a kindred concept; absent abrasion, it insists, culture lies dormant and banal. Isaiah Berlin, in a well-known 1958 formulation, contrasted "negative" freedom—a "freedom from"—with "positive" freedom: "freedom to." Though he was partial to the former and wary of the latter, he shrewdly conceded that negative freedom does not necessarily correlate with "democracy or self-government," and that, empirically, "Mill's argument for liberty as a necessary condition for human growth falls to the ground." (I here append as a note a philosophical digression, pondering the pertinence of the English empirical tradition to the American arts.)[2]

As Marx, Lenin, and Stalin were dialecticians, we should not be amazed to discover Dmitri Shostakovich explaining "freedom" to the *New York Times* in terms Georg Wilhelm Friedrich Hegel would have recognized. This was in August 1954: ten months after Nicolas Nabokov informed readers of *Encounter* that all Soviet music sounded as if "turned out by Ford or General Motors," one year before David Oistrakh and Emil Gilels would amaze Western audiences with evidence of a formidable classical music culture kept under wraps for three decades. As Shostakovich was speaking directly to Harrison Salisbury, the *Times'* Moscow bureau chief, the words can only be his—as "passed by Soviet censors."

Impressed by Shostakovich's earnest persona, which he experienced as a pedigree for "honesty and sincerity," Salisbury reported Shostakovich declaring: "The artist in Russia has more 'freedom' than the artist in the West." The reason: he enjoys, Salisbury paraphrased, "what might be described as a 'principled' relationship to society and to the party," versus a "haphazard" relationship to society, as in Western nations. He is accorded "status" and "a defined role." Questioned about restrictions, Shostakovich replied: "There is a line which is established by the Party for the general guidance of artists—a line asking of art that it be appealing to people, that it have depth and perfection of form. But this does not make Soviet composers mere automatons. Great differences of opinion continue to exist and are strenuously expressed." His Tenth Symphony had in fact just been subjected to heated debate within the Composers' Union (Salisbury reported that comparisons were made to Goya, Tchaikovsky, and Delacroix—an interesting list). Paraphrasing Shostakovich, Salisbury summarized that, in Shostakovich's view, "The Western conception of an iron hand and of rigidity of doctrine is quite wrong." Shostakovich also told Salisbury: "Who can say that my work suffered from this criticism? My works are played all over Russia. Just because one work is criticized, does not mean that orchestras stop playing the others. And I go on writing and the government goes on supporting me, and generously, too."[3] The same year, Aram Khachaturian, whose 1940 Violin Concerto Oistrakh (its dedicatee) and Leonid Kogan would champion internationally, quoted Arthur Honegger in *Sovetskaya Muzyka*: "The position of the composer in the West today is as hopeless as that of a shoe manufacturer trying to sell ladies' high button boots on the modern market." By comparison, Khachaturian continued, "the Soviet composer is an honored member of society."[4] (Khachaturian was a leading force within the Composers' Union, empowered to greatly influence Soviet musical life—an experience he proudly recounted in his memoirs.)

Such opinions naturally met with emphatic resistance. The *Times* even published a "contrasting view" alongside Salisbury's "Visit with Dmitri Shostakovich": "Music in a Cage" by Julie Whitney, who proposed as a "very serious question" whether Soviet composers "might not use their talent more successfully if they were out of the 'gilded' cage in which Shostakovich declares they are so content."

While (as I have earlier maintained) this line of speculation goes too far, the ideological and personal stress imposed by Communist cultural policies were unmentionable by Shostakovich in conversation with an American newspaper reporter. Upon hearing the first private performance of his autobiographical Eighth String Quartet in 1960, Shostakovich buried his head in his hands; the musicians left quietly. But the Eighth Quartet subsequently became his most famous, most iconic chamber work. Because we sense that it compassionately bears witness to a tragedy transcending the personal, it imparts a moral perspective. Whatever one makes of the Eighth Quartet musically—by contemporaneous Western standards, the idiom was unfashionably conservative—its self-evident meaningfulness, reinforced by encoded extra-musical allusions, contradicts Stravinsky's prickly, morally neutral art for art's sake.

That art can be morally empowering, that it can also be heartless and destructive, are complex truths. Thomas Mann, who even after Hitler could never wholly escape his infatuation with Wagner, was a peerless authority on conflicting cultural properties. He once wrote:

> Art will never be moral or virtuous in any political sense: and progress will never be able to put its trust in art. It has a fundamental tendency to unreliability and treachery; its . . . predilection for the "barbarism" that begets beauty [is] indestructible; and although some may call this predilection . . . immoral to the point of endangering the world, yet it is an imperishable fact of life, and if one wanted to eradicate this aspect of art . . . then one might well have freed the world from a serious danger; but in the process one would almost certainly have freed it from art itself.

That is from Mann's *Reflections of a Non-political Man* (1919). With the advent of the Third Reich, Mann became a "political man": he wrenched himself apart from the Germany he endorsed and embodied, and moved to Southern California. "Everything else would have meant too narrow and specific an alienation of my existence," he told a 1945 audience at the Library of Congress. "As an American I am a citizen of the world." Seven years later, having witnessed the onset of the Cold War and the Red Scare, Mann deserted the United States for Switzerland.[5]

All of this—Shostakovich's dialectical "freedom," Mann's ambivalent citizenships, American autonomy, Soviet service or servitude—contextualizes the "cultural freedom" dogma embraced by Nicolas Nabokov, Arthur Schlesinger, and John F. Kennedy. Whether naive or calculated, the simplicity of their argument—that "free artists" create wholesome art in wholesome environments—conveyed a tainted political odor where it mattered most: among Old World artists and intellectuals on the Left. It may be that in extreme cases—cases in which the past is canceled—a totalitarian regime can likewise cancel art. Perhaps something of this kind happened under Pol Pot, or Mao Tse-tung, or Kim Il Sung. But, beginning with Lenin and his formidable cultural commissar Anatoly Lunacharsky, the Soviet Union insisted on maintaining contact with Russia's traditional cultural base. And so did Stalin. Opera and ballet, Pushkin and Tolstoy were to be supported and sustained. When proletarian deviants mounted purification rites intent on destroying bourgeois habits and institutions, they were themselves liquidated. When in 1935 Serge Prokofiev decided on a "happy" ending for his *Romeo and Juliet* ballet, this exemplary socialist realist touch was overruled by party bureaucrats: Shakespeare would not be desecrated. In fact, a conservative thrust, countering "formalism," was a defining feature of Soviet aesthetics.

It was Plato, twenty-five centuries ago, who said: "Necessity is the mother of invention." There you have an account of the creative act more shrewd than any CCF "freedom" template. Artists ingeniously grapple and cope. When necessary, they devise strategies of survival. And that was what happened with Stravinsky and Shostakovich both—and also with Nicolas Nabokov.

*   *   *

When Igor Stravinsky was born in 1882, Russian classical music meant opera and ballet; the symphonic tradition—absolute music—was secondary. In fact, Stravinsky's father was a leading bass at St. Petersburg's Mariinsky Theater. Igor's early fame was ignited by three plotted ballets for Diaghilev: *The Firebird* (his tenderest score [1900]), *Petrushka* (1911), and *The Rite of Spring* (1913)—all premiered in Paris. He continued to summer in Russia through 1914, otherwise mainly residing in Switzerland. The Stravinsky family (he married in 1906) relocated to France in 1920. These early migrations generated keen nostalgia for the tang of Russian folk song and dance, inspiring a fourth ballet based on rustic wedding ceremonies. This was *Les noces* (1917)—which he later considered his favorite among his compositions.

Diaghilev's sudden death in 1929 was pivotal. Though Robert Craft, decades later, summarized Diaghilev as someone with whom Stravinsky "fought a lot," it is Diaghilev, singularly, about whom Stravinsky writes lovingly in his autobiography: "His loss moved me . . . profoundly. . . . It is only today, with the passing of the years, that one begins to realize everywhere and in everything what a terrible void was created by the disappearance of this colossal figure." Soulima Stravinsky said of the impact of Diaghilev's death on his father: "It was as if it was a brother or more, even more."[6] A blurring of personal identity— post-Russia, post-Diaghilev—is an inescapable Stravinsky motif. In Paris he maintained separate households with his wife and mistress Vera de Bosset (later his second wife). He grew remote from his children. He took French citizenship and called France his "second homeland." He regularly visited Germany. In 1937 a Chicago newspaper reported: "Stravinsky, in German, Says He's French." He left France for America in 1939. The war was not the only reason; according to Soulima, his father "couldn't cope" with his compromised domestic affairs.[7]

A new life with Vera in Los Angeles began in 1941. Like Schoenberg, with whom he never met, Stravinsky was seduced by the temperate climate. Lillian Libman, who served him in many capacities, later observed: "To think about composing required an atmosphere of peace, and every moment of all the years I knew him, that was *all* he wanted."[8] The novelist Paul Horgan, who knew the Stravinskys via the Santa Fe Opera in the 1950s, recorded that, aside from

Aldous Huxley, Christopher Isherwood, and Gerald Heard, "they had, so far as I know, no close friends with whom to have even the idlest conversation."[9] Thus left alone, Stravinsky manifested the "psychology of exile" observed by Aaron Copland and—to say the least—the condition of "freedom" extolled by Nicolas Nabokov. Concomitantly, his music aspired to an orderly, dispassionate beauty, an aesthetic of sublime equipoise. In Paris his output had included an aching Tchaikovsky reminiscence, *The Fairy's Kiss*, and a *Symphony of Psalms* poignantly redolent of Russian Orthodox ritual. By comparison, his California output eschewed nostalgia. (It is a measure of Stravinsky's stature in the 1960s that the California impresario Lawrence Morton could write in 1963 that Stravinsky had in *The Fairy's Kiss* improved on Tchaikovsky's great ballet scores: "Tchaikovsky's faults—his banalities and vulgarities and routine procedures—are composed *out* of the music, and Stravinsky's virtues are composed *into* it."[10])

A peculiarity of the Stravinsky personality was a pressing need to explain and define himself. The key texts are *Chronicle of My Life* (1936) and *The Poetics of Music*, comprising his Norton Lectures at Harvard (1939–40). That (as is now widely known) Stravinsky did not write either book adds interest: it so mattered to him to set down certain truths that he found writers—Walter Nouvel and Alexis Roland-Manuel (with assistance from Pierre Souvtchinsky), respectively—who could ideally do so.

Its combative tone is an instantly striking feature of Stravinsky's prose. In fact, he is aggrieved. Of his critics, he writes: "Their attitude certainly cannot make me deviate from my path. I shall assuredly not sacrifice my predilections and my aspirations to the demands of those who, in their blindness, do not realize that they are simply asking me to go backwards." His most famous sentences are these:

> I consider that music is by its very nature, essentially powerless to *express* anything at all, whether a feeling, an attitude of mind, a psychological mood, a phenomenon of nature, etc. . . . *Expression* has never been an inherent property of music. That is by no means the purpose of its existence. . . . [11]

> The phenomenon of music is given to us with the sole purpose of establishing an order in things . . . Its indispensable and single requirement is construction. Construction once completed, this order has been attained, and there is nothing more to be said. It would be futile to look for, or expect anything else from it.[12]

Hence the enemy of music is disorder. Writing of disruptive Romantics, Stravinsky seethes. His special nemesis is Wagnerism, whose "halcyon days . . . are past." "Pathological" in origin, the Wagnerian music drama manifests "nouveau riche smugness," "murky inanities," "adulterated religiosity," a veritable "cult of disorder."[13] A similar condition afflicts Russia. Tchaikovsky, he confesses, is "one of the few Russian composers of whom I am really fond"; his substantial exposure to the West, his adoration of Mozart, fostered aristocratic and classical virtues. But Tchaikovsky's imitators "degenerated into a mawkish lyricism." Meanwhile, with Scriabin a "new disorder . . . wormed its way into Russian thought . . . whose beginnings were marked by the success of theosophy," creating two musical Russias "which embody two kinds of disorder: conservative disorder and revolutionary disorder." Then came Stalin: "simplification," "new popularism and folklore." In a swipe at Shostakovich, he allows that the Soviet condemnation of *Lady Macbeth* was "perhaps not altogether" wrong.[14] (Decades later, Nicolas Nabokov reported from Los Angeles: "For Stravinsky, Russia is a language, which he uses with superb, gourmandlike dexterity; it is a few books; Glinka and Tchaikovsky. The rest either leaves him indifferent or arouses his anger, contempt and violent dislike.")[15]

Concomitantly, Stravinsky explicates the creative act as fundamentally autonomous. "Inspiration," he writes, "is in no way a prescribed condition . . . but rather a manifestation that is chronologically secondary." Composers do not react to feelings or surroundings, or to constraining national currents. Schoenberg, extolling instinct, spoke of canceling conscious calculation. For Stravinsky, composers pursue order and discipline; it is precisely *consciously* that they make music. Moreover, this is a universal prescription. It does not succumb to the "national" or "regional." "Universality necessarily stipulates submission to an established order."[16]

The entire polemic may be read as a survival manual in exile, with Russia the cat in the bag. The central lesson is to cleanse and purge the past—even to a point of denial, of canceled memory. The late Stravinsky scholar Richard Taruskin, tracking the many instances in which Stravinsky said and wrote things distorting his own past, has called him an inveterate liar.[17] More compassionately read, Stravinsky was a resourceful exile, furiously determined to begin anew. The Russian music with which he grew up—the operas and ballets—told stories. So music could tell no stories. He acquired an early reputation as a revolutionary and a subsequent reputation as a happy magpie, ceaselessly reinventing himself. But Stravinsky in exile needed firmer grounding than that. "It was wrong to have considered me a revolutionary," he writes. "Revolution implies a disruption of equilibrium. To speak of revolution is to speak of a temporary chaos. Now art is the contrary of chaos."[18] At all costs, the center would hold.

And so it was for Nabokov. He, too, pugilistically insisted that music was never "ideational"—a conviction deaf to the particular power of Shostakovich, whose Seventh Symphony conveyed extra-musical ideas so powerful that it rallied a city under siege. Nabokov's disdain for Wagner, his admiration for the aristocratic side of Tchaikovsky, his disparagement of a maudlin Tchaikovsky residue, his dismissal of Scriabin ("good only for highstrung adolescents"),[19] his absolute denial of Shostakovich: all echo Stravinsky's thought and writings. The ideal of the autonomous artist, transcending politics and nationalism, the notion of artistic "freedom" as a necessary condition of creativity—it is all kindred to Stravinsky and Nabokov both. In both instances, a problematic condition of rootlessness is rationalized or combated. And it all happened to rhyme with the rhetoric of "cultural freedom" that Sidney Hook was concurrently instilling within America's non-Communist Left.

One could almost say that, unbeknownst to JFK when he celebrated Stravinsky's eightieth birthday at the White House in 1962, the cultural Cold War dogma he would so elegantly adopt originated in a psychological affliction Aaron Copland had observed in the president's august dinner guest some two decades before.

*   *   *

According to Nicolas Nabokov, after Pearl Harbor was attacked and the United States entered World War II, Igor Stravinsky feared a revolution might break out in America. "'But where will I go?' [Stravinsky said] in an appalled and indignant tone."[20] Above all else, he sought refuge from the storm.

And yet in 1942, the war impinged in buffered form: Stravinsky accepted a commission from the New York Philharmonic for "a new symphony called 'La Victoire'" to celebrate the impending victory over Germany and Japan. What next transpired is documented in tangled detail by correspondence in the New York Philharmonic Archives. The Philharmonic requested a program note. Stravinsky replied: "It is well known that no program is to be sought in my musical output. . . . Sorry if this is desapointing [sic] but no story to be told, no narration and what I would say would only make yawn the majority of your public which undoubtedly expects exciting descriptions. This, indeed would be so much easier but alas . . ."

Stravinsky then asked the Philharmonic to publish a program note by the composer Ingolf Dahl. Dahl's note, duly printed in the Philharmonic program book, was itself of the species to "make yawn the majority." A specimen: "The thematic germs of this [first] movement are of ultimate condensation. They consist of the interval of the minor third (with its inversion, the major sixth) and an ascending scale fragment which forms the background to the piano solo of the middle part." But Stravinsky obliged the Philharmonic with a brief "Word," conceding: "During the process of creation in this our arduous time of sharp shifting events, time of despear [*sic*] and hope, time of continual torments, of tention [*sic*] and at last cessation, relief, my [*sic*] be all those repercussions have left traces, stamped the character of this Symphony."

The work thus described—the Symphony in Three Movements—is in fact different in tone from the Apollonian exercises Stravinsky had long pursued. Parts are indisputably militant, marchlike, propelled by harshly thrusting energies. Many writers, Dahl included, have likened it to a latter-day *Rite of Spring*. Another unmistakable influence is the swagger and muscle of big-band jazz. (Mere months later, Stravinsky completed an *Ebony* Concerto composed on commission for Woody Herman.) In Stravinsky's world-premiere recording of the Symphony in Three Movements with the New York Philharmonic, the flying syncopations of the opening measures really swing.

Stravinsky later acknowledged Broadway, boogie-woogie, and "the neon glitter of Los Angeles' boulevards" as influences on his American output. But this was nothing compared to a revelation recorded by Robert Craft in response to the question: "In what ways is the [Symphony in Three Movements] marked by world events?" Stravinsky answered:

Certain specific events excited my musical imagination. Each episode is linked in my mind with a concrete impression of the war, almost always cinematographic in origin. For instance, the beginning of the third movement is partly a musical reaction to newsreels I had seen of goose-stepping soldiers. The square march beat, the brass-band instrumentation, the grotesque crescendo in the tuba—all these are related to those repellent pictures. In spite of contrasting musical episodes, such as the canon for bassoons, the march music predominates until the fugue, the beginning of which marks the stasis and the turning point. The immobility here seems to me comic, and so, to me, was the overturned arrogance of the Germans when their machine failed at Stalingrad. The fugal exposition and the end of the Symphony are associated with the rise of the Allies, and the final, albeit too commercial, D-flat chord—instead of the expected C—is a token of my extra exuberance in the triumph. The rumba in the finale, developed from the timpani part in the introduction to the first movement, was also associated in my imagination with the movements of war machines.[21]

Although not everything Stravinsky said about himself bears scrutiny, and although not everything Craft said Stravinsky said can be taken at face value, and although Stravinsky's testimony about applying wartime "newsreels" has been discounted by his biographer Steven Walsh, the proof is in the music: as I have had occasion to confirm working with the video artist Peter Bogdanoff,

Stravinsky's movement three narrative is a fit. (To see our film: https://vimeo.com/31621069.)

Accompanied by the specified clips, this explosive finale, with its strutting marches and detonating chords, functions altogether admirably as a film score. In fact, the point of "stasis" midway through makes no apparent musical sense— it is, rather, a programmatic pivot upon which the tide of battle is reversed. Balanchine's famous setting of the Symphony in Three Movements winks at Hollywood and Broadway. But he also told his dancers to think of helicopter searches and other signatures of wartime. More recently, the conductor Valery Gergiev has called the symphony's opening flourish "an alarm" that should sound "very brutal." In the dialogue of bassoons near the opening of the finale, he hears music of "fear."[22]

In his conversation with Craft, Stravinsky added, inimitably: "Enough of this. In spite of what I have admitted, the symphony is not programmatic. Composers combine notes. That is all." But even accepting this hairpin distinction, the compositional process at hand is hardly "autonomous." Its "inspiration"—the war and its imagery—is fundamental, not a mere "manifestation that is chronologically secondary." Or is the Symphony in Three Movements a case of *waning* inspiration? Copland sensed in the American Stravinsky a composer who "copies himself." An anomaly of the Symphony is the prominence of a solo piano in movement one, and of solo harp in movement two. In fact, the first movement originated as an abandoned sketch for piano and orchestra. And movement two appropriates eerie strains created to underscore an apparition of the Virgin Mary in *The Song of Bernadette*—film music Darryl Zanuck declined to use. Stravinsky rescued these fragments—and therefore composed some passages highlighting the solo piano and solo harp in his finale. The pattern of scoring that results is a curious patchwork. And whether the mood and texture of movement two actually fit this "symphony"—for which Stravinsky considered the alternative title "Three Symphonic Movements"—is a good question.

A final frame of reference: Shostakovich, Prokofiev, and Schoenberg all responded to World War II with memorably expressive music. Prokofiev's Seventh Piano Sonata (1942) records the angry or plaintive sounds of war; it ends on a note of heroic resolution. Schoenberg, in Los Angeles, spurned the "autonomy" of exile, befriending George Gershwin, teaching his students at the University of California at Los Angeles, mentoring Hollywood's leading film composers; his *Ode to Napoleon* (1942) and *A Survivor from Warsaw* (1947) confront Hitler and the Holocaust with furious words set as *Sprechstimme*—a kind of heightened speech. Shostakovich's Piano Trio No. 2 (1944) is by comparison a subjective view, fraught or consoling, eschewing description. That his wartime voice is here so interior makes it—however Russian—the more universal.

Stravinsky, by comparison, was a poised bystander. And so he remained—until according to Robert Craft he exclaimed in anguish that his creative energies were running dry. With Craft's guidance Stravinsky tested a new methodology: the twelve-tone practice originated by Schoenberg became a fresh "strategy of survival," connecting him to a ubiquitous nontonal musical consensus. His "Cold War" compositions are therefore mainly esoteric works, whether on worldly or religious themes. A rare topical response was the two-minute *Elegy for JFK*, setting a commissioned memorial poem of four haiku stanzas by W. H. Auden. While "late Stravinsky" enjoys no settled reputation, the engine restarted. Compared to Elgar, Falla, and Sibelius—long-lived masters all of whom stopped productively composing—Stravinsky's capacity to ride the aesthetic upheavals of the twentieth century was a signature accomplishment.

Craft indispensably mediated the aging composer's relationship with the outside world. Stravinsky's conducting and recording assignments, even his compositions, were undertaken with Craft's assistance, as was the eventuality that most disturbed Stravinsky's cherished equilibrium: in 1962 he returned to Russia on invitation from the Soviet government. Perhaps predictably, Nabokov vehemently opposed this historic visit; Stravinsky had at all times crucially validated Nabokov's necessary hostility toward his former home. Isaiah Berlin, in a letter to Stuart Hampshire, described Nabokov as "hysterically anxious" that Stravinsky say no. Craft reported in September 1961 that Nabokov spent three hours with the Stravinskys in Berlin, terrifying them. Presumably, he argued that the visit was a propaganda ploy to use Stravinsky for Soviet purposes. Stravinsky was also advised by some that the excitement could prove "fatal." But as Lillian Libman sensibly recalls in her Stravinsky memoir: "*Of course* it would all be emotional (but I did not think 'fatal'), and *of course* there would be propaganda (here as well as there), but I could not see why everyone should be thrown into a state of consternation."[23]

Stravinsky, who had not set foot on Russian soil since in 1914, ultimately said yes. The contributing factors included Leonard Bernstein's 1959 visit to Russia with his New York Philharmonic, performing not only *The Rite of Spring* but also a choice neoclassical specimen: the 1924 Concerto for Piano and Winds. Two years later, Tikhon Khrennikov, the often personable head of the Composers' Union, visited Stravinsky at home in Los Angeles to convey his respects. Planning sharply accelerated once the impresario Sol Hurok, who was instrumental in securing cultural exchange between the United States and USSR, became involved. The resulting visit, in 1962, was in Libman's opinion "probably the profoundest experience of [Stravinsky's] last decade." Even Craft—who as Libman testified "always had his defenses up when the Stravinskys were involved in anything directly connected with their native country"—recorded that he was "certain that to be recognized and acclaimed as a Russian in Russia, and to be performed there, has meant more to [Stravinsky] than anything else in the years I have known him. And when Mother Russia restores her love, forty-eight years are forgiven with one suck of the breast."[24]

The Stravinsky concerts in Leningrad and Moscow included the Symphony in Three Movements, specifically requested by Kirill Kondrashin, the conductor of the Moscow Philharmonic.[25] It was obvious to all concerned that no Western nation could possibly have regarded a visit by Igor Stravinsky as so vital. In Leningrad Craft witnessed an all-night queue of one hundred people. Each individual represented a bloc of one hundred tickets. The queue was reportedly a year old and regularly checked. And Craft observed in both Stravinskys "an intense pride in everything Russian." Of Stravinsky conducting in rehearsal: "He is more buoyant than I have ever seen him." The rhythmic applause after his first Moscow concert would not stop; Stravinsky returned to the stage in his overcoat to tell the insatiable audience: "You see a very happy man." So emotional was Stravinsky in Leningrad that he decided he could not risk visiting his father's grave. Inescapably, Stravinsky and Shostakovich met. According to a widely circulated anecdote, Shostakovich expressed his well-known reverence for Stravinsky's *Symphony of Psalms*. Stravinsky, in reply, could only express his regard for Gustav Mahler, highly regarded by Shostakovich. Shostakovich later said: "I found it difficult to talk to him. We were from different planets."

In certain respects, the most remarkable event was a reception hosted by Yekaterina Furtseva, the minister of culture, and selected Soviet composers. Stravinsky rose to say:

> A man has one birthplace, one fatherland, one country—he *can* have only one country—and the place of his birth is the most important factor in his life. I regret that circumstances separated me from my fatherland, that I did not give birth to my works there and, above all, that I was not there to help the new Soviet Union create its new music. I did not leave Russia of my own will, however, even though I disliked much in my Russia and in Russia generally. Yet the right to criticize Russia is mine, because Russia is mine and because I love it, and I do not give any foreigner that right. [Anatoly Lunacharsky in fact invited Stravinsky to conduct in Russia in 1925; Stravinsky declined.][26]

To which Craft, while in Russia, added: "I.S. *does* regret his uprooting and exile more than anything else in his life, which I say not because of a few emotional speeches, though they have come from the depths, but because of the change in his whole nature here."[27]

And so a tidal wave of feeling drowned the bulwark of "objectivity" and creative "autonomy" that had been Stravinsky's survival strategy in exile. The

Russia he had condemned as anarchic in his Norton Lectures he now regarded with unaffected love and pride. The anti-Soviet polemics adopted by Nabokov, and by American propagandists to whom Stravinsky now denied "the right to criticize Russia," were erased upon contact with Russian art and Russian earth. All his life, Stravinsky had thought in Russian and spoke other languages "in translation." Returning to California, he spoke Russian almost exclusively for a period of months.

Shostakovich, visiting the United States in 1949, had been urged to defect and liberate his muse. Turning those tables, the conductor Valery Gergiev, at a 2010 New York Stravinsky festival, asked out loud: What if, like Prokofiev, Stravinsky had visited the USSR in 1927? He answered: Stravinsky would have discovered a keenness of interest in himself and his music unknown in the West, and greater resources to produce and perform it. Rooted in the St. Petersburg of his youth and young adulthood, in the Mariinsky Theater milieu of his father and of his teacher Rimsky-Korsakov, he might ultimately have composed massive operas in the Russian tradition (as Prokofiev would in 1942 compose *War and Peace* upon returning "home").[28]

Limning a final reckoning of the Stravinsky odyssey, Charles Rosen plausibly summarized around the same time: "Stravinsky followed the few years of *Petrushka, The Rite of Spring*, and *Les Noces* with a turn to neoclassicism: he continued for many decades to produce some of his finest music, but nevertheless the energetic panache of the first years had evaporated."[29] Serge Diaghilev said much the same thing to the young Nicolas Nabokov: "Stravinsky is a great composer . . . the greatest of our time . . . To me, however, his best works are those of the beginning, those which he wrote before *Pulcinella*; I mean *Petrushka, Le Sacre, Les noces*. This does not imply that I don't admire *Oedipus Rex* and adore *Apollo*; both are classically beautiful and technically perfect. Who else can write like that nowadays? But you see—" (Here Diaghilev "stopped abruptly and changed the subject.")[30]

Surely, Stravinsky is one of the most courageously resilient figures in the history of Western music. Had there been less cause for resilience—had there been no revolution to evict him—he might have left a legacy less intriguingly textured with self-denial and reinvention, more grounded in riotous elemental energies. And his polemics of exile, an unlikely source for American Cold War propaganda, would never have been needed.

＊　＊　＊

No less than Stravinsky, Shostakovich required a survival strategy: his life was at stake.

Three vectors—all of them foreign to contemporaneous Western experience—defined his pursuit and experience of the creative act. The first traced a lineage of history and tradition. In Europe Schoenberg had radically broken with past practice; then Boulez, in an Oedipal frenzy, declared even Schoenberg dead. In Soviet Russia, the Iron Curtain paradoxically preserved a living pantheon of forebears. Though its confinements were undeniably a trap, the resulting time warp could ironically act to preserve traditions grown elusive and diffuse in the free West. Shostakovich could compose heroic symphonies without seeming "old-fashioned." He also composed his set of twenty-four Preludes and Fugues inspired by Bach. The autobiographical symphonic confessions of Tchaikovsky and Mahler, Mussorgsky's panoramic empathies, Mahler's caustic or poignant ironies were all more readily accessible to him than to his colleagues abroad.

Second, Shostakovich was a people's composer. For Western modernists, audience was not a priority. But the Soviet ideal spoke to Shostakovich: he was a musical moralist for whom Stravinsky, though "maybe the most brilliant composer of the twentieth century," seemed dangerously autonomous: "he always spoke only for himself." To his close friend Isaac Glikman, Shostakovich wrote: "Stravinsky the composer, I worship. Stravinsky the thinker, I despise."[31] Shostakovich engaged in a collective artistic endeavor, partnered by the leading Russian conductors, singers, and instrumentalists.

Third, Shostakovich was a tragic victim of the state. However much his "confessions" may have contained grains of sincerity, he looked back on the thirties and forties with horror. He had feared for his life. He had kept a packed bag in readiness for his arrest.[32] Yet he ultimately responded with ingenious strategies of musical subterfuge.

The pertinent lineage is long and fascinating. In Hollywood, beginning in 1934, a "Production Code" enforced by Joseph Breen inflicted philistine censorship to which studios and directors often responded with creative ingenuity. Even before the advent of Breen, when less severe restrictions were applied, Rouben Mamoulian wittily conceived a split screen to separate unmarried lovers in the same bed in his classic 1932 film musical *Love Me Tonight*. And Shostakovich was of course far from the first composer to encode messages. When Schumann quoted Beethoven's *An die ferne Geliebte* in his Fantasy in C, when he translated his wife's initials into musical notes, he was confiding extramusical allusions. There are many other such examples. But no previous composer deployed messaging as pervasively or fundamentally—or exigently—as Shostakovich did beginning in 1953, when he first used the motif D, E-flat, C, B (in German D–S–C–H, as in "Dmitri Schostakowitsch") to situate himself in narratives characterizing his fraught time and place. Solomon Volkov has likened Shostakovich to the *yurodivy*—the Holy Fool who "has the gift to see and hear what others know nothing about. But he tells the world about his insights in an intentionally paradoxical way, in code. The plays the fool while actually being a persistent exposer of evil and injustice. . . . But he sets strict limitations, rules, and taboos for himself."[33] Partly in spite of, partly because of the personal travails Shostakovich endured, this tensile intersection of creative vectors—his nourishing attachment to a lineage of historic forebears, his principles of artistic morality, and his inventive response to a totalitarian cultural dictatorship—proved at least as artistically empowering as the autonomy of "free artists."

That beleaguered Leningraders, in the throes of a vicious Nazi siege, spontaneously stood and cheered the proud finale of Shostakovich's Seventh Symphony for more than an hour complicates the notion that music is never "ideational," "essentially powerless to *express* anything at all." Shostakovich could not compose this music while the news from the front remained bleak. Only when the tide of battle turned could he resume his symphony in a burst of energy and excitement, finishing in less than two weeks.[34]

The ending of Shostakovich's Fifth—while, like any other music, possessing no fixed meaning—plausibly imparts a different message differently delivered. Of this superficially triumphant peroration, Shostakovich reportedly told Volkov: "I think that it is clear to everyone what happens in the Fifth. The rejoicing is forced, created under threat, as in *Boris Godunov*. It's as if someone were beating you with a stick and saying, 'your business is rejoicing, your business is rejoicing' and you rise, shaky, and go marching off, muttering 'our business is rejoicing, our business is rejoicing.' . . . People who came to the premiere of the Fifth in the best of moods wept." The Soviet novelist Alexander Fadeyev wrote in his diary: "The ending does not sound like a resolution (still less feel like a triumph or victory), but rather like a punishment or vengeance on someone. A terrible emotional force, but a tragic force."[35]

Of his friend Benjamin Britten, Shostakovich remarked: "What attracts me to Britten? The strength and sincerity of his talent, its surface simplicity and the intensity of its emotional effect."[36] In his own Tenth Symphony, simplicity and intensity produce a communal rite of Aeschylean impact and dimension. Premiered in 1953 in the wake of Stalin's death, it charts a trajectory evolving from pain and terror to giddy release. Whatever one makes of the possible extra-musical meanings—whatever the pertinence of Stalin's terror—it is a symphony that begins with an avalanche of grief. The avalanche takes the form of a massive twenty-minute first movement that slowly heaves to an anguished climax, recedes, and then—for the central development—attains an even higher climax, inhumanly sustained. The first theme quotes a Mahler phrase from *The Song of Earth* setting the words "Man lies in direst need." The coda is ghostly:

wind in the graveyard. Movement two, a scherzo, is short and ferociously swift. A snare drum and military brass are deployed at maximum velocity. This devouring juggernaut of menace and fear, it has been suggested, evokes Joseph Stalin. Movement three introduces the composer's twisting four-note signature; it proves susceptible to violent inflammation. Movement four proves a brilliant romp afflicted with fierce Stalin memories. A rousing declamation of the "Shostakovich" motto comes last. Is Shostakovich dancing on Stalin's grave? Volkov: "Solzhenitsyn wrote that he wielded a sword in the hand of God to fight the evil empire. Shostakovich would never say that. But he felt that he was on earth to play an important societal and even political role."[37]

The Soviet American music historian Henry Orlov, in a memorable 1976 commentary, summarized that Shostakovich was "an artist-citizen, a thinker, philosopher, pamphleteer, poet, and preacher in music, who lived by the hardships and hopes of this world, who strove to understand, explain, shock, revile, and support." Orlov also writes: "Those born and brought up in a free society can hardly comprehend what it takes to remain honest in a police state or imagine themselves in the place of someone whose very thought of liberty puts freedom or life at stake. . . . Let us try to understand what it takes to be honest under the Damocles sword of fear, when even a look, a gesture, or a casual remark could be fatal. . . . Omnipresent supervision over every step . . . and the fear of being exposed and denounced represented only the outer aspect of this situation. An individual still capable of thinking independently lived in a stage of chronic inner doubleness." Shostakovich's formative years were notably supported by the early "golden age" of Soviet culture, when artists felt impelled to seek new paths of expression in quest of a better future. For Orlov, the final fruits of this first phase, *Lady Macbeth* (1932) and the Symphony No. 4 (1936), "show Shostakovich at the summit of inner creative freedom and reveal his true face as a composer." But, as Orlov also notes: "Although the ideals of the Revolution had been transformed into a morbid reality, Shostakovich long remained faithful to them."[38] For many listeners, Shostakovich's powers actually peaked after 1936. The crucible of World War II reanimated his genius for gravitas and empathy; in its wake came his genius for self-reflection. And all of it—the gripping fear and stoic pain, the hope and the hopelessness—was a communal, cathartic channeling of a nation's tragic doubleness.[39]

Post-Shostakovich, the Russian novelist Andrei Bitov proposed as a metaphor for Soviet cultural achievement the manner in which diamonds are formed: coal subjected to enormous pressure.[40] Sometime after, the Russian conductor Genady Rozhdestvensky was asked how to account for the Soviet achievement in music. His reply:

It's the mechanism of resistance, similar to what happens to wine. One day in France, in the Bordeaux region, I was driving in a car. On one side of the road was stony ground. On both sides, there were vineyards. It turns out that rich soil produces wine inferior to that produced on stony ground. Because in order to produce wine of the highest quality, the roots have to fight to make their way through. Its this struggle that produces a great product.

It's the same here. Resistance to the system, strengthening of ties in adversity, finding in creative activity a marvelous outlet. Fighting for survival as a person as crucial. The Soviet Union wasn't the only system to reveal these things. Every totalitarian regime secretes this phenomenon, as paradoxical as it may seem. In their opposition, their fight to defend their artistic beliefs, these people achieved awesome results. They drew their strength from it. Nevertheless, one must never never forget how many people sacrificed their lives for it.[41]

*   *   *

In the four decades following publication of Volkov's *Testimony: The Memoirs of Dmitri Shostakovich*, a formidable literature has debated Shostakovich's "messages in a bottle." That they are there no one denies. How much do they say, how much do they matter continue to arouse controversy. Less widely scrutinized is the related topic of Shostakovich and film. He scored more than two dozen movies. And here there are messages galore.

As for Prokofiev, Khachaturian, and countless other Soviet composers, scoring films for Shostakovich was first of all a source of income. The films vary widely in quality and interest. But his peak achievements marry high art with collective endeavor serving an audience of maximum size and reach. And there is a spine: his sustained collaboration with the master director Grigory Kozintsev. The manner in which their eight films mirror the Soviet cultural moment over a period of four decades is a beckoning topic. The beginning and end points—*The New Babylon* (1929) and *King Lear* (1970)—suggest a journey of memorable variety and consequence. No less than Shostakovich's concert works, it contextualizes the claims of Nicolas Nabokov and the Congress for Cultural Freedom.

An acknowledged classic of Soviet silent cinema, a cheeky product of the avant-garde twenties, *The New Babylon* is a Marxist version of the Paris Commune of 1871: heroic workers seize control of the city only to be massacred by French and German forces united by class. The Factory of the Eccentric Actor, created by Kozintsev and Leonid Trauberg (who codirected *The New Babylon*), promulgated a manic assault on cultural pretension. Their satire of Parisian decadence is populated by livid caricatures. An eccentric antipathy to linear narrative mates with the signature montage effects of Soviet silent film. The hectic pace does not preclude poetic homages to Daumier and Degas.

The New Babylon differs from other Russian silent films, also products of a feverish experimentalism, for combining social context and ideology with individualized human drama. That is, this polemical dramatization of violent class warfare is infiltrated by a gritty love story mating a fiery Communard with a hapless, placeless soldier. These characters, brilliantly enacted, are not the bold archetypes populating such Soviet silent-film landmarks as Vsevolod Pudovkin's *Mother* (1926) and Alexander Dovzhenko's *Earth* (1930). Nor is their intimacy a sentimental diversion. Rather, its shattering hopelessness meshes with the film's fierce depiction of political betrayal: the personal intermingles with the epic.

In 1929 Shostakovich was all of twenty-three years old. Four years previous, his First Symphony already encapsulated the irony and (remarkably) the pathos of his mature voice. In *The New Babylon*, his debut film score, he flaunts his enfant terrible energies. But as the film moves from satire to tragedy, his emotional range proves limitless. Omnipresent montage juxtaposes decadence with travail; Shostakovich adds a third plane of expression. When bourgeois revelers sing the Marseilles while French soldiers prepare to attack French citizens, Shostakovich responds with feigned relish, then decomposes their song with an Offenbach cancan. This compositional tour de force subverts a visceral response with a political critique. Meanwhile, the soldier himself—seething with discontent and confusion—cannot tell which side he is on. The film's jolting contradictions in content and tone jostle feeling and thought. Notwithstanding its ideological message, it does not spoon-feed. It is a propaganda tract, an aesthetic anthem, and a complex work of art. For the young Shostakovich, it was doubtless a heady learning experience. Its impact on his future development is ponderable.

The Kozintsev/Shostakovich *King Lear*, forty-one years later, is a ripe 140-minute masterpiece, a Shakespeare film to set beside any produced by Laurence Olivier or Akira Kurosawa—and as "Russian" as their adaptations are British or Japanese. It shares with *The New Babylon* a double aspect: added to Shakespeare's human drama is a social dimension inspired, in part, by *Boris Godunov*. The result is a film so necessarily vast in landscape and terrain that it fails on a home screen: to breathe, it needs the biggest possible image and the best possible sound. It would hardly be an exaggeration to suggest that Shakespeare's iconic seventeenth-century play is here conflated with Mussorgsky's iconic nineteenth-century opera. Both play and opera deal with a ruler who sins, and who dies consumed by crazed guilt. But there is a more literal resemblance, a character common to *Lear* and *Boris* and of special importance to Shostakovich: the truth-telling Fool.

In *Lear* the Fool is the king's conscience, permitted to criticize with impunity. In *Boris* the Fool alone can tell the Czar to his face that he is a murderer. Mussorgsky gives the Fool—the *yurodivy*—the last word: one of the most original endings in opera. Boris's death, however affecting, is penultimate. The culminating scene, in the Kromy Forest, shows the People—a pervasive presence—acclaim a false pretender to the throne. They march on Moscow, emptying the stage but for the Fool, who sings: "Cry, cry Russian land / Russian people / Cry." In the Kozintsev/Shostakovich *Lear*, Lear's death is witnessed by the People—a ubiquitous presence. The funeral cortege exits, the screen empties—and the Fool plays his plaintive song. It is Mussorgsky's ending, transplanted to Shakespeare's play.

Mussorgsky's Fool embodies a mass of sad, suffering humanity. So, too, does the Kozintsev/Shostakovich Fool. His centrality is such that his song also begins the movie, accompanying the credits. Then comes a trudging, placeless horde. Shostakovich's scoring of this processional echoes Mussorgsky. The beginning of Shakespeare's play is delayed fully five minutes. Doubtless, Shakespeare's dysfunctional royal family implicitly embodies a larger malaise. In the Kozintsev/Shostakovich *King Lear*, this malaise is explicit. We see it. It is epic, as vast as Russia itself. Kozintsev wrote of the ending of Shakespeare's *King Lear*: "*Lear* has no end—at least there is no finale in the play: none of the usual solemn trumpets of tragedy, or magnificent burials. The bodies, even of kings, are carried out under conditions of war; nobody even says a few elevated words. The time for words is over."[42] This dire view was also Shostakovich's view, numbed by Stalinist fear and oppression.

Reinforcing these linkages of *Lear* with *Boris* is Shostakovich's reverence for Mussorgsky. He undertook a new orchestration of *Boris Godunov*. He orchestrated Mussorgsky's *Songs and Dances of Death*. His D-minor Prelude and Fugue for solo piano sustains the poise and clarity of Bach's high example—but its vast, mournful terrain equally evokes Mussorgsky's primal choral utterances, music itself indebted to Russian liturgical chant. The refulgent closing page—an object lesson in scoring, in which every register of the modern grand piano is craftily deployed to maximize sonority—pays homage to Mussorgsky's "Great Gate at Kiev."

For Shostakovich, as for Mussorgsky, art was never for art's sake. It possessed an ethical dimension. It commented on human affairs. Pauline Fairclough, in her recent Shostakovich biography, calls Mussorgsky Shostakovich's "spiritual mentor." Shostakovich himself reportedly said of Mussorgsky:

Mussorgsky's concept is profoundly democratic. The people are the base of everything. The people are here and the rulers are there. The rule forced on the people is immoral and fundamentally anti-people. The best intentions of individuals don't count. That's Mussorgky's position and I dare hope that it is also mine.

Meaning in music—that must sound very strange for most people. Particularly in the West. It's here in Russia that the question is usually posed: What was the composer trying to say, after all? The questions are naïve, of course, but despite their naivete and crudity, they definitely merit being asked. . . . Can music make man stop and think? Can it cry out and thereby draw man's attention to various vile acts? All these questions began for me with Mussorgsky.[43]

Shostakovich identified with Shakespeare's truth-telling Fool. That is one reason Kozintsev's Fool, not Shakespeare's Albany, has the last word.

*   *   *

"We must never forget that art is not a form of propaganda; it is a form of truth," said JFK. "In free society art is not a weapon and it does not belong to the spheres of polemic and ideology. Artists are not 'engineers of the soul.'"[44] For Kennedy, political art was an oxymoron. But *The New Babylon* is artistic and political in equal measure.

Nabokov called Shostakovich "orthodox," "well-behaved," "not new or imaginative," "neither daring nor particularly new," "old-fashioned," "provincial." He claimed his music was cheapened by mass appeal. But musically encoding the death of a tyrant, for a grateful mass of listeners, is an imaginative achievement. It is not orthodox to compose a fugue conflating Bach and Mussorgsky. It is daring to mate *King Lear* with *Boris Godunov*. In 1962 the British director Peter Brook created a *King Lear* with a cold and heartless king, played by Paul Scofield, and turned it into a movie hailed as a milestone in Shakespeare interpretation. Does anyone watch Brook's *King Lear* today?

Nabokov wrote, and Stravinsky agreed, that "it is as difficult to describe the music of Shostakovitch as to describe the form and color of an oyster . . . it is shapeless in style and form and impersonal in color." He likened all Soviet music to an assembly-line product "turned out by Ford or General Motors." In fact, aligned with a pantheon of forebears beginning with Johann Sebastian Bach, fortified by a species of twentieth-century cultural populism, textured with necessary acts of creative subterfuge, Shostakovich's achievement is distinctive.

Scripted by Arthur Schlesinger, Kennedy said at Amherst: "The artist, however faithful to his personal vision of reality, becomes the last champion of the individual mind and sensibility against an intrusive society and an officious state. The great artist is thus a solitary figure. . . . [I]f art is to nourish the roots of our culture, society must set the artist free to follow his vision wherever it takes him." Buffeted by crude ideological currents, a willing or unwilling cultural bureaucrat, Shostakovich was and was not a "solitary figure." Certainly, he could never be called "the last champion of the individual mind and sensibility against an . . . officious state." But he indisputably managed to "nourish the roots" of Russian culture.

Toward the end, he reportedly told Solomon Volkov:

There were no particularly happy moments. . . . It was gray and dull and it makes me sad to think about it. . . .

I have thought that my life was replete with sorrow and that it would be hard to find a more miserable man. But when I started going over the life stories of my friends and acquaintances, I was horrified. Not one of them had an easy or a happy life. Some came to a terrible end, some died in terrible suffering, and the lives of many of them could easily be called more miserable than mine.

And that made me even sadder. I was remembering my friends and all I saw was corpses, mountains of corpses. I'm not exaggerating. I mean mountains. And the picture filled me with a horrible depression. I'm sad, I'm grieving all the time.[45]

Mstislav Rostropovich testified that when in 1974 he decided to defect: "I couldn't bring myself to tell Shostakovich. I just went with my wife to his house, and I gave him a copy of my letter to Mr. Brezhnev. He read it, and immediately started crying. He said, 'In whose hands are you leaving me to die?'"[46] One year later, Shostakovich was dead.

Vladimir Feltsman once summarized:

Everyone had to modify their behavior in order to survive. Shostakovich's life was filled with constant tension between his sense of decency and self-worth, and the necessity to compromise with the government and personally with Stalin. It took a heavy toll, but it allowed him to create his music. And, to me, this is the main duty of the artist, no matter what. It is easy to pass judgment and criticize his "compromises and weaknesses" from the comforts of our Western safe havens, but he lived his destiny as well as he could. [The composer] Alfred Schnittke once told me: "For creative people, there is no life in Russia, only destiny." Perhaps this observation applies to all really great artists in some degree.[47]

Shostakovich's thick glasses gave nothing away. However craftily or haphazardly, however unhappily, he secured a paradoxical artistic satisfaction.

CHAPTER 6

SURVIVAL STRATEGIES

Nicolas Nabokov

Vladimir Nabokov, born to cosmopolitan wealth and privilege in St. Petersburg in 1899, left Russia forever in 1919. He settled in the United States in 1940. His novels deal with the experience of exile in ways obvious and not. Humbert Humbert, in *Lolita* (1955), is a polyglot émigré who despoils a twelve-year-old New World "nymphet." He says he is "allergic to Europe," an "old and rotting world." Lolita for him evokes an irresistible prelapsarian beauty: a lost homeland. He is a predator, a murderer, a madman. Charles Kinbote, in *Pale Fire* (1962), is a polyglot émigré in whom madness takes another form. He elaborately conceives an invented past, with himself cast as a dispossessed king. "Vladimir [Nabokov's] two greatest books," writes the literary critic Edward Mendelson, "are warnings to himself, studies in the price he would have paid had he tried (somewhat as his cousin Nicolas had tried) to make real in his present-day life the vision of beauty he had seen long ago in Russia." The artworks celebrated in Nicolas's international festivals, Mendelsohn suggests, were Kinbote-like weapons in a "private campaign to regain his eastern kingdom from its usurpers."[1]

In *Speak, Memory* (1951), Vladimir remembers loneliness in Paris and Berlin, his "meager stock" of non-Russian and non-Jewish acquaintances during the interwar years, "an animal aching yearn for the still fresh reek of Russia," "an exciting sense of *rodina*, 'motherland.'" He crafts a paean to lost childhood and lost Russia, to "remote, almost legendary, almost Sumerian images of St. Petersburg and Moscow." "Give me anything on any continent resembling the

St. Petersburg countryside," he confides, "and my heart melts." But these are asides; even in autobiography, Nabokov is no more confessional than Stravinsky in his music, or Balanchine in his Stravinsky ballets. Rather, he delights in the linguistic pleasures of his medium of choice. His precision of memory and apprehension is a facet of precise and subtle language—as in Stravinsky or Balanchine, an aesthetic tour de force.

As for Nicolas, his memoirs—in *Old Friends and New Music* and *Bagazh*—are less deft, less concentrated in meaning; they are also significantly less stable in direction and self-assessment. But he does limn a prelapsarian moment: "Of the three autumn and winter seasons of my life that I spent in the Russian countryside [the] first remains clearest in my memory. . . . [T]he intense radiance, the depth and lucidity, of those few images are such that whenever they are evoked it seems as if that early part of my Russian childhood came back in all its sweetness, brilliant with a thousand mysteries and surprises."[2] Nicolas did not sublimely transcend memory after the fashion of Vladimir. Rather, like Kinbote, he invented a new narrative to suit circumstantial needs, a story in which Dmitri Shostakovich was the evil usurper. And Nicolas attempted to make his invented world real—to actually enter and participate.

Vladimir, the novelist, pursued an inward vision. Professionally, he inhabited (sometimes barely) an elite world of culture aloof from the quotidian. His personal life, his enduring marriage, was apparently stable. Nicolas, the Cold War cultural ideologue, acted out his official role in arenas large and small, private and public. As a result, he was vulnerable in ways Vladimir was not. Five marriages and a history of nervous disorders suggest a price paid.

The condition of exile demands resourceful strategizing, and such strategies are rarely predictable. Nicolas Nabokov called it "an accident of fate" that in 1940 he met Chip Bohlen at Manhattan's Mayflower Hotel. At thirty-six, Bohlen was a year younger than Nabokov—but had already been posted three times to Moscow in diplomatic service. His like-minded colleagues, not "starry-eyed about Stalin's Russia," already included George Kennan. A few years later, in postwar Germany, Nabokov was stunned by the fate of "DPs," "displaced persons," returned to Soviet Russia "to slavery and certain destruction." "My old nostalgia, my deep-rooted illness . . . left me. I knew then that my Russia, the Russia of an exile's wish-dream, had been wiped out."[3] The anti-Stalinist fervor of Bohlen and Kennan fitted his situation and mood. The connections to Arthur Schlesinger and John F. Kennedy followed in due course. Nabokov was lucky, to be sure, but his lineage and aplomb were formidable assets. And he was actually Russian. In *Bagazh* he recalled that Berlin, "a Russian-speaking native of Riga," was "fully English by adoption, by scholarship, and by training, and had never been in the Soviet Union." Bohlen had "clear answers" when questions were raised "as to the reaction of the Soviet bureaucracy to a given situation or to a particular problem."

> Yet neither Bohlen nor Berlin was even in the remotest sense Russian by *instinct*. How could they be? One of them was English, the other American. As Chip once said, "the only one among us who is gut-wise Russian is you." In other words, their reflexes, their intuition, their unconscious instinctive reactions were of necessity non-Russian, whereas mine could be gauged as such. . . . Although I never thought of myself as a "hearty Russian," Chip believed and insisted that I was one. "You've remained just as Russian as they come, brother," he would say.[4]

Did it not occur to Bohlen that a "gut-wise Russian" who happened to be a dispossessed exile might deliver tainted impressions of his childhood homeland, now distant in time and place? But then Nabokov's expertise was in music, not literature and letters—and music, especially when "modern," was and is a field typically considered esoteric by the respectful outsider.

And Nabokov himself, did he really think that Shostakovich's composer's voice was essentially "dull" and "utilitarian"? Did he harbor doubts? If his musical judgments were surely wrong, he was neither obtuse nor ignorant. Marooned in the New World, laden with *bagazh*, he discovered himself in possession of a fortuitous opportunity to fashion Cold War cultural ideology for the U.S. Department of State. To his impressive roster of intellectual and artistic friendships, he now added an international array of statesmen and their advisers. He became "generalissimo" of American cultural propaganda. But this singular vocation, which impelled a singular view of a far-away adversary, was necessarily less autonomous, and ultimately less permanent, than that of his cousin the famous novelist.

The boldest Nicolas Nabokov portrait I know is also the most speculative: a 2015 article in the *New York Review of Books* by Edward Mendelson (who though an authority on W. H. Auden did not know Nabokov personally). Mendelson writes:

> He responded to exile by opening himself as a focus of warmth and welcome, so rich in words and energy that only a few friends seem to have noticed the wound inflicted by his exile, the absence of something central, deep within himself. His intellectual integrity was passionate and unwavering, but his relations with others, though extravagantly generous, seldom seemed to have had the intimacy made possible by a focused, cohesive selfhood. . . . He said of himself in [*Bagazh*], "as Ariel says, my wish was and is 'to please.'" In his book, he de-

scribes himself and his friends in the broad strokes of a friendly caricaturist or raconteur. Everyone, including himself, lives on the surface; no one shows the outer signs of an inner life. . . .

The obscure absence at the center of himself seems to have been linked both to his good-natured polygamy and his recurring depressions that made so deep a contrast with the "light and laughter in a dark age" that gave pleasure to his friends. [His depressions] seem at times to have been episodes of chaos and melodrama. Stephen Spender . . . told of a working visit to Nabokov when he "swept all the food and the cutlery off the table in front of him and buried his head in his arms. Glass and porcelain lay broken around his feet, but he paid no attention. He was weeping uncontrollably."[5]

This is a sweeping reportrayal, but there are details in Nabokov's self-portrayal that suggestively support it. Though his memories come alive when he recalls his Russian childhood, they remain shaded with ambiguities. A nest of comforts, games, and instruction was incompletely tended. Raised by nannies, he did not enjoy a close relationship with either parent. His parents divorced when he was an infant. He heard rumors that his real father was another. He was rarely alone with his mother. The family was large and gregarious, with Russian and German branches and far-flung properties. The pertinent estates stretched from the Crimean isthmus northward to Melitopol, eastward to the Sea of Azov, and westward to the Dniepir, with additional holdings in the Crimean peninsula; houses in Simferopol, Kherson, Odessa, and Moscow; a villa on the Caucasian coast; and two Black Sea harbors—a diffusion of riches. He was presented to Serge Diaghilev as "an ephemeral relative"—his stepfather's first cousin having married Diaghilev's half-brother. His biographer Vincent Giroud mentions in passing a cousin kidnapped by the KGB and sent to a Gulag camp.[6]

Nabokov's marginally Russian birthplace, near Minsk, bordering Lithuania and Poland, made him Belorussian, and in *Bagazh* he declared himself "forever a 'Beloruss,'" even though neither side of his family had "anything to do with" Belorussia or Lithuania.[7] His articles for *Atlantic Monthly* misidentify his birthplace as St. Petersburg[8]—and it is St. Petersburg that most excited his early musical impressions. The Mariinsky Theater provoked "torrents of nostalgia." Of the theater's Imperial Ballet: "In all my association with ballet I have never seen anything approaching it in perfection." Of Fyodor Chaliapin singing Ivan's prayer in Glinka's *A Life for the Tsar*: "No one else, before or after him, has been able to evoke its moving lyricism and at the same time show a great actor's perception of its dramatic meaning." Yet, Nabokov continued, in later life he "began to react against certain obvious failings in Chaliapin's musical taste."[9] The same revisionism turned him against Scriabin and Rachmaninoff. Of Shostakovich's *yurodivy*-like hero, he wrote in 1971 that Mussorgsky was overrated in the West: "All is tentative, occasional, brilliant insights clogged by howlers of imperfection . . . burps of Wagner via Korsakov."[10] Encountering the tenor Ivan Kozlovsky singing Lenski's aria from Tchaikovsky's *Eugene Onegin* in Berlin after the war, Nabokov lamented "the awful provincial taste in delivery, its greasy outmoded sentimentality reminiscent of the worst habits of the American radio crooner."[11] One would never know from this account that Kozlovsky's Lenski was and remains to many one of the supreme achievements in Russian operatic performance; the singer's "liberties" in this famous music, evident on his classic recordings, in fact systematically shade "day" and "night" as life and death.

Russia, for the young Nabokov, was nothing less than the source of music—defined by "the continuous presence of song." Sorting it all out as of 1951, he recorded that during his "early years of exile," nostalgia "took hold of me at times with unbearable intensity." Upon settling in the United States, however, "I had a home again, a status, a country. . . . The old nostalgia, the wishful dreams that haunted me . . . died away." His Russian acquaintances began to disappear. World War II excited "a vague glimmer of hope for the fate of Russia." Instead, he found "a final cure" for nostalgia "in the bitter recognition of the hard, morbid truth." His Russia, "the Russia of an exile's wish dream," was wiped out; "all that remained of it were these tragic human beings, each one of whom had the same story to tell: misery, hunger, abuse, and violence." It has "nothing in common with what was once a real culture, a burgeoning civilization." "Another breed of men, men from a ghastly inhuman world" had taken over.[12] No less than with Stravinsky, this antipathy for what Russia had become was different from that of European and American compatriots on the anti-Communist Left. As Stephen Spender put it, he was "hard to control, for his feud with Soviet Russia, and with [Soviet] Russian music, was personal."[13]

Detached from his past, Nabokov was widely esteemed, worldly, well liked. Yet *Bagazh* is revealingly elusive. "The stories I tell in this book," he begins, are not "concerned with my own self. In one way or another, I am hiding behind each one of them. . . . I do not impose upon the reader my repetitive experiences of matrimony and of their component part, divorce. Nor do I discuss my loves or other personal affairs. They are private matters that have no place here." Midway through, he suddenly calls himself "shifty, wayward, insecure." Many are the anecdotes that evoke Nabokov as volatile, mercurial, hyperbolic. Michael Josselson, who admired and partnered him over a long period of time, in 1975 remembered (in correspondence with Sidney Hook) being tested by Nabokov's

"Chekhovian fits, tears and breast-beating one day, effusive affection the next."[14] The Polish writer Witold Gombrowicz once wrote to Nabokov: "I think you are an artistic phenomenon very difficult to assess in its exact value. The difficulty comes from your being an amalgam: you are never 'within' something, but always 'in between.' For example, you are between the spirit and the senses; between East (Russia) and West (Paris-Rome); between music and the theater; between music and words; between culture and primitivism; between art and life, etc., and there always is something in you that is a pretext for something else."[15]

A window of sorts on Nabokov's inner turmoil, undisclosed in *Bagazh*, was his relationship to the Catholic theologian/philosopher Jacques Maritain. Vincent Giroud writes that Nabokov experienced "a deep personal and religious crisis" in France in the 1920s—and that, according to the conductor/composer Igor Markevitch, it was Maritain who rescued Nabokov from the temptation of suicide. Nabokov was then a regular participant in the salon Maritain kept with his Russian wife, Raissa, on the outskirts of Paris. A charismatic, worldly presence, an ardent music lover and dedicated aesthetician, Maritain influenced Stravinsky's neoclassicism and its intellectual moorings. Though Maritain's passion for music was imprecise, his predilections were clear. He disliked thundering climaxes and definitive cadences. He avowed art that was "radiant" and "self-standing," elevating and purifying, a striving for perfection. He did not endorse communism, nihilism, surrealism, or dada. Creative expression was trans- or postnational. It more depended on inward resource than outward circumstance. It was based in faith. Nabokov did not experience the fervent conversion to Russian Orthodoxy that overcame Stravinsky in France in the twenties. But Maritain's stabilizing influence buttressed Nabokov's espousal of musical idioms that counteracted "nationalistic chauvinism or parochialism." It could only have supported his allegiance to the cosmopolitan/religious Stravinsky, not to mention his aversion to the Soviet atheist Shostakovich.[16]

In the context of exile and displacement, Nabokov's leadership role with the Congress for Cultural Freedom furnished a life anchor—for a time. As its propagandist in chief, he in effect amalgamated the "cultural freedom" rhetoric of Sidney Hook and Arthur Schlesinger with a Stravinskyan insistence on creative "autonomy." But then the CCF became a source of confusion and shame. As early as 1955, the literary critic William Empson furiously denounced *Encounter* as an organ of American propaganda pretending to be British.[17] As of 1966, when CIA funding for the CCF was conclusively documented and acknowledged, not only did Nabokov know with certainty that he had been living a lie—so did everyone else. His argument that the same CIA propaganda initiative could and should have been mounted overtly—that an informational "Marshall Plan" would have made more sense—was and remains debatable; as defenders of the CIA have pointed out, many in Congress would have resisted applying federal funds to promoting modernist music and art. In any event, Nabokov resigned his CCF position in May 1966—weeks after the *New York Times* specifically mentioned the Congress and *Encounter* as CIA beneficiaries. His resignation was formally accepted the following September. Though he insisted the Congress had "never knowingly received support, directly or indirectly, from any secret source," he had at the very least long suspected something of the kind. To his CCF colleague Robert Oppenheimer he confided, in November, that he felt he had been made a target for public slander.[18] Beyond a doubt, the personal toll of the 1966 disclosures was great. (I reference the case of Elliott Carter in a note.)[19] Schlesinger, for one, felt they shortened Nabokov's life.[20]

A final ingredient in Nabokov's mercurial journey—his improvised career in exile—was his submerged vocation as a composer. Rachmaninoff in exile had to reconfigure his musical activities to emphasize concertizing over composition—it generated income. Nabokov's reconfiguration—his metamorphosis into America's generalissimo of Cold War cultural propaganda—likewise penalized the creative act. Might his early prominence as the composer of the *Ode*, as produced by Diaghilev, and of *Union Pacific*, as danced by Colonel de Basil's Ballets Russes, have led to comparably visible subsequent achievements? Did he have adequate opportunity to find out? Or was he too much "in between"? A widely read review of his 1965 *Don Quixote* score for Balanchine—the most noticed of his later compositions—was written by Andrew Porter in the *New Yorker:* "There is nothing, alas, that can be done about Nicolas Nabokov's wretched score, which lays a deadening hand on the evening. It is short-breathed, repetitive, feeble in its little attempts to achieve vivacity by recourse to a trumpet solo or a gong stroke."[21] Porter embraced the high modernism of Nabokov's friend and beneficiary Elliott Carter. Nabokov did, too—but not in his own composer's heart.

*   *   *

A sizable body of recent scholarly literature positions the CIA, via its cultural propaganda efforts, as an advocate for high modernist visual and musical styles—in particular, the abstract expressionists and serialists. The idea is that the Cold War impelled or supported a species of fierce individualism, rejecting alignment with the political Right (McCarthy) or Left (Communists), and equally rebuffing "midcult." The resulting aesthetic is relatively unencumbered by past practice. In the case of nontonal musical composition, it is also "scientific," recondite, necessarily elitist. The music historian Richard Taruskin, a crucial voice, writes:

> The status of twelve-tone music as a no-spin zone, a haven of political non-alignment and implicit resistance in the postwar world, was widely touted and accepted from the start, both in Europe, where it could be seen to embody the "neither/nor" option . . . opposing Cold War powers, and in America, where Aaron Copland, for one, sought refuge in it when called to account for his erst-while political engagements. These were among the factors determining seri-alism's seeming natural selection . . . as a musical lingua franca. . . . They were what ultimately made the utopian extension into "total" serialism—the use of neutral, cultural unburdened algorithms to control an ever greater number of musical parameters in addition to pitch [as influentially practiced by Milton Babbitt in the US and Pierre Boulez abroad]—so compelling."[22] (For Copland's odyssey, see my pages 124–27.)

Though Nicolas Nabokov, too, stressed the "autonomy" of the "free artist," he does not really fit this postwar paradigm, however much it may have inflected other CIA-funded operations. His Stravinskyan aesthetic base was modernist, but the high-modernist extension into esoteric, mathematical methodologies was not for him. Nor was he disposed to endorse Germanic intensities, whether cerebral or emotive. At the Paris festival, as we have seen, the visual arts com-ponent eschewed the likes of Jackson Pollack and Mark Rothko. It was mainly the avant-garde chamber concerts, curated by Fred Goldbeck, that embraced composers whom Taruskin and others align with a Cold War sensibility. This list notably includes Charles Ives, whose *Concord* Sonata was sampled on Gold-beck's series, and whose thorny musical vocabulary was read (and misread) as protomodernist by his midcentury advocates. So distant was Nabokov from the world of the *Concord* Sonata that in a 1952 letter to Leopold Stokowski, he misspelled the composer's name as "Yves."[23]

A highlight of Nabokov's 1954 Rome festival, as we have seen, was the Eu-ropean premiere of Elliott Carter's First String Quartet. The festival repertoire also prominently featured several twelve-tone works. Frances Stonor Saunders, in *The Cultural Cold War*, cites the Rome festival to support her argument that the CIA advanced cutting-edge high modernism. But the festival's advisory board comprised Stravinsky, Benjamin Britten, Samuel Barger, Luigi Dallapiccola, Darius Milhaud, Frank Martin, Arthur Honegger, and Virgil Thomson—among whom only Dallapiccola could be called a high-modernist priest. Nabokov was never an ardent advocate of nontonal composition. Pierre Boulez, who was, once wrote to him: "The worst thing is that you seem to think that the situation [composers isolated from one another] can be improved by these congresses. What stupidity! What do you think is resolved through muddy waffling, by gathering a few puppets together in a well staked-out cesspit. They may be able to enjoy the quality of each others' sweat; nothing more fruitful."[24]

In fact, Nabokov's emphasis on artistic independence predates the Cold War. Its origins, as we have seen, go back to Stravinsky's polemics of the 1930s and forties, and to the experience of emigration. Though their survival strategies prioritized the condition of "freedom," neither Stravinsky nor Nabokov was kindred to Ives or Pollack, Babbitt or Boulez. A counterexample is Daryl Dayton, who as music adviser to the United States Information Agency (USIA) in the 1970s wrote:

> For the past several years we have projected the image of Charles Ives, as the great American musical pioneer, the first American to work outside the European musical mainstream, the first to develop a truly American musical profile. . . . We have disseminated thousands of recordings and scores of Ives' music. . . . We have sponsored distinguished lecturers, both American and foreign, in illustrated programs of Ives' music. We have held special "Charles Ives Music Weeks" in such cities as Lisbon, Sao Paulo, Athens, Mexico, D.F., Paris, Bucharest.[25]

This plausible initiative, more logical than CIA-funded performances of *Billy Budd* and *Wozzeck* (as in Paris in 1952), could never have come from Nabokov.

If Nabokov's advocacy of Elliott Carter seems not to fit this picture, an explanation was offered by the American composer Martin Brody. In 2001 Brody served as a composer in residence at the American Academy in Rome, where his predecessors included Nicolas Nabokov. Scouring the academy archives, Brody surmised:

> For all of 1953–54, Nicolas Nabokov, Secretary-General of the Congress of Cultural Freedom and impresario of the Rome Festival, was also Resident Composer at the American Academy in Rome. Carter was also a Fellow of the Academy during the same year. After its re-opening shortly after the war, the American Academy in Rome became a hotbed of US cultural diplomacy, known as the third American Embassy, alongside the US embassies in Italy and the Holy See. The Academy's Director Laurance Roberts and his wife Isabel held court, with Nabokov often at their side, as premiere US cultural ambassadors in the Eternal City, then a site of intense anti-Communist and soft power machinations. While mingling in this heady atmosphere, and aided by his long time friend Nabokov, Carter wove his own tight set of professional networks—one that provided him with varies forms of encouragement and support for years to come.
>
> Carter served as a trusted confidante to Secretary-General Nabokov, who . . . saw himself as a chameleon-like double agent (politics and art) and an old school

humanist, whose musical tastes were colored as much by personal affinities as shifting compositional aesthetic or political expediency. His big gamble on the avant-garde in Rome was a one-off affair with messy results. But even as his strategies as a political operator and cultural impresario morphed repeatedly over the ensuing years, his loyalty to Carter and Stravinsky endured for the remainder of his life.[26]

As this credible snapshot attests, Nabokov's gift for charming personal accommodation could trump or at least mediate his intellectual and aesthetics predilections. The most stubborn of his aversions remained toward the Soviet side of things. But these, too, proved susceptible to change.

*   *   *

In 1967 the Congress for Cultural Freedom was reconstituted as the International Association for Cultural Freedom and continued to exist with funding from the Ford Foundation. Nabokov's attentions had by then refocused on overseeing the Berlin Festival (1963–66), in which capacity he discovered himself bonding with an unlikely friend: Pyotr Abrassimov, the Soviet ambassador, whom he regularly visited in East Berlin. Abrassimov urged Nabokov to visit Russia and see for himself what it had become. In 1962 the prospect of Stravinsky visiting Russia had driven Nabokov to fevered opposition. Two years later, however, his anti-Communist ardor was fading. Michael Josselson was vexed and dissuaded Nabokov from taking up Abrassimov's offer. "You could become an unwitting instrument of Soviet policy in Germany," he warned.[27] Three years after that, with the Congress disbanded, Nabokov said yes. The dates of this startling volte-face were June 21 to July 1, 1967.[28]

He began in Moscow, a city he never knew, and detested it. "In me there's not a shadow of a tremor, not a whiff of an emotion, or even the slightest nostalgia," he recorded in *Bagazh*. "Only irritation and impatience." In an unpublished travel diary, he described "an uncouth, disoriented, unfinished and utterly bewildering city.... Thank God! I am a foreigner here. A foreigner *everywhere*." To a correspondent, he wrote that he "hated the Kremlin and its empty churches: coloured wards with gilded cupolas."

But his various visits with composers he had vilified were absorbing and entertaining. Like everyone else, he adored the warmth of Aram Khachaturian. He found Yekaterina Furtseva, the Soviet minister of culture, charming. He heard and perused music by young composers—Edison Denisov, Alfred Schnittke, Boris Tishchenko, Valentin Silvestrov—that was "some of the most advanced" he had ever encountered. (He nonetheless considered it "indispensable" that they travel West.) Mstislav Rostropovich invited him to an eventful birthday party at his dacha, where he encountered the conductor Gennady Rozhdestvensky—and also Dmitri Shostakovich and his wife. "Poor, poor sick man," Nabokov wrote in his diary. He also observed that Shostakovich did not appear to bear any grudge, not even for their Waldorf Astoria confrontation in 1949. He did not appreciate that Shostakovich's amenability was chronic and meaningless. (In *Testimony* Shostakovich would reportedly say: "There can be no friendship with famous humanists. We are poles apart, they and I. I don't trust any of them and not one of them has ever done anything good for me. I do not acknowledge their right to question me. They do not have the moral right and they dare not lecture me.")[29]

The main event could only be the city whose poetic external beauty, marrying pastel European architecture with Russian winters and white nights, instilled an artistic intelligence unique in the world: St. Petersburg, now Leningrad. He found it "a traumatic experience." It "angered" him. "I knew in my mind that I would not find what I had left there," he reminisced on French television, "but I couldn't help looking for something that was no longer present."

Bagazh ends with an exquisitely conflicted "letter to a friendly ambassador" — Abrassimov. It deserves copious citation:

> I fretted to go to Leningrad. I told you I would fret. You cannot possibly understand why, my friend. You have a land to which you belong . . . But I? I have nothing. I'm like a Jew in the early Diaspora, praying for "next year in Jerusalem." My Jerusalem is St. Petersburg. And I know it will never happen, it cannot possibly happen, and yet I pray for it deep down in my unconscious.
>
> Because . . . because, as you yourself once said in your direct, pragmatic way, this is the culture to which I and my whole family, with all of its atavisms, belong. This is the culture that nurtured us and the likes of us in our Russian Diaspora.
> . . .
> There it was, all of it, intact or reconstructed with infinite love and care by its inhabitants: the "Queen of the North" standing proudly on the shores of the Neva. . . . Splendid, spacious, airy, curiously absent-minded, yet the most extraordinary city human beings have ever conceived and built! . . .
>
> I did tell you that it appeared to me as if it were a shell. The content of that shell—its spirit, its soul . . . was gone, gone forever. . . .
>
> Do remember (*please do!*) that I will remain forever grateful to you and to Slava Rostropovich for bringing about the homecoming of an old Petersburzhets.
>
> And maybe someday we will go crayfishing in Lake Kroman. Could I bring my three sons—Ivan, the Russian; Peter, the American; and Alexander, the Frenchman? Notice that all of them have old Russian tsarist names. But then you yourself bear the name of not just the most fearsome tsar of Russia, but the inventor of my northern capital.

For Stravinsky, in 1962, Russia opened floodgates of memory and belonging. For Nabokov, in 1967, the floodgates opened but—he insisted—proved resistible.

The ensuing final decade, according to Vincent Giroud, was "one of the happiest" of Nabokov's life. His fifth marriage, to the young French photographer Dominique Cibiel (today well known as Dominique Nabokov), proved enduring; it "brought him an element of emotional stability he had lacked."[30] Auden, who believed that Nabokov had failed to fulfill his creative gift because "he cannot bear to be long enough alone," pressed him into composing an opera based on Shakespeare's *Love's Labour's Lost* for which Auden and Chester Kallmann—as they had for Stravinsky's *The Rake's Progress*—wrote the libretto. According to Edward Mendelson, it was characteristic of Auden to "mask sympathy with brusqueness." Mendelson also has written: "Auden seems to have used Shakespeare's plot as a gently instructive allegory of Nabokov's career and the direction Auden thought it should not take: as the opera begins, the king and his courtiers hope to build an enlightened community, but they are distracted by love until, at the end, a sudden revelation of mortality startles them into a year of voluntary, contemplative solitude."[31] Relatively unencumbered with other responsibilities, Nabokov experienced composing the opera as "a continuous pleasure." He characterized the music as "tonal, non-experimental, and consistently melodic," detached "from any school of aesthetic ideology."[32] *Love's Labour's Lost* was premiered in Brussels in 1973, followed by performances in Berlin. When subsequent productions did not materialize, Nabokov seemingly bore the disappointment with equanimity. He next completed his *Memoirs of a Russian Cosmopolitan*, begun in the 1950s, published in 1975 first in German, then (somewhat abridged) in English as *Bagazh*.

Meanwhile, partly thanks to the always helpful Arthur Schlesinger, Nabokov undertook a series of remunerative professional opportunities. But he could not land the job he craved: running the new Kennedy Center for the Performing Arts in Washington, DC. His correspondence with Schlesinger on this topic discloses intense mutual frustration.[33] Schlesinger remained close to the Kennedy family. The center marked the posthumous culmination of a presidential advocacy campaign to which Nabokov and Schlesinger had vitally contributed. The trip to Russia, whatever its disappointments, had doubtless laid some Nabokov demons to rest. He was positioned to put behind him his tendentious Cold War vocation and pursue what might have proved his highest and most impassioned calling—not as a composer or propagandist, but as a world impresario in the hallowed tradition of Serge Diaghilev. A Nabokov-led Kennedy Center might have eclipsed the contemporaneous efforts of Lincoln Center and Carnegie Hall, and rivaled Harvey Lichtenstein's Brooklyn Academy of Music as a national and even international hub for cultural enterprise and innovation.

He befriended Teddy Kollek and discovered in Jerusalem "the only city I really love," visiting five times beginning in 1973.[34] But his health was failing. The end came on April 6, 1978—the day on which Stravinsky had died seven years earlier. Schlesinger wrote to his four children:

> We saw Nicolas just a week ago. He was in fine form, full of plans for the future, and said he was going into the hospital on Monday for 'routine surgery" (prostate). The doctor forgot to have him given antibiotics after the operation; he ran a terribly high temperature; and the strain was too much for a weak heart. I am filled not only with grief but with rage. He was one of my dearest friends, and one of the dearest friends of all our family, for more than thirty years.[35]

The main speaker at a memorial tribute the following January at the Institute for Advanced Study was George Kennan, who rose to the occasion with a eulogy both tender and reflective. He said in part:

> I approach this task with hesitation, almost with apology. I was indeed a friend of Nicolas Nabokov—a friend, that is, in the terms of that international-cosmopolitan world to which each of us, though in different ways, belonged. And yet I wonder whether others of you have not also had, upon the death of a friend, the feeling I have now: the sudden realization of how little you have really known that friend— how much you have taken for granted—how content you have been to accept the outward personality, what Freud called the *persona*, in place of the real person. . . .
>
> [Nicolas] went through life tossing off to every side bits and pieces of himself; of his wit, his enthusiasms, his friendships, his loves—tossing them off generously, recklessly, without reflection and without remorse. Each of us who thought of ourselves as his friends (and there were a great many of us) had a small part in this lavishly-dispense bounty. The result was that, aside from his music and his books, the whole of him was probably not left in any single place. But he was not the first man to express himself in such a manner; and who is to say, after all, that the sum total of these contributions, entering like everything else into that great stream of time and forgetfulness that sooner or later embraces and absorbs all that any of us has to offer, was any the less significant for the open-handed and joyous manner in which its component parts were flung to the winds of sociability, of friendship, and of affection?[36]

It is pertinent to remember, in calibrating this and other such "international-cosmopolitan" Cold War friendships, that during the seventeen years Kennan partnered with Nicolas Nabokov at the Congress for Cultural Freedom, he knew that the CIA was on board. So did Arthur Schlesinger. So, doubtless, did Sidney

Hook. Nabokov, according to his own testimony, did not. How much, exactly, did each of them know and not know? It is impossible to say. But there can be little doubt that Nabokov's closest associates kept information from him.

As with Stravinsky, Nabokov left no instructions for burial, and a proper resting place was far from obvious. Dominique decided on the picturesque Alsatian village of Kolbsheim, one of his "elective homes," where Jacques and Raissa Maritain were buried. A Russian Orthodox priest presided.

*   *   *

In 1978 Nabokov's Soviet ideological adversary Tikhon Khrennikov remained alive and well at age sixty-five. Like J. Edgar Hoover or Talleyrand, he was an inveterate survivor. Having been born in 1913, he never knew the feverish experimentalism of the twenties; rather, he grew up under Stalin. Shortly before his death in 1948, Zhdanov appointed Khrennikov to become secretary of the Composers' Union—a post he retained until the USSR collapsed in 1991. A hard-liner at first, he softened under Khrushchev. He also remained a successful composer who broke no rules. In 1959 he visited the United States, leading a delegation including Shostakovich. It was he who subsequently hosted and invited Stravinsky and Nabokov in 1962 and 1968. In his later years—he died in 2007—he expressed hostility toward perestroika and admiration for Stalin.

It was Khrennikov's frequent contention that he ensured that "no composers were killed" during the purges. Though Shostakovich reportedly challenged this contention in *Testimony*, Khrennikov's expertise at promoting composers' interests, and shielding them from anti-Semitism (his own wife was Jewish) and other political blights, is well established. The St. Petersburg–born American music historian Boris Schwarz found Khrennikov "at times cold and officious, particularly when it came to politically sensitive situations," but "friendly and cooperative" in "personal dealings." Schwarz also wrote: "The Composers' Union profited immensely by his political acumen and his excellent relations with the Kremlin leaders."[37] Kiril Tomoff's book-length investigation of the Composers' Union, accessing Soviet archives, portrays Khrennikov as a master operator who typically succeeded in insulating professional expertise from ideological intrusion. "From preserving their right to keep a car to saving them from expulsion . . . , Khrennikov's brokerage was a significant point of articulation between the fields of resource allocation, party politics, and music production"; the union was enabled "to shield even those Union members who were disciplined from the most dangerous consequences."[38] The late pianist Alexander Toradze, whose father was a leading Soviet Georgian composer, recalled Khrennikov as an affable activist. He added that if Khrennikov felt antipathetic to the modernism of Stravinsky's Concerto for Piano and Winds, so did the vast majority of Soviet musicians when Bernstein brought the work to Moscow and Leningrad in 1959.[39]

But it is the infamous 1948 antiformalist decree—reprinted (as we have seen) in *Politics* with Nabokov's commentary that spring—for which Khrennikov will always be chiefly remembered; it was his job to enforce it.

> The Central Committee of the Communist Party of the Soviet Union considers that the opera, *Great Friendship* . . . is unsound . . . the composer [Vano Muradeli] did not utilize the wealth of folk melodies, songs, and turns and dance motifs in which the creative art of the peoples of the USSR is so rich. . . .
>
> In the field of symphonic and operatic composition matters are especially bad. We are speaking of composers who confined themselves to the formalist anti-public trend. This trend has found its fullest manifestation in the works of such composers as comrades D. Shostakovich, S. Prokofiev, A. Khachaturian . . . and others, in whose compositions the formalist distortions, the anti-democratic tendencies in music, . . . are especially graphically represented.
>
> Characteristic of such music are the negation of the basic principles of classical music; a sermon for atonality, dissonance and disharmony, as if this were an expression of "progress" and "innovation" . . . a passion for confused, neuropathic combinations which transform music into cacophony, into a chaotic piling up of sounds. This music reeks strongly of the spirit of the contemporary modernist bourgeois music of Europe and America. . . .
>
> In defiance of the best traditions of Russian and Western classical music, [composers] have shut themselves off in a narrow circle of specialists and musical gourmands, have lowered the high social role of music and narrowed its meaning, limiting it to a satisfaction of the distorted tastes of aesthetic individualists.

Stripped of jargon and hyperbole, this diatribe reads as an assault on modernist principles and predilections that today are no longer taken for granted. Moreover, Kiril Tomoff, in a post-Soviet archival investigation, has refuted the conventional wisdom that explains the 1948 resolution as part of a tidal, top-down ideological campaign; the complex backstory he reconstructs includes intraprofessional discord between warring composers and aesthetic precepts.[40] Not only do Nabokov's writings of the fifties and sixties mischaracterize the workings of Soviet music; they embody an alternative dogma, almost a mirror image. He supports art for art's sake. He insists on originality and innovation. He is impatient with mass audiences. He denounces political art with its intended "high social role." He denies the very possibility of "ideational" content as a component of musical composition. He disparages appropriated folk sources cheapened by popular appeal. He mistrusts synergistic marriages of Western art music with non-Western traditions. He embraces a sanitizing fissure between art and life: great music, as per Stravinsky, is autonomous, and so is the creative act.

A vast scholarly literature correlates modernism with the Cold War politics of anti-Communism. Modernism also aligns with the repudiation of "kitsch" and "midcult" by mid-twentieth-century critics like Clement Greenberg and Dwight Macdonald. Though Nabokov fits both these scenarios, how much his modernist credo—how much modernism, generally—is a function of the psychology of exile is a fascinating question. The first half of the twentieth century was ruptured by seismic upheavals: the Russian Revolution, the fascist tide, the Second World War. Just before that, fin de siècle ferment, especially in Vienna, was a modernist seedbed. Marginalized and otherwise dislocated artists and intellectuals broke with the past. Meanwhile, itinerancy became a new norm. Modernist icons who wound up in countries not their own included (in addition to Schoenberg and Stravinsky) such seminal innovators as James Joyce, Pablo Picasso, and Wassily Kandinsky. And there was Diaghilev in France, for Nabokov as of 1951 "the center of a very healthy and profoundly creative internationalism (or 'rootless cosmopolitanism' as it is now termed on the other side of the Oder)."[41]

A cost analysis for modernism is as yet untabulated. There is no consensus. But undoubtedly, there were musical costs of consequence. The high modernism of Pierre Boulez and Karlheinz Stockhausen, Milton Babbitt and Elliott Carter added nothing to the mainstream musical canon. By this criterion, Western classical music forged into a cul-de-sac. The grand concert narrative beginning with Bach dissipated. The last man standing was Dmitri Shostakovich. The standard repertoire symphonies, performed the world over, terminate with his No. 10.

Did John F. Kennedy fully believe the Cold War "cultural freedom" dogma he eloquently embraced? It is impossible to say. Did Nicolas Nabokov ever attain perspective, however privately, on the bipolar doctrinal counterpoint in which he partook? His charmed sophistication notwithstanding, was he finally a victim of a form of post-traumatic stress? Evicted from his homeland, he inferred the annulment of the aristocratic intelligentsia with which he identified and which he explicitly regarded as the necessary source of Russian culture. Shostakovich's creative stature invalidated Nabokov's worldview, his very identity. And so he could neither see nor hear—and fabricated a cartoon of "Soviet music." No one blew the whistle, because he was a certified expert. A privileged witness, he was actually empowered to "make it up"—and he did. Circumstantial evidence—the party edicts, the purges, the gulags—supported Nabokov, as did Cold War fear, paranoia, and ignorance. Trapped in exile, he insisted on a criterion of originality: newness for its own sake. In retrospect, that is something that can sever what JFK called "the root of art." Kennedy's contention that the "creative impulse" depended upon the oxygen of "free societies" was just Nabokovian hot air.

Stravinsky, in Moscow, said: "A man has one birthplace, one fatherland, one country—he *can* have only one country—and the place of his birth is the most important factor in his life." Whatever one makes of this grand pronouncement, his Russian birthplace, twenty-five miles west of St. Petersburg, was ultimately paramount for Stravinsky. And Nicolas Nabokov? George Kennan observed that he was born "along the western border of Russia proper—at the corner of where Lithuania, Poland, and what is now known as Byelorussia meet. All of this area then belonged formally to the Russian Empire, but none of it was entirely typical of Russia. And this relationship to Russia of the locus of birth—near it but not entirely of it—seems to me symbolic of his own relationship to that country throughout his life."[42]

CHAPTER 7

COLD WAR MUSIC, EAST AND WEST

In '46, when I was a delegate to the Congress of Antifascist Women, I happened to speak with an English actress, who had been forbidden to approach our delegation. But she boldly made her way over to us regardless, and struck up a conversation with the Soviet women. While she was talking to me about the arts, she couldn't keep herself from looking downwards, at my chest, and eventually she asked me: "What did you get that medal for?" I told her that it was a medal given to Stalin Prize laureates. "For what?" she asked. "For my work in the role of Nadezhda Durova," I replied. "I was also awarded something for my theatre work," she went on. "What did they give you?" I asked her. After a moment's hesitation, she dipped into her handbag and pulled out something drab-looking, small and flat, a kind of powder box. "That's how they reward us performers."

Comrades, this is dreadful. They reward their artists with powder boxes. This shows that as far as they're concerned, the arts are a mere distraction, a kind of amusement, a decadent form of escapism. But on our tunics, we proudly bear the medal of Stalin Prize laureates, a medal portraying our great leader, Stalin—Stalin who is leading all the peoples forward, Stalin the fighter for peace. We feel that we are a people of the state, if I can put it like that. We carry out the tasks of the state, and we build up that state.

That actress smiled at me, with a hint of envy, realizing that we were a different kind of people.

This 1951 testimony, by the actress Vera Maretskaya, affirms the high importance of culture in Soviet Russia.[1] It also affirms the high importance of Stalinist

ideology—a priority sometimes in conflict with cultural achievement, sometimes not. It is cited by the historian Marina Frolova-Walker at the head of her
revelatory 2016 study, *Stalin's Music Prize: Soviet Culture and Politics*—a book whose
findings would greatly have surprised Nicolas Nabokov, Arthur Schlesinger, and
John F. Kennedy. They point toward a more sophisticated, more comprehensive
picture of Soviet musical life, and of East/West contradictions and resemblances
revealed or concealed by the cultural Cold War.

For first-place composers, the Stalin Music Prize, awarded from 1941 to
1954, conferred publication, performances, and 100,000 rubles—a lavish sum.
(Manual workers averaged 300 rubles a month, heads of university depart-
ments 1,500 rubles monthly.) The winners were recommended by a consulta-
tive panel comprising both musicians of distinction and musical bureaucrats.
Stenographic records of the proceedings survive. Studying these documents,
Frolova-Walker made two discoveries. The first was that the decision-making
process, though multilayered and subject to Stalin's approval, was as much
bottom-up as top-down; when musicians and bureaucrats disagreed, the outcome could go either way. The second was that ideology was not necessarily
determinant. Though the bureaucrats applied rigid socialist realist criteria,
some compositions nevertheless won purely on musical merit. At the same
time, it was frequently observed by the deliberators that the prize did not designate "best piece"; rather, its intention was to designate the best piece fulfilling
criteria insisting on communal uplift and popular appeal.

So it was that the first three first-prize compositions, in 1941, included
Shostakovich's Piano Quintet, a neoclassical work bereft of social or political
connotations; it was accurately assessed as a major contribution to the Russian chamber repertoire that warranted acknowledgment. Shostakovich won
a first or second prize four more times—in 1942 for the Seventh Symphony, in
1946 for the Second Piano Trio, in 1950 for *Song of the Forests* and the film score
The Fall of Berlin, and in 1952 for Ten Poems for chorus. The 1950 prize, following the 1948 antiformalist decree, was purely political; Shostakovich himself,
as a panelist, actually requested that these works not be honored. Two Shostakovich compositions that were passed over, the Eighth and Tenth Symphonies,
were of far greater consequence. The debate on the former work was so charged
that the composer was invited to supply an additional piano performance of
his own (which was found more ideologically appealing—more "tragic," less
"pessimistic" in tone—than Evgeny Mravinsky's premiere performance with
the Leningrad Philharmonic). Both symphonies were criticized—not unintel-
ligibly—for their discouraging density, complexity, and darkness. (The Second
Piano Trio, though a winner, was also predominantly dark, but was considered
more tuneful. For an ideologically hostile response to Shostakovich's Eighth

Symphony, it would be hard to top the *New York Herald-Tribune* review of the work's 1944 New York Philharmonic broadcast by a composer/critic closely associated with Nicolas Nabokov: Virgil Thomson.)[2]

One learns from Frolova-Walker that Shostakovich thought the Stalin Prizes a bad idea: an intrusion. But once he became an active participant in 1947—a tenure interrupted while he was in disfavor from 1948 to 1951—he was outspoken and controversial. He did what he could to instill integrity, to "both play the game and remain true to himself." He sometimes succeeded, and sometimes—as with his efforts to secure a prize for the Jewish Mieczysław Weinberg, who deserved one—did not.[3]

Frolova-Walker summarizes that the Stalin Prizes—awarded in Musical Composition, Musical Performance, Musicology, and "Non-Musicians in Production or Performance," as well as a host of nonmusical fields—played "a crucial role" in shaping Soviet cultural life.[4] The panelists were frequently artists of distinction: the directors Konstantin Stanislavsky and Vladimir Nemirovich-Danchenko, the sculptor Vera Mukhina, the éminence grise composer Nikolai Myaskovsky. Stalin himself was a hands-on participant who voraciously read the submissions in literature and notably intervened on awards for books, paintings, sculpture, and architecture. His role in the music awards is less documented: an ambiguity. Tikhon Khrennikov, who represented music at several Politburo meetings, recorded:

> I saw Stalin only at the meetings of the Committee for Lenin and Stalin prizes, during the discussion of nominated candidates. This only took place on four occasions, the last in 1952. He participated in the discussions of musical works and other artistic and literary works, as well as work in the area of science and technology. I always listened very attentively to what he said and how he said it. Stalin revealed a complete knowledge of the subject; he must have found the time to familiarize himself with the nominated works, because I witnessed several times how he caught out celebrated academics when scientific studies were discussed. Stalin sometimes agreed to accept proposals that were at odds with his own. He was a most intelligent man, and never entered into long polemics and with anyone except [Alexander] Fadeyev, who dared to argue with the leader. Let us be frank: we feared and worshipped him together with the rest of our people, who had won such a terrible war.[5]

Khrennikov also credited Stalin with remarkable histrionic abilities—to, for instance, feign anger in order to achieve a desired Politburo result.[6]

Frolova-Walker shows that, as music betrayed less ideological clarity than other art forms, the winners represented a higher standard, more greatly influenced by expert opinion. Of Shostakovich she concludes:

Hearing Shostakovich's voice at the [Stalin Prize] meetings can leave us asking the same questions that we pose after listening to his music. Was he being sincere or ironic? Principled or cynical? Fearless or cautious? It seems he was, at various times, all these things. But the one thing he never did was to keep silent. He could have done so . . . Shostakovich's interventions . . . give us a glimpse of a fiery public temperament that could not conform to professional etiquette or delicacy, nor to hypocrisy or tedium. Shostakovich clearly had a strong desire to participate in public life, and following this compulsion sometimes allowed him to make a principled stand, or to help out friends, and at other times drew him into shabby compromises. . . . Once he had accepted the mantle of a public figure, he could not slip it off and on at will. But it was surely that same public temperament that shaped much of his music. Without that innate need to speak up, to interfere, whether to take a stand or to find official approval, we wouldn't have had either the Seventh or the Thirteen Symphony [protesting anti-Semitism via Yevtushenko's "Babi Yar"], nor, on the other side, *Song of the Forests* or the Twelfth Symphony ["The Year 1917"].

She adds: "Whatever we think of Shostakovich's [musical] Stalin eulogies, they succeeded at least in forcing his former detractors to change their ways." When *The Fall of Berlin* was to receive a film award, Stalin made certain that Shostakovich's score was duly acknowledged.[7]

In parallel with Frolova-Walker, the American historian Kiril Tomoff studied the internal history of the Union of Soviet Composers and in 2006 reached similar conclusions.

In the Soviet cultural world, artistic expertise mattered. It afforded professional musicians the agency to construct a musical culture that appealed to audiences at home and abroad. . . . Perhaps most remarkable, composers of all kinds came to occupy a particularly elite position in Soviet society. . . . The Composers' Union was decidedly not an autonomous institution. Party leaders always could and sometimes did intervene in the music world. Nevertheless, the Union's eventual monopoly of musical expertise allowed music professionals to maneuver within the system.

The bona fide "Soviet cultural elite" that Nicolas Nabokov denied could possibly exist is in Tomoff's study shown to apply nonideological standards of expertise while mainly running its own affairs. The Composers' Union "was governed by a specific type of expertise—the ability to create and interpret new Soviet music." It oversaw the admission of new members and maintained "a vast creative apparatus to enable and oversee . . . creative work." It fashioned and preserved a complex material infrastructure. It furnished emergency loans, health-care payments, and housing assistance. It maintained idyllic creative resorts available to members as many as four months out of the year. It sponsored forums for composers and musicologists, with important proceedings published in *Sovetskaia muzyka*. It was subject to ideological currents that were, however, "fluid, mutable, and fundamentally dependent on institutional practices for sensible definition"; socialist realism was not a single governing template. "Though self-conscious modernist experimentation was not viable," the resulting musical output—characterized by Nabokov as a gray morass of assembly-line uniformity—was "nevertheless . . . strikingly diverse."[8]

Stravinsky, a free man in Los Angeles, claimed to relish and require his autonomy. But at times he contemplated leaving: he commensurately resented and deplored his invisibility.

* * *

Boris Schwarz's landmark English-language study *Music and Musical Life in Soviet Russia, 1917–1970* neither utilizes nor acknowledges Nabokov's many pertinent writings. Rather, his purview is nonideological. The picture he draws is complex and by no means unsympathetic to what Nicolas Slonimsky once called "the most remarkable experiment in music history—in which the code of aesthetics is formulated according to a rigid political ideology."[9] A necessary leitmotif is the Soviet push to inculcate classical music for the widest possible audience. More recently, archival research of a kind inaccessible to Schwarz has amplified understanding of this popularizing impulse. The same impulse was pervasive in the United States, where it was called "music appreciation." The resulting similarities and differences further delineate a picture of Russian musical life at variance with Cold War wisdom. In fact, the quest for a new audience is embedded in a larger picture of surprising Soviet/American analogies. In both the Soviet Union and the United States, the twenties were a decade of compositional experimentation. During the thirties, composers retrenched. Wedded to social purpose, a simplified, more "accessible" idiom was pursued. A neoclassicist aesthetic arose. During the wartime forties, robust patriotic music mattered. After the war, at least for some, came a music of disillusionment.

The "new audience" was in both countries a phenomenon both ideological and demographic. Comprising legions of upwardly mobile untutored listeners, it was in America a product of "the new middle classes." The Soviet term was "the people," notably including peasants morphing into an urban proletariat. East and West, their cultural cravings, whether for learning, respectability, or both, were guided and reinforced from above. In Russia the teacher was the state. American pedagogy was supplied by a nexus of commercial interests headed by the Radio Corporation of American and the National Broadcasting Company, both led by a phenomenally entrepreneurial Russian immigrant: David Sarnoff. Stalin and Sarnoff pursued different strategies and priorities. The Soviets stressed Marxist praxis: how to make music. The Americans stressed consumption: broadcasts and recordings. In Russia the repertoire of choice, shaped by ideological considerations, was often Russian. In the United States, remarkably, it was never American, always Russian and European; the goal in part was to maximize profit with the most familiar, most easily appreciated merchandise.

Here Frolova-Walker's findings about the Stalin Prize are writ large: Soviet musical life resists generalization. It did not chart a monolithic continuum. And the varied forces shaping its trajectory, for thirteen years, were both top-down and bottom-up. For instance, the grassroots thrust toward active participation in a nation's musical life was notably stronger than any comparable American initiative.

Here is George Marek, who in 1950 became manager of artists and repertoire at RCA Victor, and vice president/general manager seven years later: "You can enjoy a Beethoven symphony without being able to read notes, without knowing who Beethoven was, when he lived, or what he tried to express." Shielding novices from "commentaries and explanations which . . . have tended to make music an intellectual exercise," Marek counseled: "There are no critics around, no musical analysts, no wise men who know the symphony by heart. . . . [I]t is up to the composer to entertain us." In his inaugural 1940 music column for *Good Housekeeping* magazine, he wrote: "You needn't dig or look for 'meaning.' . . . You need only listen." Marek's *Good Housekeeping Guide to Musical Enjoyment* (1949) signifies the homemaker's migration from the spinet to the family phonograph. Though Marek was born in Vienna in 1902, it was never Hausmusik, but radio and recordings that had made the United States the world's "most musical nation" as of 1940. Olin Downes, chief music critic for the *New York Times* and a bellwether for popular sentiment, purveyed a modulated version of the same message: "The listener does not have to be a tutored man or a person technically versed in the intricacies of the art of composition to understand perfectly well what the orchestra [is] saying to him." And here is Sinclair Lewis, whose *Babbitt* (1922) caustically limns a typical midwestern family: "Against the wall was a piano, but no one used it save [the Babbitts' ten-year-old daughter] Rinka. The hard briskness of the phonograph" contented the Babbitts.[10]

Before glancing at the pertinent Soviet status quo, consider Henry Krehbiel, the "dean" of New York City's music critics before World War I and the author of a rigorous primer, *How to Listen to Music*, reprinted thirty times between 1896 and 1924. Assessing "the majority of the hearers in our concert-rooms," Krehbiel groaned: "They are there to adventure a journey into a realm whose beauties do not disclose themselves to the senses alone, but whose perception requires a cooperation of all the finer faculties; yet of this they seem to know nothing . . . 'hearing they hear not, neither do they understand.'" In the same volume, pondering gargantuan amateur choral festivals and competitions that once seemed characteristically American, he discovered a democratic performance genre "of necessity unselfish and creative of sympathy. . . . Amateur choir-singing is not older anywhere than in the United States. . . . A little reflection will show this fact, which seems somewhat startling at first blush, to be entirely natural. Large singing societies are of necessity made up of amateurs, and the want of professional musicians in America compelled the people to enlist amateurs at a time when in Europe choral activity rested on the church, theater and institute choristers, who were practically professionals." Krehbiel espoused active listening and music making. Broadcasts and recordings were for him a nascent marginal accessory.[11]

And so to the USSR, where amateur choruses, orchestras, and even opera companies were a remarkable early feature of Soviet music. In Moscow and Petrograd/Leningrad alone, tens of thousands of workers participated in amateur performances during the twenties. Every factory had its own music club: minimally, a string band or choir. Leningrad's Putilov factory founded an opera studio in 1927. Elsewhere, a 1928 workers' production of *Fidelio* featured an ideologically refreshed ending. If this fully staged Beethoven opera was hardly typical, the ideal of musical proletarians (also to be found in German factories partial to Hanns Eisler's revolutionary songs) was widespread. In all Nabokov's accounts, the Revolution marked an impoverished new beginning, absent the intelligentsia. But the intelligentsia, traditionally, had espoused the social and cultural betterment of peasants and workers. "People's Houses," widely important beginning in 1911, offered inexpensive workers' concerts; related efforts tackled musical illiteracy. In fact, the Revolution both alienated and seduced the intelligentsia; many of those who stayed (including Old Bolsheviks) entered into a bargain that went bad. Like other features of Soviet music, cultural popularization was a thread begun decades earlier, amplified under Lenin, then twisted by Stalinist vicissitudes to come.[12]

At the top, Russian ideologues rewrote music history for mass consumption, rebranding epochs and composers. The United States, comparably, had music appreciation bibles with such titles as *The Victor Book of the Symphony*, *The Victor Book of the Opera*, *The Victor Book of Concertos*, *The Victor Book of Musical Fun*,

Form in Music, and *What We Hear in Music*—all RCA products, as was the monthly *Victor Record Review*. This top-down instruction, which maintained energy and prominence through the 1950s, was of course neither compulsory nor ideological. Rather, its "free society" beneficiaries were American consumers subjected to a combination of savvy salesmanship and sincere middlebrow enthusiasms. The crucial significance of RCA Victor recordings was of course a leitmotif, as in the following remarkable propaganda specimen: "The importance to music of modern methods of reproducing sound is parallel to that of the printing press to literature, philosophy, and the whole sum of the world's knowledge. There is this vital difference: Books preserve in cold type the great thoughts of the ages, priceless even though disembodied, but electronical reproduction actually re-creates the living organism of music, giving it voice and movement and compelling vitality."

Basically, a pantheon of dead European masters was endorsed, if rarely as exclusively as by George Marek, whose curriculum extolled no composer later than Wagner and Verdi. The great composers were variously recanonized for mass consumption. The most startling aspect of this exercise was their eclipse by certain great performers, invariably immigrant conductors and instrumentalists famous in the United States. The flagship enterprise was *Toscanini and Great Music* (1938) by the prominent *New York Herald-Tribune* music critic Lawrence Gilman. It abetted an RCA/NBC promotional juggernaut binding "great music" with the deified conductor of the newly formed NBC Symphony, and previous chief conductor of the Metropolitan Opera and New York Philharmonic: Arturo Toscanini. Gilman's threefold purpose was to elucidate "Toscanini the priest of music, and . . . certain masterworks that he reveals, and the significance of their interaction for the democratic culture of our time." Toscanini's "unexampled weekly concerts" over NBC signified "a new extension and significance to our ideas concerning the democratization of musical culture." He was "the most illustrious conductor who ever lived," a "vehicle of revelation" whose fame— eclipsing that of all and any composers—"is probably without parallel in the annals of music." Preaching to grateful New Worlders—"we who have heard him oftenest, and have known him, as an artist, longest and best"—Gilman commensurately reconsidered Haydn, Beethoven, Schubert, Brahms, Wagner, Debussy, and Sibelius, each allotted a chapter. Thus, "The Real Haydn" distinguished "the old and conventional picture of him as essentially a light-hearted classic in a periwig who, oddly enough, was always in good spirits" from a "true picture," illuminated by Toscanini, of "a master of poignant and affecting musical speech." Haydn, the pious bourgeois of foolish legend, disappears. The Toscanini cult was a fascinating illustration of what Dwight Macdonald called

"midcult"—a cultural stratum feeding on the prestige of high culture but water-
ing it down for mass consumption.[13]

The entirety of music appreciation was dismissed by Virgil Thomson, who
succeeded Gilman at the *Herald-Tribune* in 1940, as a commercial "racket." Concurrently, it provoked Aaron Copland to his single most memorable utterance:

> Very often I get the impression that audiences seem to think that the endless
> repetition of a small body of entrenched masterworks is all that is required for a
> ripe musical culture. . . . Needless to say, I have no quarrel with masterpieces. I
> think I revere and enjoy them as well as the next fellow. But when they are used,
> unwittingly perhaps, to stifle contemporary effort in our own country, then I
> am almost tempted to take the most extreme view and say that we should be
> better off without them![14]

The Soviets, by comparison, were heavier-handed, with lists of wholesome
and decadent composers and, eventually, approved and forbidden compositions. Initially, Lenin and his impressive cultural minister, Anatoly Lunacharsky,
discouraged a sharp break with the past. Both of them, and also Leon Trotsky,
were grounded in "bourgeois" Western culture, which the Soviet state would
assimilate and respect en route to new norms. Lunacharsky rejected radical
proletarian demands to shut the Bolshoi and Mariinsky Theaters. Instead, the
Soviets in 1928 founded Moscow's first permanent orchestra. A snapshot of
cosmopolitan Soviet musical life in Leningrad was furnished by a Soviet music historian in 1963, comparing five landmark modernist operatic premieres
in Berlin and Leningrad (at the Mariinsky). Franz Schreker's *Der Ferne Klang*,
Berg's *Wozzeck*, Stravinsky's *Pulcinella* and *Renard*, and Prokofiev's *Love for the Three
Oranges* were first given in Berlin in 1925 and 1926; in Leningrad the pertinent
years were 1925, 1926, and 1927.[15] Twentieth-century symphonic repertoire in
Moscow and Leningrad prior to 1936 included Bartók, Berg, Bliss, Casella, Falla,
Hindemith, Honegger, Janáček, Krenek, Malipiero, Milhaud, Pfitzner, Poulenc,
Ravel, Reger, Respighi, Satie, Schreker, Richard Strauss, and Szymanowski. Of
Schoenberg, Soviet audiences heard both the gargantuan *Gurrelieder* and the
twelve-tone Variations for Orchestra. The Stravinsky repertoire was copious,
including (among other works) *The Rite of Spring*, *The Nightingale*, *Mavra*, *Ragtime*,
Symphonies of Wind Instruments, *Oedipus Rex*, *Apollo*, and the Concerto for Piano
and Winds. The participating conductors included such leading European new
music advocates as Ernest Ansermet, Erich Kleiber, Otto Klemperer, and Alexander von Zemlinsky, alongside the likes of Fritz Busch, Oskar Fried, Jascha
Horenstein, Clemens Krauss, Pierre Monteux, Artur Rodzinski, George Szell,
Vaclav Talich, Bruno Walter, and Felix Weingartner.[16] The significance of these

lists is not merely that they contradict every picture drawn by Nicolas Nabokov of a radically diminished Soviet musical culture, crippled by totalitarian restrictions on "freedom," or that they refute the logic of John F. Kennedy's equation of high artistic attainment with "free artists" and "free societies"; they notably document symphonic and operatic norms more progressive than those of New York City—where the repertoire predilections of Kleiber and Klemperer proved unwelcome at the New York Philharmonic, and the stage works of Schreker, Berg, Stravinsky, and Prokofiev were unknown at the Metropolitan Opera.

Soviet rebranding of the "great composers," while vigorous, was not initially preemptive. Beethoven and Mussorgsky were obvious ideological favorites, the former for his "democratic" and "revolutionary" propensities, the latter for his fervent allegiance to "the masses." Bach and Mozart were typically rationalized as progressive factors, the former for counteracting Catholic "gloom," the latter for embodying rising bourgeois revolt against "the dying culture of the feudal classes." Haydn (whom Lawrence Gilman, as we have observed, denied was a mere "pious bourgeois") was not to blame for his necessary dependency on aristocratic patronage; rather, he was like Mozart part of a progressive "Third Estate." Wagner, recently the object of a Silver Age cult, was a personal favorite of Lenin's. Even "decadent" Romantics like Chopin and Schumann, prone to despondency and pessimism, proved susceptible to ideological support.[17]

The turning point, of course, was Stalin and his retreat from the West. The general outcome was a punishing insularity, especially after the 1948 antiformalist resolution. In terms of repertoire, new Western music was prohibited. Russian music was prioritized, except for outbursts of opprobrium and cancellation. When the Tchaikovsky centenary was celebrated in 1940, his monarchism and homosexuality were sidestepped. Musicological scholarship turned infantile and inane. And, beginning in the late 1930s, there were purges that destabilized such institutions as the Moscow Philharmonic, whose leadership suffered continual flux.[18] That Shostakovich managed to persevere, that his stream of creative achievement remained uninterrupted, is a tortuous feat of survival we have already explored.

Meanwhile, the ongoing emphasis on Russian music was by no means crudely ideological. In 1948, for instance, the Composers' Union helped draft a Moscow Philharmonic concert series highlighting outstanding Soviet compositions of the past thirty years. Concurrently, a bureau was created to develop a three-year plan to increase the exposure of new Soviet music; the resulting list included twenty-one new symphonic works, twenty-five rarely performed works from the past, and seven new chamber music compositions.[19] American composers, by comparison, complained from the sidelines that they had no influence over the Eurocentric orientation of the nation's most prominent institutions of classical music.

A recent attempt to freshly apply archival resources to a summary of "Soviet musical identity" through 1953, by Pauline Fairclough, tracks a narrative from "cosmopolitan" conditions, through 1936, to a new and hermetic Russian nationalism under Stalin. As with Frolova-Walker, her findings prove unpredictable. She cautions that antiformalist cultural arbiters were not necessarily "insincere" when campaigning for people-friendly musical institutions and compositions, that there is less evidence of top-down demands than might be assumed, and that musical bureaucrats doubtless "did their best to self-regulate in order to avoid censure." Summarizing the period of maximum Iron Curtain constriction, 1948 to 1953, she writes:

> A great deal of music was kept out but, on the other hand, there was a regular supply of new Soviet music brought in, and in this sense, Soviet audiences had access to a lot of "new" music, even if their diet was a restricted one. If Soviet musical culture can be viewed as a "museum" at all, it was one with very active curators, able deftly to replace Bach with Glinka, Wagner with Tchaikovsky, and Stravinsky with Szymanowski as required. Though never entirely static, it was most certainly carefully controlled and monitored and in that sense, was a true microcosm of the society it served.[20]

Ian Wellens, in *Music on the Frontline: Nicolas Nabokov's Struggle against Communism and Middlebrow Culture* (2002), conjectures that Nabokov's scorching delineation of "middlebrow" Stalinist aesthetics was heavily indebted to the writings of Dwight Macdonald and such like-minded culture critics as Clement Greenberg. But American musical midcult remains a better fit for the misgivings expressed by Macdonald, Greenberg, and other soured observers of the cultural home front. During decades when the iconic representative of American classical music was an Italian conductor purveying the dead European masters, Shostakovich—a composer—was the reigning Soviet musical figurehead, however embattled. He was served by the "great performers," not the other way around. When David Oistrakh, Mstislav Rostropovich, and Evgeny Mravinsky toured the United States, they showcased Shostakovich's First Violin Concerto, his First Cello Concerto, his Eighth Symphony. Van Cliburn, in Moscow, showcased Russian music: Tchaikovsky and Rachmaninoff—with Samuel Barber's Piano Sonata, itself indebted to Prokofiev, an insignificant footnote.

*   *   *

If Shostakovich furnishes a compelling embodiment of the Soviet quest for a new audience, the commensurate American embodiment was the most famous, most popular, most influential American concert composer. Shostakovich's symphonies proved compelling statements of national identity. So did Aaron Copland's signature ballets. Copland was also a pedagogue whose books and lectures sought to counteract the banalities of music appreciation. And he was a de facto music historian whose accounts of American musical history—most notably *Our New Music* (1941)—aspired to promote an American canon superseding in emphasis the dead European masters. As the "dean" of American composers, he played a leadership role in some ways comparable to the Soviet Composers' Union, urging his colleagues to attend to new listeners, and advocating their pertinence to a nation's life, and to artistic privileges and prerogatives.

As it happens, Stravinsky was Copland's favorite twentieth-century composer, his hero from his student years in Paris with Nadia Boulanger. At the same time, like many others he was chiefly amazed by Stravinsky's early output; he found the later Stravinsky beset by "mannerisms" and "somewhat cold-blooded."[21] And as Copland sought to wield wide influence and do his share in support of human betterment, Shostakovich, though Stravinsky's antipode, became an ambiguous yet indispensable second influence. They first met at the Waldorf Astoria peace conference in 1949. In 1960, visiting the Soviet Union, Copland spent an evening at home with Shostakovich and his family and later remarked, "He loves music with a kind of innocent joy I have rarely seen in a famous composer. Music must have been a great solace to him in the tough days." In a 1946 lecture, he praised Shostakovich as a composer with "a personal note all his own and enormous facility and brilliance," though "not a deep thinker, not strikingly original by comparison with Stravinsky, and sometimes unnecessarily trite." But the populist in Copland—a propensity more acquired than native—was inescapably directed to Shostakovich's capacity to "speak of serious matters in a musical language that had a marked profile and a wide appeal."[22]

That Copland thus absorbed two such antithetical models produced complex ramifications. His populism, however synthetic, anchored his fame. But when Roger Sessions quipped that "Aaron is more talented than he realized,"[23] he voiced a professional sentiment widely shared: that Copland was essentially a modernist—a "formalist"—who had vitiated his style as an act of social conscience.

Amplifying other resemblances linking Soviet and American music in the decades after World War I—and confuting binary Cold War wisdom—the

Copland and Shostakovich careers track concurrently. They were born only six years apart. In the twenties, they were cheeky and experimental. Copland was known as a wild man who emptied concert rooms with his Piano Variations (1930). As with so many American artists and intellectuals, the human tragedy of the Great Depression impelled him to reconsider. A 1932 visit to Mexico, with its "revolutionary" artists and intellectuals, proved formative; he returned frequently in the thirties and forties. (In 1959 Shostakovich received a hero's welcome in Mexico City.) "Mexico turned out to be even grander than I expected," Copland reported. "The best is the people—there's nothing remotely like them in Europe, nothing in them is striving to be bourgeois. It wasn't the music that I heard there, or the dances that attracted me so much as the spirit of the place. In some inexplicable way, one felt the electric sense of suddenly knowing the essence of a people—their humanity, their dignity and unique charm." He also wrote: "When I was in Mexico I was a little envious of the opportunity composers have to serve their country in a musical way. When one has done that, one can compose with real joy. Here in the U.S.A. we composers have no possibility of directing the musical affairs of the nation—on the contrary, I have the impression that more and more we are working in a vacuum."[24] This was when Copland composed *Billy the Kid* (1938), *Rodeo* (1942), and *Appalachian Spring* (1944). These ballets, instantly popular as concert works, not only convey wholesome imagery of a striving, celebratory America; they enunciate a newly considered musical idiom. Of "the job of the forties," Copland wrote: "The radio and phonograph have given us listeners whose sheer numbers in themselves create a special problem." The solution? "To find a musical style which satisfies both us and them."

> The new musical audiences will have to have music that they can comprehend. That is axiomatic. It must therefore be simple and direct. But there is no reason why it should not be a music that exploits all those new devices discovered during the first years of the twentieth century. Above all, it must be fresh in feeling. . . . To write a music that is both simple and direct and is at the same time great music is a goal worthy of the efforts of the best minds in music.[25]

That such pronouncements echoed Soviet aesthetic priorities was not coincidental: Copland's milieu was packed with party members and fellow travelers. In 1934 he addressed a Communist picnic in Minnesota. The same year, he composed a revolutionary workers' song, "Into the Streets May First"; it won a competition sponsored by *The New Masses*. Three years later came a "play opera for school children," *The Second Hurricane*, modeled after the didactic Marxist "Lehrstücke" (learning pieces) of Bertolt Brecht. Hanns Eisler's militant workers' songs were an inspiration for the Composers Collective, whose Manhattan meet-ings Eisler and Copland attended. Concurrently, Copland supported the Com-munist presidential ticket in 1936. In 1948 he backed the pro-Soviet Henry Wal-lace for president. Cognizant of the outstanding film scores of Shostakovich and Prokofiev, among others abroad, he resolved to tackle Hollywood. His first effort, to get the hang of it, was *The City*, a documentary for the 1939 World's Fair; scripted by Lewis Mumford, it showed happy workers living and laboring in government-created "new cities." In Hollywood Copland scored *Of Mice and Men* (1939), *Our Town* (1940), and the *Red Pony* (1949)—and also the pro-Soviet *The North Star* (1943). His uncharacteristically robust Symphony No. 3 (1944–46) betrayed kinship with the war symphonies of Shostakovich. When the Soviet Composers' Union promulgated its antiformalist resolution of 1948, Copland remarked: "They [Shostakovich et al.] were rebuked for failing to realize that their musical audience had expanded enormously in the last several years and that composers can no longer continue to write only for a few initiates."[26] Though employed by the U.S. State Department as a cultural ambassador in 1941 and 1947, he was—to say the least—out of step with U.S. cultural Cold War propaganda.

And he proved out of step with America. American workers did not sing "Into the Streets" and American schoolchildren did not perform *The Second Hurricane*. William Wyler altered Copland's highbrow score for *The Heiress* (1949). Though he received an Academy Award for music adulterated by another hand (Wyler had Copland's assistant Nathan Van Cleave interpolate a maudlin arrange-ment of "Plaisir d'amour"), Copland departed Hollywood never to return. His speech at the 1949 Waldorf peace conference (which we have already sampled) revealed an unhappy frame of mind. Copland was no longer unabashedly pro-Soviet; neither was he disposed to defend American foreign policy. Mainly, he complained that the Cold War made it difficult for him to compose.

> Lately I've been thinking that the cold war is almost worse for art than the real thing—for it permeates the atmosphere with fear and anxiety. An artist can function at his best only in a vital and healthy environment for the simple reason that the very act of creation is an affirmative gesture. An artist fighting in a war for a cause he holds just has something affirmative he can believe in. That art-ist, if he can stay alive, can create art. But throw him into a mood of suspicion, ill-will and dread that typifies the cold war attitude and he'll create nothing.[27]

Copland's discontent nonetheless found musical expression in his first twelve-tone work: a Piano Quartet (1950) that made no effort to please the "new audi-ence" he had so assiduously befriended. Yet of all his compositions, it may be the one most influenced by Shostakovich: the spare, bitter polyphony of the opening

Adagio; the *scherzando, delicato* grotesquerie of the central Allegro, are "fear and anxiety" markers atypical of Copland. His friend Harold Clurman likened the affect of this little-known chamber music to "the quiet preceding or following an atom bomb attack. The work is the voice of our inner fear."

During the ensuing decade, the State Department stopped asking Copland to go abroad. His *Fanfare for the Common Man* was dropped from the Eisenhower inauguration at the insistence of congressional Republicans. And on May 26, 1953, he was compelled to testify before Senator Joseph McCarthy's Permanent Subcommittee on Investigations. McCarthy and his aide Roy Cohn were so poorly prepared—they had no idea who Aaron Copland was—that they failed to clinch his past relations with Communists, Communist causes, and Communist organizations. McCarthy expressed consternation that the Department of State "selected you as a lecturer when we have many other people available as lecturers. . . . We must find out why a man of this tremendous activity in Communist fronts would be selected." When Senator Karl Mundt was bewildered by Copland's assertion that "musicians make music out of feelings aroused out of public events," Copland amplified: "A musician, when he writes his notes, makes his music out of emotions and you can't create music unless you are moved by events." Igor Stravinsky's notion of creative autonomy, embraced by Nicolas Nabokov, the CIA, and the Kennedy White House, was thus disavowed by America's iconic composer of classical music.

After all that, Copland was cut adrift. He assured the State Department in 1953: "I have since March 1949 rigorously confined myself to purely musical matters."[28] His musical language vacillated between tonality (as in the Violin Sonata of 1968) and a confrontational atonality. He said that his nontonal *Connotations*, premiered at the New York Philharmonic's inaugural Lincoln Center concert in 1962, expressed contemporary "tension" and "desperation." His valedictory Piano Fantasy (1957) was an epic revisitation of the modernist Piano Variations that began his mature compositional odyssey twenty-seven years before. He stopped composing in the early 1970s. He died on the sidelines in 1990.

Aaron Copland's relationship to the America he courted and served is a cyclic saga of modernist insularity, populist ardor, and renewed estrangement. Shostakovich and Stravinsky, deeper talents, proved more resilient.

* * *

In 1941 Nabokov asserted that Copland was a better composer than Shostakovich.[29] At the 1952 Paris festival of "Twentieth Century Masterpieces," Copland was represented by *El salón México* and his Clarinet Concerto (performed twice, as set to dance by Jerome Robbins as *The Pied Piper*); of Shostakovich (as we have already observed), only a suite from *Lady Macbeth* was heard. More than untenable, Nabokov's opinion that Copland surpassed Shostakovich was implausible—a flaw fatal to effective propaganda.

Something else that proved untenable to American propaganda efforts was the spectacle of McCarthyism, viewed from abroad. It made a mockery of American culture. It threatened the credibility of the Congress for Cultural Freedom's emphasis on "free artists" in a "free society." It also served as a reminder why the CIA chose to remain a covert messenger.

Worse: McCarthy split the American partner of the Paris-based CCF: Sidney Hook's American Committee for Cultural Freedom. Many anti-Communist New York intellectuals noisily supported the thrust of McCarthy's surveillance, regardless of his methods. When the ACCF met at the Waldorf Astoria in 1952, the writer/activist Max Eastman accused liberals who saw McCarthy as a greater threat than Communism of "divided loyalty." Arthur Schlesinger, who was hissed at an ACCF forum, complained of "some sickness in certain sectors of the New York intellectuals." He told Nabokov: "The whole thing left a very bad taste in my mouth and considerably diminished my enthusiasm for the Congress [for Cultural Freedom] which, in this country, at least, has become an instrument for these bastards."[30]

With the death of Stalin in 1953, however, a new cultural initiative rapidly evolved outside the precincts of the CIA. The crucial participants were not dueling propagandists and spymasters, but composers and performers from both sides of the Iron Curtain. Transcending the complexities of covert action, it would prove a better way of warming the Cold War and celebrating American artistic achievement.

CHAPTER 8

ENTER CULTURAL EXCHANGE

Russia's relationship with the West traces a centuries-old dialectic of hostility and engagement, rejection and imitation. From the start, these countervailing forces intensified under Soviet rule. The new government earnestly cared what others thought of the "great experiment," and not least in the realm of culture. At the same time, currents of mistrust and insularity discouraged contacts with the West.

As early as 1922, an exhibit of avant-garde Soviet art electrified Berlin. VOKS—a "Society for Cultural Ties Abroad"—was formed in 1925. Led by Leon Trotsky's sister Olga Kameneva, it successfully mobilized the intelligentsia to work with sympathetic foreigners in propagating positive impressions of Soviet achievement. Though embattled and underfunded, VOKS dynamically sustained a window on the outside world until Kameneva's ouster in 1929.[1]

Democratizing and reforming Western high cultural traditions remained a Soviet priority—as in science and technology, aggressive competition with Western Europe and the United States was built-in component. The Soviet strategy was to broker a rapprochement with the intelligentsia, imposing Stalinist discipline but also assimilating traditional values (Russian writers and thinkers had typically laid emphasis on pursuing a better society for all). As "engineers of the soul," Soviet artists were to fulfill a pedagogical mission for the largest possible audience. The distinctive outcome was intended to combine wide dissemination with the repudiation of capitalist mistakes: commercialized culture for the marketplace, modernist culture for decadent elites.

The triumphant early success of Russian performing artists in international musical competitions—Lev Oborin's first prize at the first Chopin International Piano Competition in 1927, David Oistrakh's first prize at the first Queen Elisabeth Competition in 1937, Emil Gilels's first prize in the second Queen Elisabeth Competition in 1938—fortified Soviet claims to musical supremacy. So did the early Western popularity of Shostakovich's symphonies, and of his opera *Lady Macbeth*. Once Nikita Khrushchev took over in 1953, xenophobia was no longer an obstacle to sending Soviet artists abroad. And Khrushchev was an enthusiastic believer that Soviet prowess would "bury the West."[2] (In *Virtuosi Abroad* [2016], Kiril Tomoff argues that Khrushchev's reckless, self-defeating overconfidence in the Soviet system was partly a product of internationally validated musical achievements.)

A dozen years before Khrushchev's ascendance, the Russian Ministry of Information entered into discussions with the British Ministries of Economic Warfare to bring the Bolshoi Ballet to London. For the British, this was a propaganda initiative to coax Soviet citizens "out of their ring-fence" to experience "normal" life in Britain. Mikhail Krapchenko, chair of the Soviet Committee on Arts Affairs, was more than interested. The plan floundered in 1946 when the Bolshoi insisted on sending 250 personnel and new sets fitted to the Covent Garden stage. Meanwhile, in 1944, Krapchenko reported that his committee hoped to host the conductors Otto Klemperer, Leopold Stokowski, and Arturo Toscanini; the violinists Jascha Heifetz and Yehudi Menuhin; the pianist Vladimir Horowitz; and the soprano Lily Pons. Menuhin came in November 1945. Horowitz sent a telegram expressing interest. Krapchenko also proposed that Serge Koussevitzky tour Russia with his Boston Symphony Orchestra in exchange for having Evgeny Mravinsky, conductor of the Leningrad Philharmonic, guest conduct the Boston Symphony in Boston. And Alfred Wallenstein requested permission to tour Russia with his Los Angeles Philharmonic. That none of this came to pass, except for Menuhin's visit, seems mainly due to Stalin's swift retreat from cooperation with the Allies at war's end.[3] Another initiative, by the American-Soviet Music Society (in which Koussevitzky was a central force) arranged for two singers from the Kiev State Opera to perform in the United States in 1946. Following a New York City appearance, their tour was abandoned when they refused to register as foreign agents, as demanded by the U.S. government.[4]

Once Stalin was gone, Gilels, Oistrakh, and Mstislav Rostropovich played in the United States in 1955 and 1956. The Bolshoi Ballet came for eight weeks in

1959 and returned in 1962. Sviatoslav Richter made his American debut in 1960, the Kirov Ballet in 1961, the Leningrad Philharmonic in 1962. Amid a deluge of further Soviet visits, that of the Bolshoi Opera, in 1975, was another landmark cultural event.

The sheer frisson of these visitations, as from another planet, is impossible to recapture. Even Khrushchev harbored indistinct impressions of life in the United States. "It is hard for us now to imagine how distant we were from each other and how little we understood each other," wrote Sergei Khrushchev of his father's Geneva meeting with Dwight Eisenhower in 1955. "Diplomats and intelligence agents supplied their leaders with information, of course, but that was not enough to gain an understanding of the other side. We had to look into each other's eyes." The Bolshoi prima ballerina Galina Ulanova, who was a loyal Soviet artist accustomed to comforts and acclaim, and who deservedly became a cult figure in the West, confessed in 1959: "We knew so little about the outside world, and we were just amazed by the scale of the country. All those huge stores five and six floors high, with all these clothes on sale, and entire apartments on display—we just didn't have anything like that." The choreographer Igor Moiseyev, whose folk ensemble toured America in 1961, said: "I'm amazed that all your workers are fat and all your millionaires are thin."[5]

The amazement was mutual. When Oistrakh appeared at Carnegie Hall with Dmitri Mitropoulos and the New York Philharmonic on December 29, 1955, his vehicle was the Shostakovich Violin Concerto No. 1: a work not yet heard in Moscow. The occasion was historic. Responding to the ovation, Mitropoulos held the score aloft. He also recorded it with Oistrakh. A year earlier, Mitropoulos and the Philharmonic had made the first Western recording of Shostakovich's Tenth Symphony: a tremendous reading. (In Paris, Nicolas Nabokov continued to denigrate Shostakovich as a hack and stooge.) Richter's American debut was so long and keenly anticipated that it comprised a marathon series of ten concerts at Carnegie Hall, most spaced only days apart, spanning music by twelve composers—and all of it recorded live by Columbia Records. When Rostropovich's singular interpretation of the Dvořák Cello Concerto was broadcast nationally by the New York Philharmonic in 1965, its expressive liberties ignited a national conversation. I am old enough to recall that Dvořák broadcast. I also heard Oistrakh, Gilels, and Richter, among others, as visiting Soviet artists. As these memories remain vivid, the following account is necessarily personal.

*   *   *

The crown jewel of Soviet classical music was not merely unknown in the United States; it was unknown even by reputation. This was the Leningrad

Philharmonic, an instrument unique in the world. Its conductor since 1938, Evgeny Mravinsky, rarely conducted other orchestras. A towering martinet who in bearing and gesture evoked the impersonal severity of a Byzantine gargoyle, he drilled the players unstintingly. His authority and rehearsal prerogatives were absolute. More than any Western conductor, he enjoyed a close relationship with living symphonic composers of world consequence: he led first performances of Prokofiev's Sixth Symphony and of Shostakovich's Fifth, Sixth, Eighth, Ninth, Tenth, and Twelfth. The orchestra plausibly regarded its hall as acoustically supreme. Though beginning in 1956 it toured in Western Europe, it had never visited the United States before the fall of 1962.

In New York, I heard a program comprising Mozart's Violin Concerto No. 5 with Oistrakh, a Myaskovsky symphony, and Tchaikovsky's Fifth. "The Death of Tybalt" from Prokofiev's *Romeo and Juliet* was an encore. (This concert, in White Plains, was conducted by the young Genady Rozhdestvensky—but the orchestra was Mravinsky's.) I listened in a state of shock. The entire ensemble vibrated with color. The horn vibratos and tight, bright trumpet timbres were new to me. The orchestra's glory was its string choir. The violins played with a wealth of nuance I had not imagined possible. The dynamic range of the whole group, from threaded wisps to sonic avalanches, was unique in my experience. In Prokofiev the palette of the Leningrad Philharmonic, in its myriad dimensions, was more "Romantic," less "modern," than the Western norm. In Mozart its *espressivo* grew exquisitely refined. In Tchaikovsky the Leningrad sound was, as I instantly and unforgettably realized, Tchaikovsky's sound, revealed to my ears for the first time. (The most titanic Tchaikovsky performance I know is Rozhdestvensky's 1960 performance of *Francesca da Rimini* with the Leningrad Philharmonic at the Edinburg Festival. You can hear it on YouTube.)

For Harold Schonberg, the chief music critic of the *New York Times*, Cold War rivalries never died. In a review, he patronized Mravinsky, lecturing him on up-to-date Mozart interpretation. (Schonberg's response to the "old-fashioned" Bolshoi Opera, thirteen years later, was the same. It would be a mistake to imagine that American critics of Soviet artists were more generous or less threatened than Soviet critics in their assessment of visiting Americans.)[6] In the seventies, the Leningrad Philharmonic lost key members to defection, including any number of Jewish string players. I got to know Lazar Gosman, who wound up in the St. Louis Symphony. He told me that when Mravinsky read Schonberg's review, he announced he would never return to the United States—and he never did. Gosman also told me that in St. Louis he was amazed to discover the musicians heading for their cars after concerts. In Leningrad the orchestra members would congregate postconcert to drink and decompress. The Leningrad concertmaster,

Viktor Liberman, became concertmaster of the Amsterdam Concertgebouw Orchestra. He told Russian acquaintances[7] that he did not fully appreciate the quasi-religious solemnity of Mravinsky's rehearsals and concerts until he left. In Leningrad, rehearsals and concerts were never casual occasions.

Only gradually did Mravinsky's studio and live recordings become readily available to me. I discovered, on further acquaintance, that he was not a conductor for all seasons. And the orchestra's singularity could seem too much of a good thing. But it had no successors. Today's St. Petersburg Philharmonic sounds generic in comparison.

I also heard Kirill Kondrashin conduct his Moscow Philharmonic at Carnegie Hall in 1965. It was no Leningrad Philharmonic. The strings were exceptional. The winds and brass were not world-class. The Bolshoi Opera orchestra, at the Metropolitan Opera House for one month in 1975, was another matter. It produced warmer, more fragrant music than any I had previously heard emanate from that pit. The company also disclosed a core of big-voiced singers who instantly established international careers. The repertoire was all-Russian. In Prokofiev's *The Gambler*, as directed by Boris Pokrovsky, the Bolshoi produced an ensemble of singing actors no Western house could rival. In Tchaikovsky—*Eugene Onegin* and *Pique Dame*—a shared tradition of performance buoyed the proceedings. In *Boris Godunov*, tradition produced a Disney rendering that seemed old-fashioned and stale.

Mainly, however, my experience of Soviet classical music was an experience of pianists, arriving in droves. Gilels, more than Richter, was for me. He commanded the biggest, most colorful of all keyboard signatures. He was at all times larger than life, heedlessly expressive. But he suffered greatly as a Soviet artist. Other pianists, fed up with being told what, when, and where they could perform, fled to the West with stories of unimaginable indignities and insanities. Two whom I came to know were Vladimir Feltsman and the late Alexander Toradze. They resented being trained as Soviet musical athletes, groomed to win the international piano competitions in which the Russian excelled. But their musical preparation, at the Moscow Conservatory, was more personal and comprehensive than in any Western music school; from an early age they were accepted into a ripe community of musicians. They also attained a higher level of cultural and intellectual awareness than was (or is) the Western norm. And they benefited from a native repertoire including important twentieth-century and contemporary composers. Toradze specialized in Prokofiev, Shostakovich, and Stravinsky; he was also closely associated with the late Georgian composer Giya Kancheli. Feltsman, whose affinities are Germanic, forged a close personal and professional relationship with Alfred Schnittke, for many the leading Soviet composer of the post-Shostakovich generation. The late American pianist John Browning, who well knew the competition circuit, once summarized: "If the Russians don't come, the general standards are not nearly as good. . . . You know, they're ready to give concerts at the age of fifteen—they're truly ready."[8]

In one obvious respect, cultural exchange was a Russian failure: the departures of Toradze (1983) and Feltsman (1987); of Rudolf Nureyev (1961); of Vladimir Ashkenazy (1963); of Rostropovich and his wife, the soprano Galina Vishnevskaya (1974); and of Mikhail Baryshnikov (1974) were world news. But these artists, and others who remained Soviet, conveyed a caliber of cultural life surpassing in many respects an American classical music culture that had (and has) never outgrown a Eurocentric bias. More fundamentally, however, Russian cultural exchange in the realm of music, whatever its intent, sealed a commonality of purpose. The abiding message was not the propaganda claim "we are better," but the human realization "we are all the same." Differences registered less than did similarities. And the same held true of state-supported musical diplomacy as transmitted from West to East.

* * *

Aside from Menuhin's 1945 visit, the first North American musicians to visit Soviet Russia after World War II were the African American singers comprising Robert Breen's touring *Porgy and Bess* company, in 1955, and the Canadian pianist Glenn Gould, in 1957. Van Cliburn's unanticipated victory in Moscow's International Tchaikovsky Competition came in 1958.

It retrospect, it is notable that none of these visits was supported by either the Canadian or the U.S. government. *Porgy and Bess* is one of America's highest creative achievement in classical music. Gould and Cliburn were the two biggest North American keyboard talents of their generation. And all three visits impacted momentously.

Gershwin's achievement, as of 1955, was not appreciated by American-born classical musicians. They viewed him as a gifted dilettante. His concert works were pigeon-holed as "pops" repertoire. His great opera was not given by American opera companies. The reasons are complex: modernism was a factor and so was institutional racism.[9] But foreign-born classical musicians recognized Gershwin's genius. This was true, in America, of Jascha Heifetz, Otto Klemperer, Fritz Reiner, Arnold Schoenberg, and countless others. And it was true of Europeans, including Dmitri Shostakovich. In fact, the Soviet Union had a love affair with Gershwin dating back to the 1930s, when Alexander Tsfasman toured the Soviet Union with his jazz band; their pièce de résistance was *Rhapsody in Blue*. In 1945 *Porgy and Bess* was performed in Moscow (with piano and drums); Shostakovich called it "magnificent" and drew comparisons to Borodin and Mussorgsky.[10] A year later, both Leningrad's Mali and Moscow's Stanislavski theater requested performing parts only to discover that the lack of copyright protection for foreign authors could spell trouble. Breen's *Porgy* production triumphantly toured Europe, the Mediterranean, and Latin America with State Department support beginning in 1952. But when he proposed that State further underwrite performances in Moscow and Leningrad, the answer was no. The Russian ambassador to the United States, Andrei Vishinsky, favored this project, as did the American ambassador to the Soviet Union, Chip Bohlen. Breen was told that the State Department's limited budget for cultural exchange could not afford another $400,000. He reacted with undisguised anger. The real reason, he suspected, was misguided apprehension: that the opera's depiction of African American squalor could be used against American interests.[11] In fact, State Department anxiety about possible Soviet machinations is an early leitmotif of the cultural exchange narrative. It was even surmised that, as Russian audiences were "controlled," they might hiss Americans off the stage.[12]

And so the tour proceeded with a precariously tight subsidy from the Russians themselves. Not only did Gershwin's opera triumph (no other American concert or stage work more powerfully depicts fraught human relationships within a morally sensitized community); the cast members proved irrepressible American ambassadors, whether extemporizing a jam session in the supper room of Leningrad's Astoria Hotel or performing arias in five languages at a Russian dinner concert alongside Bolshoi artists. Bohlen later recalled: "The cast created a problem for the Russians. The freewheeling actors rebelled at being guided everywhere they went. They wandered out alone and refused to go on tours. They always attracted large numbers of curious Russians, who, after decades of propaganda, found it difficult to believe there were well-dressed, well-educated black Americans." Bohlen also said: "Of the cultural, educational, and scientific exchanges that followed the relaxations of tension after [the 1955 Geneva Conference], the one that stands out most vividly in my memory is *Porgy and Bess*."[13]

Two years later, Gould's chiseled polyphonic clarity, his rangy intellect and repertoire, his eccentric personal habits stunned musical Russia. According to a much-told story, the first half of his Moscow debut recital was sparsely attended; many phone calls were made; the second half was packed. At an impromptu master class, Gould played and discussed twelve-tone and atonal music by Schoenberg, Berg, Webern, and Krenek, all of it new to his eager listeners. His permanent influence on Russian performers surpassed that of any visitor to come.

Cliburn's impact was pandemonious: broader and more legendary. The So-viets had created an international piano competition studded with big-name jurors: Gilels, Richter, Heinrich Neuhaus, Alexander Goldenweiser. A Soviet winner was naturally anticipated (the favorite being Lev Vlasenko). Out of nowhere, a twenty-three-year-old, six-foot-four Texan with a mop of frizzy blond hair overwhelmed the field. Gilels embraced Cliburn backstage. Richter called him "a genius—a word I do not use lightly." Khachaturian said: "You find a virtuoso like this once or twice in a century." Khrushchev, who necessarily ap-proved the surprise verdict, threw his arms around the Cliburn beanpole. While the Cold War context doubtless varnished this irresistible saga, Cliburn's first-prize performance of Rachmaninoff's Third Piano Concerto remains a reading for the ages.[14]

In Washington it was well understood that Soviet musical competitors were beneficiaries of exemplary state-funded conservatories that spared no expense preparing and deploying artistic athletes. Cliburn, a graduate of New York's Juil-liard School, set out for Moscow with an unpaid telephone bill; when the State Department said no, the Martha Baird Rockefeller Foundation helped him to meet his Russian costs. At the time, discussion of cultural exchange with the Soviets was ongoing. Some in the State Department worried that the resulting propaganda exchange would favor the cagey Russians. In 1956 and 1958, the Boston Symphony and Philadelphia Orchestra toured the USSR with patchwork government funding. The milestone was the 1958 Lacy-Zarubin Agreement, which put the State Department in charge of U.S.-Soviet exchanges "in the Cultural, Technical, and Educational Fields"—a rubric including performing arts, science and technology, agriculture, medicine and public health, radio and television, motion pictures, exhibitions, publications, athletics, scholarly research, and tourism. In the field of music and dance, on the Russian side the state would handle everything. On the American side, government would part-ner private-sector impresarios, among whom the Russian-born Sol Hurok—a personage of legendary proportions—was and remained a crucial asset.

Ensuring principles of reciprocity and mutual benefit, the agreement ad-dressed a multiplicity of objectives both spoken and not. For the United States, it pursued President Eisenhower's push for "people to people" contacts to en-hance mutual knowledge and understanding. The Americans did not conceal their concomitant intention to promote evolutionary change within the So-viet system. For the Soviets, bilateral agreements handsomely established an equal footing with the United States. Lacy-Zarubin would also showcase Soviet achievement, earn foreign currency, placate a growing demand for foreign travel and exposure, and—not least important—facilitate access to American science and technology.

In the realm of culture, the first American beneficiary—in August 1959—was the New York Philharmonic. Its visit would recontextualize the aims and achievements of Nicolas Nabokov and the Congress for Cultural Freedom virtually overnight.

*   *   *

Born outside of Boston in 1918 to Ukrainian Jewish immigrants, Leonard Bernstein was the youngest music director in the orchestra's 117-year history and the first to be native to the United States. He was also a wildly successful Broadway composer and a popular, even glamorous, television pedagogue. His obsession was making American classical music truly American—finding, championing, and helping to create an American canon to supplement the European masterpieces that still anchored the repertoire of every American orchestra and opera company. His qualifications for cultural diplomacy were as self-evident as they were comprehensive. Even so, the State Department was nervous. Every member of the Philharmonic received a twenty-eight-page booklet (including a six-page bibliography), *So You're Going to Russia*. Its intent was to equip visitors with facts and observations to spread "the American message of good-will"—a message, that is, of American superiority.[15] As it turned out, all such admonitions and instructions were irrelevant. In Moscow, Leningrad, and Kiev, Bernstein proved not only wholly independent, but completely unpredictable.

Many if not most accounts of this New York Philharmonic tour describe a concerted act of provocation. Early on, Bernstein was asked not to program one of the American works he had scheduled: Charles Ives's *The Unanswered Question*. According to whom? Bernstein asked. "Experts," he was told. The State Department's Hans Tuch, a witness to this exchange, vividly recalls Bernstein's retort: "He said 'Fuck you!,' got up, and walked out."[16] Bernstein proceeded not only to perform the five-minute Ives piece; he encored it.[17] He also conducted Stravinsky's Concerto for Piano and Winds even though it was not listed ahead of time. His reading of Shostakovich's Fifth Symphony controversially sped up the ending. A wild reception compelled the composer (whatever he may have thought) to stride quickly to the podium and awkwardly shake the conductor's hand. And, famously, Bernstein violated Soviet concert decorum by speaking from the stage. When criticized for doing so, he decided he had not talked enough. But the biggest surprise Bernstein pulled was inviting Boris Pasternak, the disgraced Russian author, to his final concert. A year before, Pasternak had been prohibited from accepting a Nobel Prize. He not only came to the concert—his first public appearance since the Nobel scandal and his expulsion from the Writers' Union—but hosted Bernstein in his dacha while the world watched.

Nearly every retelling of this story highlights an account of the first Moscow concert—with the Ives piece, plus the Stravinsky Piano Concerto and *The Rite of Spring*—by Alexandr Medvedev in *Sovetskaya Kultura*.[18] Medvedev called Bernstein's spoken comments "immodest" and objected to the repetition of *The Unanswered Question* after "a ripple of cool applause." And he characterized the concert as "some kind of show being played under the title 'Bernstein Raises the Iron Curtain in Music'." Bernstein himself called the review "an unforgivable lie and in the most worst possible taste." He claimed that the applause after the Ives was emphatic, not "cold" (a contention supported by the *New York Times'* correspondent). And he added: "Every word printed is official one way or another. I take this as very important." Humphrey Burton, in his authorized Bernstein biography, calls Medvedev's notice "a stinging attack," a "party line."

But Bernstein clearly enjoyed himself in Russia. As elsewhere abroad, he was mobbed by young people. Grinning broadly, he had his hair cut in full view of an entertained crowd. He visited with Russian relatives—his father's younger brother and his brother's son—then belatedly brought his father to Moscow to visit some more. As for the reviews, they were far better than the ones Bernstein was accustomed to receiving in New York City. Both the violinist Leonid Kogan and the composer Dmitri Kabalevsky contributed paeans of praise. Kabalevsky reported about the final concert that he "emphatically" preferred Bernstein's ebullient ending to Shostakovich's Fifth to the usual solemnity. One also learns from his account that the audience applauded both the second and the third movements, that the final ovation was "screamed," and that every member of the orchestra received a bouquet.

As for Medvedev's review, it begins by calling Bernstein "a great musician" who "swept the public away." As a lecturer, he found Bernstein "unsuccessful" and "somewhat presumptuous." He took issue with Bernstein's assertion that *The Rite of Spring* had not been performed in the Soviet Union for more than thirty years; he himself had heard it a year before in Tallinn, excerpts were performed at dance concerts in Leningrad and Kiev, and many in the audience brought along the score. He considered the Stravinsky concerto "cold," "dry," and "lifeless"—a specimen from "a tragic period in his creativity." He closed: "Such are my impressions of the concert. I could not help expressing them. We are glad to welcome here a guest from a country of great musical traditions. We find much value in the art of the Americans, and we welcome this. But hospitality should not keep us from telling the truth, even if it is not always to the liking of our guests."

In retrospect, two things seem most significant about this review. The first is that its "insincerity" cannot be assumed—the Cold War notion that Soviet judgments were typically ideological was a two-way street full of mutual mis-readings. And, second, Medvedev's misgivings about the content and "pre-sumptuous" tone of Bernstein's spoken commentary would be familiar to any New York concertgoer in 1959. His script lectured: "I want very much to make it possible for you to hear Stravinsky (whom I consider a very great Russian composer and a great international artist), and I think you must hear more than one aspect of Stravinsky."

Alexander Toradze, who knew Medvedev well, remembers him "very posi-tively." He adds: "In 1959, virtually no one in Russia liked the Stravinsky Con-certo for Piano and Winds"—a view supported by another Soviet-trained pia-nist, Alexei Lubimov, who attended Bernstein's concerts at the age of fifteen and was transported by Ives's *The Unanswered Question*. In later years, both Toradze and Lubimov became prominent exponents of the Stravinsky concerto—as did the legendary Maria Yudina, for whom Seymour Lipkin's performance of the concerto with Bernstein was a watershed experience.[19]

Free-spirited, irrepressible, Bernstein in Russia extolled American music and critiqued Soviet restraints. But his fundamental sermon was ecumenical. On the last full day of his visit, he taped a one-hour lecture/concert for American televi-sion; his Moscow audience was furnished with a printed translation. Illustrating the popularity of Russian music in American popular song, he sampled "Full Moon and Empty Arms" (after Rachmaninoff) and "Tonight We Love" (after Tchaikovsky). But his main exercise was to juxtapose excerpts from Copland's *Billy the Kid* and Shostakovich's Seventh Symphony and discover fundamental similarities mirroring "the similarity of our two great peoples."

> What have we discovered? . . . Just this: everything we have heard points to our common youth, our affection for our primitive past, our emotional expansive-ness, our sense of fun, our frankness, our tremendous vigor and the endless variety with our two countries. Your music and ours are the artistic products of two very similar peoples—peoples who are natural friends, who belong together and who must not let suspicions and fears and prejudices keep them apart. This is what I have come to feel in these few weeks that I have been your guest, and I deeply hope that you feel the same.[20]

Moscow (eight concerts), Leningrad (six), and Kiev (four) were the final stops on a Bernstein/New York Philharmonic tour also including Greece, Turkey,

Lebanon, and Warsaw as well as Western Europe. Upon returning to the United States, Bernstein spoke at a press conference in Washington, DC, advocating increased funding for cultural exchange.

Vladimir Feltsman recalls talking to Bernstein in 1987 about the Philharmonic's Russian visit. "His most vivid and precious memory was meeting and spending time with Pasternak. 'Great man. He is imprinted in my brain,' he said." Feltsman added: "Bernstein's visit to Russia was very important at that particular time. The scent of freedom was beguiling and irresistible."[21] In fact, Bernstein in Russia was the very embodiment of the Congress for Cultural Freedom ideal: a "free artist" representing a "free society." So flamboyant was his ardor that he implausibly placed Copland on the same high pedestal as Shostakovich and praised American concert music in the same breath as Shostakovich, Tchaikovsky, and Rachmaninoff. Bernstein was in fact more greatly appreciated in Soviet Russia than in Manhattan (or Berlin or London). Americans and Europeans widely questioned his depth and maturity in this nascent stage of his podium career, which would peak in future decades when his dream of a great American concert repertoire had faded to insignificance.

* * *

The five-year sequence *Porgy*-Gould-Cliburn-Bernstein, however fortuitous, was a milestone in Cold War propaganda. These visits, and their concomitant itineraries outside Russia, impressed the world that the young North American continent had over the course of the twentieth century produced art and artists of the highest consequence. Juxtaposed with the ongoing festival activities of the Congress for Cultural Freedom, they also dramatized the increasing incongruity of Nicolas Nabokov in his capacity as chief Cold War cultural propagandist. It was fully three years after Bernstein's Russian visit that Nabokov—still the exiled aristocrat, angry at Soviet usurpers—"hysterically" implored Stravinsky not to go to Moscow. Bernstein, plainly, was a true believer in the New World. Nabokov's cultural base was and remained Russian and European. His 1952 Paris festival now seemed a weird extravagance, unknowable in cost, oblique in purpose, its American works few and oddly chosen.

Nabokov's writings from this period do not mention Cliburn's victory or Bernstein's Soviet visit. (He detested both Rachmaninoff's Third Piano Concerto and Shostakovich's Fifth Symphony—the twin vehicles of conquest.) Recalling his first Berlin Festival of 1964, he wrote in *Bagazh*: "I was offered Kirill Kondrashin whom I had never heard of and who then, like Rostropovich, was largely unknown outside the USSR."[22] But American music lovers knew both these names. Kondrashin was Cliburn's memorable accompanist at the

Tchaikovsky competition. Cliburn took him to New York, where he conducted Cliburn's best-selling RCA recordings; he also toured with Cliburn to other American cities and made additional symphonic recordings for RCA. As for Rostropovich, he was already a musical celebrity in the United States. Nabokov, not a brand name, was chiefly known to Soviet musicians for humiliating Shostakovich in Manhattan in 1949. Vladimir Feltsman—himself a U.S. propaganda asset as the most prominent musical "refusenik" and a frequent guest of U.S. ambassador Arthur Hartman—comments: "Nabokov was a paid political operator, shameless in his actions and methods, not a sympathetic personality. A small dog barking at an elephant."[23]

Bernstein's cultural diplomacy was ongoing. At his 1959 DC press conference, he said, "If military strength is a nation's right arm, culture is its left arm, closer to the heart. . . . You can always touch people with music."[24] In 1966 he wrote and hosted a New York Philharmonic Young People's Concert to celebrate Shostakovich's sixtieth birthday. Addressing a national television audience, he contradicted a decade of CIA "cultural freedom" ideology when he said:

> In these days of musical experimentation, with new fads chasing each other in and out of the concert halls, a composer like Shostakovich can be easily put down. After all he's basically a traditional Russian composer, a true son of Tchaikovsky—and no matter how modern he ever gets, he never loses that tradition. So the music is always in some way old-fashioned—or at least what critics and musical intellectuals like to call old-fashioned. But they're forgetting the most important thing—he's a genius: a real authentic genius, and there aren't too many of those around any more.[25]

With the wisdom of hindsight, it is easy to appreciate the many reasons Bernstein was better equipped to pursue American foreign policy objectives than Nabokov. That he was not a pedigreed anti-Communist was by no means irrelevant. The "fellow travelers" at the Waldorf Astoria in 1949 had included the thirty-year-old Bernstein. He was also one of the American musicians who warmly welcomed Shostakovich via cable. And he was thereupon duly identified as a "security risk" and blacklisted by CBS.

The post-Bernstein deluge of American musical artists visiting the Soviet Union under State Department sponsorship included the Cleveland Orchestra and a host of jazz ensembles, including those of Benny Goodman (a naive and anachronistic first choice, because Russians knew jazz—a topic I pursue in a note),[26] Duke Ellington, Earl Hines, and Dave Brubeck. So far as Russia's classical musicians were concerned, the most important visitor was a dance company: George Balanchine's New York City Ballet, in 1962. The repertoire included *Agon* (1957), setting a nontonal Stravinsky score wholly unknown to Soviet audiences. Balanchine's central pas de deux featured Arthur Mitchell and Allegra Kent, Mitchell being the company's one African American soloist. For Russian audiences, *Agon* was a milestone discovery. Balanchine's *Episodes* (1959), setting music by Webern, was if anything even more tumultuously received. In New York, according to the *Times'* John Martin, this was found "perhaps the most puzzling avant-garde works in the repertory"; Webern's aphoristic Five Pieces, Op. 10, often provoked nervous titters—but not in Moscow or Leningrad. The biggest ovations, night after night, were never for the dancers, but for the master choreographer, punctuated by rhythmic shouts of *Spa-si-bo! Spa-si-bo!* The company's farewell performance was said by Bolshoi personnel to have ignited the greatest ovation ever recalled in that theater. Solomon Volkov attended performances in Leningrad. "Older people hated it. 'The Americans aren't dancing; they're solving algebra problems with their feet.' But the young saw in Balanchine's productions the heights that the Petersburg cultural avant-garde could have reached if it had not been crushed by the Soviet authorities." When a Radio Moscow interviewer welcomed Balanchine to Moscow, "home of the classic ballet," he famously retorted, "I beg your pardon. Russia is the home of romantic ballet. The home of classic ballet is now America." In the 1950s, the CIA had balked at supporting a City Ballet tour to Russia in fear that the company would seem insignificant compared to the Bolshoi and Kirov. In fact, Russian audiences understood better than Americans that Balanchine had created the supreme American performing arts institution.[27]

The termination of the Congress for Cultural Freedom in 1966 and Nabokov's capitulatory return to Russia a year later proved more than timely. Cultural exchange had by then eclipsed the CCF as a foreign-policy instrument. Within the CCF itself, the spirit of détente had ultimately prodded Michael Josselson toward dialogue with the East. Concurrently, Vietnam and the Nixon presidency enraged the artists and intellectuals the CCF was supposed to woo.

Cultural exchange hung on—to a degree. As late in the day as 1986, Vladimir Horowitz's return to Russia, supported by President Ronald Reagan and U.S. ambassador Arthur Hartman, perceptibly allayed Cold War tensions inflamed by American airstrikes against Libya, then a Soviet ally. Russia had recently rejected tours by the Philadelphia Orchestra and Dave Brubeck. They relented for Horowitz. To his intense frustration, Hartman discovered the State Department nonetheless indifferent to the opportunity at hand.[28] And the Russians initially refused to televise a Moscow recital otherwise viewed throughout the world. The most lionized concert pianist of his generation, a surviving exemplar of Russian Romantic traditions facing extinction, Horowitz, at age eighty-three, had not visited his homeland since leaving in 1925. Once he had been heard, the mood changed to one of intense interest and gratitude. Horowitz wound up on Soviet TV after all. He played Scriabin's piano. He visited Tchaikovsky's house. He reunited with members of his family. Mikhail Gorbachev was after all a man of culture.

Upon returning home, Vladimir Horowitz was awarded a Medal of Freedom at a White House ceremony. President Reagan called him "an emissary of good will to the people of the Soviet Union." Some seventeen months later, on December 8, 1987, the Reagan White House hosted Van Cliburn. The occasion was a visit by Mikhail Gorbachev. The diplomatic side of things was not going well. At the evening's end, Gorbachev and his wife, Raisa, sang "Moscow Nights," launched by Cliburn at the piano. The next day, their impromptu performance made headlines around the world—and Reagan and Gorbachev began negotiations on the most ambitious arms-control treaty in history.[29]

And yet cultural diplomacy between the United States and Russia dissipated with the waning of the Cold War and termination of the Soviet Union in 1991. The late Hans Tuch, who served in Moscow for the State Department during the tenure of Ambassador Llewellyn Thompson, recalled:

> The State Department gradually came around to thinking that cultural exchange with the Soviet Union was a good thing. We in Moscow were influential in convincing them that this was a good way of penetrating Russia. I for one was unable to establish the necessary relationships. It was people like Isaac Stern, when he came to Moscow, who made the relationships and included me. Also, Sol Hurok was instrumental—I give him enormous credit for fostering cultural exchange. His aims were exactly what we wanted to accomplish. We couldn't do it by ourselves. Ambassador Thompson was very much in favor, he backed me and my colleagues completely. I was totally divorced from what the CIA was doing—if I had any kind of relationship with them, it would have been the end of my usefulness in Moscow.[30]

As deputy director of Soviet and Eastern European affairs, director of the Office of European Affairs, and director of European Affairs for the United States Information Agency from 1979 to 1983, Leonard Baldyga was the USIA's principal negotiator of cultural and scientific agreements with the Soviet bloc from 1979 to 1983.[31] When Baldyga was named Director of European affairs for the second time in 1992, he was given $1.2 million to staff and open posts in each of the former Soviet republics. To his frustration, none of the money was designated for cultural programming. A year later, Mstislav Rostropovich performed in Moscow's Red Square for an audience of one hundred thousand, conducting the National Symphony Orchestra of Washington, DC (of which he was music director). They were joined by the Washington Choral Arts Society, which took part in Prokofiev's *Alexander Nevsky* cantata. The Choral Arts Society had unsuccessfully petitioned the State Department and USIA for $100,000 to help subsidize for the trip. Baldyga paid the $100,000 out of his own European area budget.[32]

William Kiehl, who served in Moscow for the State Department's Bureau of Educational and Cultural Affairs, a few years ago recalled: "In the waning days of the U.S. Information Agency [that is, in 1999], there was no money or interest in 'cultural exchanges.' When we survivors realized what the future of public diplomacy would be, we could not wait to get out of the failing structure. I left ECA under fire. . . . I decided it wasn't worth staying on in a meaningless job in State."[33]

CULTURE, THE STATE, AND THE "PROPAGANDA OF FREEDOM"

Of Van Cliburn's victory in the 1958 Tchaikovsky International Piano Competition, Dmitri Shostakovich, serving as competition chairman, said: "We, for our part, are extremely happy that this outstanding young American artist earned his first wide and entirely deserved recognition among us here in Moscow." Shostakovich's claim was resented in the United States. As recently as 2019, an American historian decreed "Shostakovich was wrong."[1] But Shostakovich was right. Recalled today (as in my previous chapter), this most famous musical tale of the cultural Cold War remains a stirring affirmation of how an irresistibly personable young American beat the odds in Soviet Russia. Revisited in detail (in my pages to come), it also registers as an ambiguous and cautionary commentary on cultural conditions in the two nations then and now.

The Russians launched Sputnik in October 1957, shocking the West. They had as well just successfully fired an intercontinental missile before anyone else. They announced their new Tchaikovsky competition in the same breath. At the time, the most prominent music competition was the Queen Elisabeth, in Brussels. The first two winners, in 1938 and 1939, were Emil Gilels and David Oistrakh. When the competition resumed after World War II, in 1952, an American, Leon Fleisher, took first prize—but no Russians competed. Four years later, the Russians returned—and Vladimir Ashkenazy won. At Warsaw's Chopin competition, the first winner, in 1927, was Lev Oborin. In four subsequent

Chopin competitions, the first or second prize was taken by a Russian four times. The Soviet threat in music seemed nearly undeflectable.

The reigning piano pedagogue at New York City's Juilliard School was also Russian: Rosina Lhevinne. According to a story too good to be true, yet told by an eyewitness, she read the Tchaikovsky competition brochure, walked to a window, and said softly, half to herself: "Van." He had already won the most important American competition, the Leventritt, in 1954. But it was a stubbornly private affair. Edgar M. Leventritt had been a New York attorney of German Jewish descent, a skilled amateur musician whose friends included Rudolf Serkin. A major pedagogue in addition to his high standing as a concert pianist, Serkin wielded formidable influence as a Leventritt juror. Musically, he was a strict literalist. That a pianist as incorrigibly Romantic as Cliburn could win the Leventritt bespoke a talent of inordinate dimension. Cliburn's Leventritt dates had now come and gone. He had no recording contract. As Lhevinne instantly intuited, the Tchaikovsky competition, with repertoire requirements favoring music Cliburn ardently and unaffectedly loved, was an opportunity to astound the musical world. In fact, she may already have privately gleaned that her one-of-a-kind Van would bewilder and overwhelm the Russians as he could never bestir his fellow Americans.

From the day he arrived in Moscow, Van Cliburn inhabited a dream come true. No clairvoyant could have negotiated every aspect of his visit as sublimely. Upon landing, he asked to be taken first to the Church of St. Basil. Standing in snowy Red Square at night, he thought his heart would stop. He called the Russians "my people" and said, "I've never felt so at home anywhere in my life." It became swiftly evident that this was actually true. Back in the United States, his hero's welcome included a "Van Cliburn Day" ticker-tape parade down Fifth Avenue, a meeting with President Eisenhower (who, however, had been notably slow to congratulate him on his victory), a *Person to Person* TV interview with Edward R. Murrow, and a guest appearance on *What's My Line?* Cliburn more than tolerated these signatures of celebrity. His precocious aplomb, at age twenty-three, seemed absolute. But, privately, he was cracking under the pressure.[2]

Already in Moscow, behind the scenes, Cliburn had been viewed with concern by Washington as a possible Soviet tool. The State Department (which as we have seen had passed on supporting *Porgy and Bess* in Russia, or helping Cliburn with his expenses) mistrusted Cliburn's enthusiasm for Russia; there was even speculation, according to a secret telegram, that he "may have been approached" by the Soviets to do their bidding. The FBI expressed concern about apparent homosexual tendencies. In both Moscow and New York, Cliburn continued to praise the Russians unstintingly. He bristled, at times, that Eisenhower—who met with him for only twelve minutes and, like Vice President Nixon, was too busy to attend his DC performance at Constitution Hall—so little appreciated his victory in comparison to Khrushchev and Georgy Malenkov. (The FBI recorded him telling his New York manager that he intended to remain in Russia indefinitely and that "if Eisenhower wants to see me, he knows where he can find me.") At the same time, Cliburn's patriotic streak, a product of his Texas upbringing, remained in play. On *What's My Line?*, addressing a vast national television audience, he volunteered: "I've said it before, and I'll say it again, that the debt of gratitude that I owe is to the United States because, after all, where was I born, where did I come from, and where did I get the advantages?" More frequently, he said, "Ya lyublyu Moskvu" (I love Moscow).[3] Conditioned by Cold War anxiety and mistrust, the U.S. government was slow to apprehend it all—both the opportunity at hand and future opportunities that therefore beckoned. The Americans, it would ensue, had more to gain via cultural exchange, and much less to lose, than did the Russians.

And so it happened that Van Cliburn discovered himself not as at home in America as in Moscow. The Russians had feted him, first of all, as a musician. To the Americans, he was first of all a phenomenon. As Howard Taubman wrote in the *Times*: "Over and over again, the question . . . has been: 'Is this Van Cliburn really that good?'" It was rumored that the Russians had engineered a grand propaganda coup. Wonderfully, the evidence that Cliburn was really that good survives. In fact, it has never been so readily available. Soviet films of his Moscow performances are sitting on YouTube. The one to watch first is the Rachmaninoff Third. I have had occasion to describe it before:

> Americans associated this big, densely embroidered concerto with Vladimir Horowitz, for whom it showcased his febrile, piledriving virtuosity. Cliburn's treatment is majestically expansive, never hectic or distorted. Horowitz is the more brilliant colorist; his blinding speed and mercurial nuance evoke Rachmaninoff himself. . . . Cliburn's fingers never brag. His tone is not kaleidoscopably varied, but invariably round, burnished, unforced. The long lines he intuits sing beautifully of sadness and nostalgia. His course is steady and far-sighted. Its current heaves upward in great concentrated waves, slowing the pace, weighting the climaxes. The first-movement cadenza, the concerto's central storm-point, an upheaval of expanding force and sonority, builds with utter sureness; Cliburn simply lets it come. The tidal altitude and breadth of its crest are dizzying. The long descent is equally thorough; to begin the coda, the first theme returns dazed and spent.[4]

It must be added that Kirill Kondrashin, leading his Moscow Philharmonic, is a peerless accompanist. Cliburn's Moscow performances of the Rachmaninoff Second, Brahms Second, and Grieg concertos, in 1960 and 1962, were again memorably partnered by Kondrashin. The Grieg is really a work too fragile for the expansive grandeur with which it is invested; but they get away with it. In 1960 in Moscow, as well, Cliburn made a profoundly felt concert recording of the Rachmaninoff Second Piano Sonata that eclipses any of the many solo recordings he undertook at home.

That Cliburn brought Kondrashin with him to New York in 1958 for his American concerto performances might be written off as a sentimental gesture. And Cliburn was a complexly sentimental man who willingly confided his addiction to nostalgia and resistance to growing old. (Cliburn sent Kondrashin back to Moscow in 1958 with a silver Tiffany table service and a life-size FAO Schwarz Russian bear—a typical gesture of generosity. He also, inimitably, brought Kondrashin with him, and also his own parents, when he met President Eisenhower at the Oval Office; only Cliburn had been invited.)[5] But if Kondrashin was doubtless a talisman, he was also more than that. RCA Victor did not notice and proceeded to record Cliburn with Fritz Reiner, whose severity of disposition and musical temperament yielded predictably hollow results. Cliburn's career slipped steadily; he became a hinterlands exotic, dazzling audiences with his enduring charm and lingering reputation. Countless musicians (including Kondrashin, according to his memoirs) counseled Cliburn to expand his range of affinity, to enlarge his cultural base. Then, in 1978, he retired at the age of forty-five. When I met him in Fort Worth in 1989, he seemed a man outwardly at peace with himself, endearing yet courteously and resolutely private. He was in fact about to return to the stage. His Philadelphia Orchestra performance of the Tchaikovsky First Concerto that year was memorably beautiful; Donal Henahan's review in the *Times* was a favorable yawn. He then played the same music in Moscow. John Ardoin of the *Dallas Morning News*, a critic more reliable than Henahan, went with him and wrote:

> The adulation was unbelievable—much more intense than for Vladimir Horowitz in 1986. Crowds of admirers gathered outside Van's hotel room at every hour of the day and night—people with flowers, and with photographs and other memorabilia from 1958. . . . [T]he performance itself—of the Tchaikovsky concerto at the first Moscow concert—showed how an audience can work on an artist. Cliburn takes such strength from an audience—if it's there, he will absorb it. As exciting as the Philadelphia performance had been, the Moscow performance was unlike anything I'd ever heard. It was one of the great events of my life.[6]

Cliburn's return to Russia attracted scant attention in the New York press that had lavishly feted him as America's Sputnik thirty-one years before. Another American pianist who visited the USSR more than once was Byron Janis, whom the State Department first sent in 1960, in part to show that Cliburn was not alone. As it happened, Francis Gary Powers's spy plane had recently been shot down, and tensions were running high—even in the concert hall. Janis was nonetheless invited back in 1962. He later recalled of his Moscow debut:

> At the end of the concert pandemonium broke loose. Audience members thronged the edge of the stage, some weeping. The cheers and applause were deafening, lasting some twenty minutes. Seeing the tears of joy and gratitude streaking down those faces that only a short time earlier had been twisted in hate, made me understand more deeply than ever the power and mystery of music. Thanks to music, I was no longer the enemy. I was a human being, just like them. I blinked back tears of my own as I heard one woman shout, "You make us love America."

Of his 1962 Moscow audience, Janis wrote: "The electrifying response . . . was something I'd never experienced anywhere before."[7] Janis recalls Kirill Kondrashin, with whom he performed in both 1960 and 1962, as "one of the best accompanists in the world, and for me a great conductor." He also remembers requesting an opportunity to perform with Yevgeny Mravinsky and the Leningrad Philharmonic and being told: "We're very sorry, but Mravinsky will not take orders from anyone."[8]

Certainly, the Russian oxygen that Cliburn craved conveyed an invigoration of ambience and tradition. And the Russian embrace was personal. Nikita Khrushchev (who had to secretly approve Cliburn's first prize when others around him were urging that it be shared with a Russian) struck up a genuine friendship; his 1962 home movies show Cliburn mingling with the Khrushchevs at their dacha as if part of an extended family. In DC in 1958, it was the Russians, not the Americans, who threw a lavish party for him after his Constitution Hall concert. Cliburn was more than aware that Eisenhower's pleasure in his victory, while real, was shallow by comparison. A crucial additional factor, binding Cliburn to the Soviets, was the Russian listening public.

Like his friend Nicolas Nabokov, Isaiah Berlin was early exiled from the Russian Empire. But he became well and truly British—and could look back with appreciation, as in 2000 when he wrote of Soviet audiences:

> These are perhaps not far removed from the kind of popular audiences for which Euripides and Shakespeare wrote. . . . [T]hey still look on the world with the

shrewd imagination and the unspoiled eye of intelligent children, the ideal public of the novelist, the dramatist and the poet . . . and it is probable that it is the absence of precisely this popular response that has made the art of England and France often seem mannered, anaemic, and artificial.

The principal hope of a new flowering of the liberated Russian genius lies in the still unexhausted vitality, the omnivorous curiosity, the astonishingly undiminished moral and intellectual appetite of this most imaginative and least narrow of peoples.[9]

Kiril Tomoff, recalling the starting point of his revisionist 2006 study of the Union of Soviet Composers, wrote of a 1990 sojourn in Leningrad: "As I took advantage of what to me were shockingly low ticket prices for world-class orchestral and operatic performances night after night, I was struck by the prominent and important place that such music held for the large, multigenerational audiences in attendance, night after night."[10] In New York City today, the best audiences—at Russian films, concerts of Russian music, exhibits of Russian art—are Russian. They also patronize Russian-language theater en famille. Their capacity for knowing engagement impacts onstage and off. Most, one supposes, fled the Soviet Union. They are products of a cultural inheritance that, *pace* Nabokov, more than survived Lenin, Stalin, Khrushchev, and Brezhnev.

To be sure, cultural diplomacy enabled Soviet musicians to discover American freedoms: a revelation. It also apprised American musicians of the potency of a Russian musical milieu embracing composers, performers, pedagogues, students, and listeners, a hungry community more keenly engaged, more appreciative, more inquisitive than any back home. By the midsixties, prevalent Cold War notions of Soviet life—the lockdown inferred by Hannah Arendt in her landmark 1951 study *The Origins of Totalitarianism*, the "system of total terror" depicted by Sidney Hook, the "perfectly dead, closed society" envisioned by Dwight Macdonald, the hollowed culture described by Nicolas Nabokov—were rapidly dispelled for those who cared to notice.[11] But during his period of employment by the U.S. government, Nabokov's perceptions were at all times circumscribed by Cold War antinomies. His Arendt-like notion of an iron-clad Soviet "totalitarianism," echoed by JFK and countless others, both skewed his assumptions about Soviet culture and fed a "fight to the death" mentality demanding ultimate allegiance to one side or the other. His allotted roles as chronicler and propagandist proved contradictory and mutually misbegotten.

As we have had occasion to observe, Dmitri Shostakovich told Harrison Salisbury: "The artist in Russia has more 'freedom' than the artist in the West." That is: the Soviet artist is supported by the state and by a community of culture both of which confer honor and purpose. The artist in America, by comparison, is free not to matter. Shostakovich's comparison is of course simplified and overdrawn; no Western composer feared for his life as he did. And yet even though Van Cliburn seemingly died a reasonably contented man in 2013, his artistic fate does not wholly escape Shostakovich's stark paradigm.

*   *   *

It was four years after Cliburn's victory, and three years after Bernstein's tour, that John F. Kennedy delivered his Amherst address, declaiming: "I see little of more importance to the future of our country and our civilization than full recognition of the place of the artist." He concluded: "I look forward to an America which commands respect throughout the world not only for its strength but for its civilization as well."

A month later, President Kennedy was dead. A memorial concert—Mahler's *Resurrection* Symphony—was conducted by Leonard Bernstein. Bernstein led a similar tribute to the dead Robert Kennedy in 1968. He had more than shared John Kennedy's aspirations for an American civilization to set beside the cultural inheritance of older nations. Fellow Harvard alumni, they first met when Kennedy was a U.S. senator. The night before the Kennedy inauguration, Bernstein was the only classical musician to have been invited by Frank Sinatra to his star-studded gala at the National Guard Armory; he composed and conducted a fanfare for the occasion. The Kennedy and Bernstein families socialized at the White House. The National Cultural Center for which the president was crusading, Jacqueline hoped, would secure Bernstein as artistic director. Three days after the assassination, Bernstein spoke to an audience of eleven thousand at Madison Square Garden, where a United Jewish Appeal benefit had been transformed into a wake. "I know of no musician in this country who did not love John F. Kennedy," he said. "American artists have for three years looked to the White House with unaccustomed confidence and warmth. We loved him for the honor in which he held art, in which he held every creative impulse of the human mind, whether it was expressed in words, or notes, or paints, or mathematical symbols."[12]

Eventually, however, Bernstein's orchestra of choice became the Vienna Philharmonic. It was far too late, he had discovered, to amass an American concert canon. Even American popular music, which he had adored, had in his opinion lost its way. So had Bernstein: when in 1970 he and his wife hosted a benefit for the Black Panthers, they were savagely ridiculed by Tom Wolfe in *New York* magazine for succumbing to "radical chic." His 1973 Norton Lectures at Harvard railed against "mediocrity and art-mongering" that "increasingly uglify our lives." Asking "Whither music in our time?" he could not accept Schoenberg's twelve-tone system. In Stravinsky's embarrassed response to direct emotional expression he discovered (*pace* Stravinsky) a paradoxical Romantic poignancy, "speaking for all of us frightened children." The twentieth century's musical prophet, for him, was Gustav Mahler, whose Ninth Symphony, his "last will and testament," showed in its morbidities "that ours is the century of death" and verily declared "the death of society, of our Faustian culture." Shadowing Bernstein's many disappointments was the war in Vietnam. The White House, where he had joined Kennedy to honor Pablo Casals and Igor Stravinsky, was occupied by Lyndon Johnson, then Richard Nixon. The youthfully sanguine American Bernstein had come and gone; he was now a disenchanted outsider.[13]

As for John Kennedy's dream of an American civilization honored and embraced by the state, the National Endowment of the Arts (NEA) and the National Endowment of the Humanities (NEH)—twin initiatives to dedicate federal funds to American arts and learning for their own sake—were created in 1965. The Public Broadcasting System and National Public Radio, both intermingling public and private support, began operation in 1969 and 1971. The Kennedy Center for the Performing Arts opened in 1971. These initiatives mark a notable departure. That said, Bernstein said no to Mrs. Kennedy's Kennedy Center offer—and there was no one else of comparable stature for the job. American public radio and television never attained anything like the penetration or ideals pursued by state-supported cultural programming abroad—or, for that matter, early American commercial radio and TV; compared to the work of such broadcast pioneers as Bernstein and Bernard Herrmann, PBS's *Great Performances* proved merely generic. That American audiences were thereby impoverished was an unforeseen discovery of Cold War cultural exchange. As for the endowments, they have weathered gusts of congressional incomprehension to secure a relatively firm place in the DC bureaucracy, however tiny their allocations. Meanwhile, just as the WPA arts projects were spurred by mass unemployment and ended when jobs returned, cultural exchange at the State Department was essentially abandoned with the dissipation of the Cold War.

When Andrew Carnegie built Carnegie Hall in 1891, he insisted that it pay for itself; the arts, he assumed, would support themselves if properly pursued. This American myth has never wholly died—government support for the arts remains an exogenous European tradition. To be sure, government support can breed indolence and ideological strangulation. But only those Americans who work in the arts can fully appreciate the crippling burden imposed, and the distortions encountered, when arts institutions must less dedicate time and manpower to programming than to fund-raising from private individuals and corporations.

Michael Josselson, defending the Congress for Cultural Freedom after the CIA cover was blown, wrote to Stephen Spender in 1967: "We can all deplore that there has never been, and is not now, and is not even in the offing an American ministry of culture. . . . In the absence of such a body, or of sufficient European or American sources of funds, the alternatives then, as you know, were to do nothing or take the [CIA] money and do freely what we felt was right with it. When the Congress supported arts festivals, . . . do you think that this was just some kind of window-dressing?"[14] Today, American civic life suffers from a failure of arts advocacy at every level: public schools, private schools, and colleges prioritize other forms of learning.

In retrospect, it is easy enough to spot an essential flaw in Kennedy's arts advocacy. To be sure, by binding arts advocacy to the "long twilight struggle" with Communism, he was partly seeking a political strategy to advance a nonpolitical goal. Nonetheless, linked to an urgent campaign to defeat Soviet Russia, the campaign for an ennobling "American civilization" embraced by the state was burdened with special pleading. Commensurately, its logic was distorted by an imposed propaganda of freedom. Promulgated in its most extreme form by Nicolas Nabokov, American cultural dogma held that liberal democracy is the ideal form of government; that free societies foster free artists; that only free artists create great art; that the creative act, born in freedom, is autonomous; that music, being autonomously conceived, means nothing beyond itself; that totalitarian states necessarily shackle great art; that Shostakovich was not a great (or even a distinguished) composer; that all Soviet music, strangled by dogma, sounded the same. To which President Kennedy added that all great artists, being free, are motivated by "concern for justice." How much more simple, sensible, and prescient was Aaron Copland's plea at the 1949 Waldorf Astoria Peace Conference: "All of us are aware of how powerful an agent art can be in giving all humanity a sense of togetherness. How unfortunate it is that our lawmakers have so little conception of the way in which the work of our composers, painters, and writers might be used in order to draw closer bonds between our own people and those of other nations."[15]

Kennedy's hortatory eloquence alternated with styles of espousal poisoned by what Frances Stonor Saunders, in her history of the Congress for Cultural Freedom, called "the kind of language which petrified reality, and which was one of the contributing factors of the Cold War (on both sides)."[16] The resulting freedom ideology was lent plausibility by militant Cold War fervor in combination with the blaze of optimism emanating from a youthful White House. It proved most credible in the United States, where principles of freedom formed a Cold War bedrock, and in the Soviet Union, where a dissident scent of freedom was to many irresistible. In Western Europe and Latin America, toward which it was directed by the CCF, the propaganda of freedom could only have rung false among artists and intellectuals on the Left who were its primary targets. And it naturally excited rebuttals at least as extreme.

There is no need to here attempt a scorecard in assessing cultural Cold War credit and blame. If the Russian campaign against formalism was not always insincere and simplistic, its trappings and tactics were frequently brutal. The United States, to say the least, did not jail, purge, or murder its composers, writers, and painters. But both sides misperceived the other. And both, punitively or unwittingly, imposed or sanctioned conditions frustrating to creativity.

Once Stalin's death made possible the robust mutual practice of cultural exchange, the CCF propaganda of freedom, though still pursued by the CIA, lost pertinence. Rather than targeting the non-Communist Left in Europe and Latin America, American diplomatic objectives were now directly served by seeking maximum mutual exposure between Russia and the United States. To what degree cultural exchange leveraged the demise of the USSR is an excellent question. For the Russians, it backfired when Soviet visitors, however policed, saw America with their own eyes. In his voluminous 2003 history of the cultural Cold War, David Caute plausibly summarizes: "Was the defeat of the Soviet system primarily 'economic?' . . . Or did the Soviet leviathan succumb to the heart-stopping weight of its own military armour? These were certainly powerful factors, yet the mortal 'stroke' which finally buried Soviet Communism was arguably moral, intellectual, and cultural as well as economic and technological."[17]

*   *   *

My account of the propaganda of freedom does not aspire to judge the Congress for Cultural Freedom in the round, or to assess the CIA's covert Cold War propaganda efforts generally. Though others have done so, such a call can only be subjective. The range of CCF activities was great. Their net impact was not subject to any objective empirical calculation.

Arthur Schlesinger, looking back in the 1980s, opined: "Of all the CIA's expenditures, the Congress for Cultural Freedom seemed its most worthwhile and successful." Sidney Hook, a CCF participant as remote from Nabokov as Schlesinger, Kennan, and Bohlen were close, viewed such CCF journals as *Encounter* and *Preuves* as its "greatest achievement" amid other activities irrelevant to the task at hand. Vincent Giroud, in his admiring Nabokov biography, opines that the congress "fulfilled much of its original political purpose—countering the Communist influence, especially among Western intellectual milieus."[18] Former CIA director Richard Helms called the CCF the standout among the agency's "long-lived successes . . . [in] Cold War cover political action."[19] Michael Josselson, after it all fell apart, reflected in a 1967 letter: "The first question is: does the end justify the means? . . . I myself change my mind about it every day and have been doing so, painfully. . . . In theory, the answer is certainly No. As far as my own personal experience goes, the answer is also No, for I have paid dearly, both physically and spiritually. But if I had not taken the responsibility of saying Yes, there would have been no Congress nor any of its unique achievements . . . this long record of accomplishment does seem to me to justify the means in this case."[20]

The two best-known studies of the CCF, by Hugh Wilford and Frances Stonor Saunders, both stress the deleterious effects of covert sponsorship and management. Wilford's *The Mighty Wurlitzer* is, on balance, a notably nonpolemical study of Cold War covert action. He concludes:

> Was the cost worth it? The United States eventually won the Cold War struggle . . . , but how much this victory had to do with government-funded psychological warfare measures, as opposed to the spontaneous appeal of consumer capitalism or factors internal to the communist bloc, is very much open to question. . . . CIA front operations in the Cold War blighted individual careers and lives; their eventual exposure stained the reputation of the nation itself. Cultural diplomacy, the winning of hearts and minds, should be left to overt government agencies and genuine, nongovernment organizations.[21]

Saunders, in *The Cultural Cold War*, lays greater stress than Wilford on CIA machinations. Her conclusion, titled "A Bad Bargain," reads in part, "The democratic process which western cultural Cold Warriors rushed to legitimize was undermined by its own lack of candor. The 'freedom' it purveyed was compromised, unfree, in the sense that it was anchored to the contradictory imperative of 'the necessary lie.'" If Nabokov, assuming he was innocent of CIA support, is exempt from this critique, what Saunders says next impugns him: "Pursuing an absolutist idea of freedom, they ended up by offering another ideology, a 'freedomism' or a narcissism of freedom." She heads her epilogue by quoting the U.S. intelligence officer David Bruce: "Some people's minds freeze."[22]

A third CCF study, less well known, is Peter Coleman's *The Liberal Conspiracy: The Congress for Cultural Freedom and the Struggle for the Mind of Postwar Europe*. It reads as an act of CCF advocacy. Coleman stresses the scope and diversity of CCF activities; his fifteen pages of appendixes valuably itemize CCF conferences and books. He concludes:

> The achievement of the Congress for Cultural Freedom was in its time to have
> placed some severe limits on the advantages of Stalinist Russia. Today almost
> everyone . . . agrees with the Congress's once lonely assessment of Soviet totali-
> tarianism, and in particular of the Soviet failure to accept human rights. . . . In
> contributing in so brilliant and timely a way to this public awareness throughout
> the world in a period of great danger, the Congress for Cultural Freedom was a
> historic success.[23]

Whatever one makes of this brave cause-and-effect extrapolation, certainly
the CCF "assessment of 'Soviet totalitarianism'" was, as in Nabokov's case,
distorted and exaggerated by ideology and ignorance.

If the effects of the CCF were ultimately controversial and ambiguous, the
same cannot be said of cultural exchange. It worked. In *Cultural Exchange and
the Cold War* (2003), Yale Richmond, long a foreign service officer in Moscow,
stresses the degree to which

> the end of the Cold War and the collapse of communism were consequences
> of Soviet contacts and exchanges with the West, and with the United States in
> particular, over the thirty-five years that followed the death of Joseph Stalin in
> 1953. Moreover, those exchanges in culture, education, information, science,
> and technology were conducted by the United States openly for the most part,
> under agreements concluded with the Soviet government, and at a cost that was
> miniscule in comparison with U.S. expenditures on defense and intelligence
> over the same period of time.

Richmond emphasizes the resulting "increase in Western influence among the
people in Russia who count—the intelligentsia. . . . Concerned mainly with
Moscow's ability to project its power abroad, Washington underestimated its
ability to influence the Soviet intelligentsia, and through them the entire nation."[24] Because he persisted in regarding the Russian intelligentsia as extinct,
because he resisted visiting the Soviet Union to see for himself, this was an
outcome necessarily unforeseen by Nicolas Nabokov.

That Richmond, Leonard Baldyga, and others at State favored cultural diplomacy over covert action is not surprising. But George Kennan, a CIA insider
and long a staunch defender of the agency, ultimately reached the same opinion.
"Operations of this [covert] nature are not in character for this country," he said
in 1985. "I regret today, in light of the experience of the intervening years, that
the decision was taken." Kennan also wrote:

> I personally attach high importance to cultural contact as a means of combating
> the negative impressions about this country that mark so much of world opinion.

What we have to do, of course, is to show the outside world both that we have a cultural life and that we care something about it—that we care enough about it, in fact, to give it encouragement and support here at home, and to see that it is enriched by acquaintance with similar activity elsewhere. If these impressions could only be conveyed with enough force and success to countries beyond our borders, I for my part would willingly trade the entire remaining inventory of political propaganda for the results that could be achieved by such means alone.[25]

*   *   *

The story told in this book is in many respects a strange one. The questions that it poses are answerable and not. A lingering mystery is John F. Kennedy's role. He was a thinker and a reader (especially of history and biography). He liked poetry and memorized a lot of it. His idealism was authentic and his aspirational rhetoric sincere. His respect for learning, gradually acquired, impelled a 1956 Harvard commencement address decrying the schism between politicians and intellectuals ultimately conjoined by "a common framework . . . we call liberty." Kennedy's "core philosophy," observes Fredrik Logevall in his superb *JFK* (2020), was predicated on the rights of the individual grounded in Greek thought, Christian morality, and American political philosophy.[26]

But by inclination and experience John Kennedy was not remotely an aesthete. He grew up in a family that played touch football, never chamber music. When in 1960 *Musical America* magazine asked the two presidential candidates to answer a series of questions about the place of music in American diplomacy, and the advisability of government arts subsidies, Richard Nixon's was the more sophisticated, more substantive response, transcending cant and politics with such observations as: "Although [music] is almost a universal tongue it has always been the foremost form of expression for folklore and the passions of nationalism." Nixon promised an advisory council "that not only would resolve the questions you have raised in the field of music, but provide a firm base for expansion of all the arts and American participation in them in the future." Kennedy's statement, by comparison, was chauvinistic and evasive. It read in part:

Babbitry is behind us. We live in an era of impressive artistic achievement. Our painters, sculptors, musicians, dancers, and dramatists are the envy of the world. . . .

The climate in which art thrives is a delicate climate. It must foster individual work by sensitive persons. And it is of real importance that the Government not disturb this climate by meddlesome incursions, or limitations on the free play of mind.

But if the Government must not interfere, it can give a lead.[27]

Whence his subsequent call for a more civilized America in which artists would assume privileged roles?

In retrospect, the story of Igor Stravinsky's White House dinner furnishes some clues. Nicolas Nabokov's initial proposal that Stravinsky be honored was not delivered to the president; it was addressed to the first lady. And it was Mrs. Kennedy, as we have seen, who hosted Nabokov's first White House visit; the president did not even appear. It is apparent, from the history of this event, that Kennedy had little or no idea who Stravinsky was. And—as we have seen—when he arose to speak, he referenced his wife.

In February 1962, Mrs. Kennedy took American television viewers on a tour of the White House. She said, "It's so important . . . the setting in which the presidency is presented to the world, to foreign visitors. The American people should be proud of it. We have such a great civilization. So many foreigners don't realize it."[28] Kennedy would subsequently echo this sentiment.

Mrs. Kennedy's first guest at the White House had been George Balanchine, on January 25, 1961. The two of them met alone. She sought advice on how she could help support the arts. Three months later, Balanchine participated in a panel in Washington on the subject "If I Were President." He said he would only want to be president if Jacqueline Kennedy were first lady. He subsequently wrote to her, urging her to take on the role of "spiritual savior" of America.

> I don't mean in a religious sense, but I mean to distinguish between material things and things of the spirit—art, beauty. No one else can take care of these things. You alone can—if you will.
>
> Your husband is necessarily busy with serious international problems and cannot be expected to worry too much about the nation's art and culture. But woman is always the inspiration. Man takes care of the material things and woman takes care of the soul.[29]

Jacqueline Kennedy was in fact an avid Russophile. Balanchine actually likened her to Catherine the Great, Russia's first great patron of the arts.[30] As first lady, she advocated a Department of Culture—an American culture ministry. She admired her husband's appreciation of excellence in human endeavor, and doubtless played to that. She accompanied him to the Bolshoi Ballet's November 13, 1962, DC performance of *Swan Lake* (the president left after act 2, but not before congratulating the dancers backstage); she also accompanied her four-year-old daughter, a dance student, to a Bolshoi rehearsal, and with the president hosted Bolshoi soloists at the White House.[31] (Weeks before, on October 23, Nikita Khrushchev had attended *Boris Godunov* at the Bolshoi Opera in order to hear the American bass-baritone George London sing the title role. Both this visit and Kennedy's appearance at *Swan Lake* were ameliorative gestures during and just after the Cuban missile crisis.) In later life, as Jacqueline Onassis, she was an editor. The books she oversaw included her own *In the Russian Style*, Edvard Radzinsky's *The Last Tsar: The Life and Death of Nicholas II*, prose works by Nina Berberova, and the paperback edition of *Balanchine's Tchaikovsky: Interviews with George Balanchine* by Solomon Volkov. Her acquaintances included Radzinsky, Volkov, Yevgeny Yevtushenko, Andrei Voznesensky, Rudolf Nureyev, and Mikhail Baryshnikov.[32]

Rather than by personal knowledge and predilection, John Kennedy's arts advocacy was to some degree doubtless inspired by his wife. This connection could help explain both his surprising ardor and the innocence with which he inhabited Nabokov's fantasy of thriving democratic free artists and inconsequential Soviet artistic slaves.

Another retrospective explanation of Kennedy's cultural pronouncements— why he said what he did and what he actually knew or thought—is simpler yet far more ponderable. By 1962 the propaganda of freedom was an inert residue of an earlier Cold War phase, in which Stalin's postwar clampdown was observed with dismay. It was during this period that George Orwell wrote *Animal Farm* (1945) and *Nineteen Eighty-Four* (1949)—and the view of Stalin's Russia was formidably Orwellian. In fact, both books were regarded by the CIA as prime propaganda assets. (And both books were made into movies with the participation of the CIA. In the case of *Animal Farm*, the agency, whose covert influence in Hollywood was ongoing, itself secretly initiated, financed, and distributed the 1954 cartoon film version. The CIA's Howard Hunt was instrumental in setting in motion the 1956 film version of *Nineteen Eighty-Four.*) Invoking Big Brother, doublethink, Thought Police, Newspeak, memory holes, and unpersons, Orwell portrayed a totalitarian nightworld truly inimical to art. (In his preface to *Animal Farm*, he opined that without "intellectual freedom," our "characteristic Western culture could only doubtfully exist." In 1946 he pronounced "the atmosphere of totalitarianism" to be "deadly to any kind of prose writer.")[33] What is more, Stalin's renewed isolationism ensured ignorance of what life in Soviet Russia was really like. As we have seen, as late as 1958–59, some in the State Department worried that Van Cliburn had been turned into a spy and that "controlled" Soviet audiences would whistle Western performers off the stage if cultural diplomacy were attempted.

But by the end of the fifties, cultural and intellectual exchange between the United States and the Soviet Union had for many already dispelled Cold War assumptions. It became apparent that Khrushchev was no Stalin. The Hungarian Revolution of 1956, and its violent suppression, soured enthusiasm for

Communism on the European Left. Daniel Bell, in 1960, declared "the end of ideology." The pages of *Encounter* tracked a sea change. As early as 1951, the Hungarian-American polymath Michael Polanyi complained that "too many people are still glaring at each other through the angry masks of obsolete ideologies." Another eminent CCF insider, Ignazio Silone, wrote in 1954 that "we all know the myth of the liberating power of the proletariat has dissolved." Peter Wiles, an expert on Soviet economics, reported in *Encounter* in 1956 that Polish intellectuals had never succumbed to dogma; they "just ducked under for six years" and reemerged as "ordinary Western people with a straightforward Western understanding of events in their own country and abroad, and normal Western taste." The same year, the British political writer Nora Beloff, returning from Russia, told *Encounter* readers she was struck "that [Moscow's] intellectual elite should remain at the end of it all so very unsubdued—Orwell may well have been wrong."[34] Meanwhile, Michael Josselson absorbed that the founding premises of the CCF were no longer valid and began retooling.

By comparison, Kennedy's *Look* magazine article of December 18, 1962, seems a remnant of Orwellian thought. "We know that a totalitarian society can promote the arts in its own way—that it can arrange for splendid productions of opera and ballet, as it can arrange for the restoration of ancient and historic buildings," Kennedy wrote. "But art means more than the resuscitation of the past." These sentences were drafted less than two months after Yevgeny Mravinsky and his peerless Leningrad Philharmonic stunned a Carnegie Hall audience with their apocalyptic rendition of Shostakovich's Symphony No. 8.

In his Amherst speech of 1963, citing Stalin, reading words drafted by Arthur Schlesinger, Kennedy declared: "We must never forget that art is not a form of propaganda; it is a form of truth. . . . In free society art is not a weapon and it does not belong to the spheres of polemic and ideology. Artists are not 'engineers of the soul.' It may be different elsewhere. But democratic society—in it, the highest duty of the writer, the composer, the artist is to remain true to himself and to let the chips fall where they may. In serving his vision of the truth, the artist best serves his nation." Is that necessarily how artists best serve the nation? Truly, it is "different elsewhere." Next door to the United States, magnificent political muralists were a defining product of the Mexican Revolution—and when Shostakovich visited Mexico in 1959, he was greeted with acclaim, not mistrust. The Kennedy administration had ceremoniously initiated an Alliance for Progress with the nations of Central and South America, dedicated to fresh efforts at understanding and support. How did Mexico's artists and intellectuals (among whom Carlos Fuentes, though by no means a Communist, was barred from the United States during Kennedy's presidency) process a cultural

Cold War propaganda campaign impugning political art as false and craven? (Fuentes called the United States "very good at understanding itself, and very bad at understanding others.") As for Russia, Kiril Tomoff's scrupulously researched 2006 study of Soviet musical culture matter-of-factly states: "The Soviets inherited a broad commitment to musical culture, but music became, if anything, even more significant in the Soviet period. . . . Musicians were held up alongside pilots and polar explorers as exemplary heroes for a new generation of Soviet citizens. In fact, all the arts were extremely important to the Soviet system, which conceived of artists as indispensable agents of enlightenment and ideological education. . . . they were engineers of human souls. And they performed this task well enough to warrant the elite status afforded them."[35]

In human affairs, what becomes obvious in hindsight may be invisible in the moment—and the propaganda of freedom stayed intact. Nicolas Nabokov clung to his implausible vision of a Soviet cultural wasteland as a seeming psychological necessity. Could it be that something similar was also true for the White House, the State Department, and the CIA? Was there—as Lewis Mumford put it in 1964—a "catatonic Cold War trance that has so long held our country in its rigid grip"?[36] What the historian Michael Geyer terms "national imaginaries" may suggest a pertinent psychological undercurrent. "A sense of superiority is deeply invested in these imaginaries," Geyer writes, "and so too is a sense of inferiority."[37] Is it not plausible to read a sense of national inferiority into Kennedy's cultural exhortations—and a countervailing boastfulness claiming superiority to Soviet cultural shackles?

When in 1958 *Encounter* magazine refused to publish Dwight Macdonald's "America! America!," Nabokov and others insisted that what Macdonald had to say contradicted American interests. Here is an excerpt: "When one hears Europeans complaining about the Americanisation of Europe, one wishes they could spend a few weeks over here and get a load of the real thing. Even the Soviet Russians, for all their ruthlessness barely covered by the fig of ideology, seem to speak a more common language with other peoples than we do."[38] Whether this assertion was overstated or not, it cannot be denied that Kennedy was speaking an American language that sounded out of touch with cultural realities abroad.

If this line of thought seems contradicted by the worldliness of the Kennedy White House, the testimony of Nikita Khrushchev's son provides a further perspective. Sergei Khrushchev was twenty-three years old when Van Cliburn was first a guest at the family dacha in 1959. Thirty-two years later, he moved to the United States and became a senior fellow at Brown University, uniquely positioned to testify to a chasm of misunderstanding during his father's tenure as first secretary of the Communist Party. Asked by Brown University's Watson Institute for International Studies, "What was the Cuban missile crisis from the Soviet perspective?" he answered:

> Each great power has their obligation to protect all their allies. . . . When Castro proclaimed he joined the Soviet bloc, he put this obligation on my father's shoulders. So Cuba became to the Soviet Union the same as Berlin to the US . . . a small piece of land very deep inside hostile territory. If you could not protect this small piece of land, . . . your allies would not trust you. So Khrushchev decided to send missiles there as a diplomatic message: don't invade Cuba—we are serious. He did not understand at that time that American mentality was different. Europeans, Soviets, all their history had enemies at the gate. . . . For Americans, each such threat was like a shock. . . . Americans thought it was end of the world . . . as if there would be [an] apocalypse.[39]

Finally, it is doubtless pertinent that, whereas Khrushchev eagerly toured the United States as a leader of state (I cite a piquant anecdote in a note)[40] and proved mettlesome and inquisitive, Kennedy visited Soviet Russia as a Harvard undergraduate for only a few days in 1939; he found it "crude, backward, and hopelessly bureaucratic" (but enjoyed his dinner with future ambassador Charles Bohlen).[41] A conclusive reckoning of the provenance of his cultural pronouncements should perhaps begin with beginnings: he was a child of entitlement and privilege, leavened by discipline and the personal hardships of fickle health and an older brother's death. His dedication to public service was early and true. His respect for learning and intellect was sure. But his circumscribed milieu, and circumscribed cultural awareness, notably impacted on his sluggish response to exigent civil rights demands. In the realm of foreign policy, he was an original Cold Warrior who did not altogether outgrow the zealous anti-Communism he espoused as a senator, with its postwar picture of a Soviet "slave state of the worst sort."[42] That is: his was not an upbringing conducive to understanding what it felt like to be an oppressed Black American, or an inflamed Mexican muralist, or a great Soviet composer. The same sense of entitlement may have been glimpsed by Alfred Kazin when in Fall 1961 he prophetically surmised:

> The most significant side of Kennedy as intellectual seems to lie not in his public cultivation of the "intellectual" style that is now admired in the highest echelons, but in the fact that, as a would-be intellectual who happens to be President of the US, his natural tendency may be to identify the US with a crusade, a cause, with "liberty" . . . He has been left free by his immense power to adopt a cause forged out of his energy and the depths of his restless ambition.[43]

As this account has shown, mutual miscomprehension was a central motif of the cultural Cold War.

* * *

"No idea is more fundamental to Americans' sense of themselves as individuals and as a nation than freedom," writes Eric Foner in *The Story of American Freedom* (1998). "The central term in our political vocabulary, 'freedom'—or 'liberty,' with which it is almost always used interchangeably—is deeply embedded in the documentary record of our history and the language of everyday life. The Declaration of Independence lists liberty among mankind's inalienable rights; the Constitution announces as its purpose to secure liberty's blessings." But, as Foner continues, the meanings of "freedom" are ever elusive and changeable. What is more: whatever freedom may mean to Americans at any given moment, it is in every case imperfectly realized.

In no period of American history was freedom more clarion than during the Cold War. The "free world," juxtaposed with "totalitarianism," might include Iran and Guatemala, where the CIA staged coups to install friendly governments. It might harbor a climate of fear: the Red Scare. No matter: "Every domestic political initiative, it seemed, from John F. Kennedy's decision to send a man to the moon to more mundane proposals for manpower development or highway construction were promoted in the fulsome language of freedom. Freedom emerged as the 'masterword' in critical writing on American culture."[44]

That ideals of freedom may shrink to cant is itself a facile proposition: those ideals remain American fundaments not without noble intentions and robust practical benefits. Even the story I have told in this book bristles with American idealism. And yet—to summarize—the Congress for Cultural Freedom, as chief cultural propaganda arm of the U.S. government during the Cold War, embraced a propaganda of freedom asserting (among other things) that only "free artists" in "free societies" produce great art, and that in "totalitarian" states, genuine creativity is not possible. The sources of this doctrine, surprisingly, included a "psychology of exile" experienced by Igor Stravinsky and Nicolas Nabokov, for whom it was a survival strategy. From its inception, the doctrine was plainly counterfactual. Nabokov believed in it because he had to. Others—notably Kennedy and Arthur Schlesinger—believed in it for reasons we can only surmise; ideology, politics, and naïveté were all pertinent factors. It seems unlikely that the propaganda of freedom was particularly credible for its most intended audience: the non-Communist Left in Western Europe and Latin America. Certainly, its most conspicuous product, Nabokov's 1952 Paris festival, was on balance an expensive mistake. Here, Sidney Hook's verdict is precisely correct: it more served Nabokov's interests than the nation's. In the latter stages of the Cold War, cultural exchange proved a better propaganda instrument than the CCF. It also, by virtue of achieving some degree of mutual acquaintance, disproved the claims of the propaganda of freedom about as thoroughly as anything could.

That Nabokov's Paris festival may have advanced his professional prospects by no means implies insincerity. Rather it was driven by a surfeit of enthusiasm for the culture he loved, and by a convenient conviction that the music of Igor Stravinsky could help defeat Communism. His visit to Soviet Russia in 1967 seemingly becalmed his exile's trauma. It is a pity he could not land the post-CCF position he most hoped would be his. Purged of ideological zeal and intent, his impresario's panache, and stellar international network of artists and intellectuals, might have produced a national cultural center surpassing the more localized performing arts venue the Kennedy Center became.

To what extent Nabokov truly believed that the Soviets had annulled the prerevolutionary intelligentsia remains unknowable. He would not have been aware of what we now know—that Soviet musicians, rather than becoming puppets, were engaged in a complex symbiosis with the regime. They were used and abused, at times ruthlessly. They also enjoyed considerable genuine authority—not least because the Soviet prioritization of culture was genuine. If they lacked the "freedom" of creative autonomy, they were empowered in other ways. A wink at the Congress for Cultural Freedom is here irresistible—the CIA, too, used artists and intellectuals to further the interests of the state.

As for Stravinsky and Shostakovich: The late Saul Bellow, in a 1975 interview, distinguished between two kinds of writers. "Great-public writers" see themselves as "spokesmen for a national conscience. They address grand issues of social justice and political concern." Bellow cited as examples Theodore Dreiser, Charles Dickens, Emil Zola, Upton Sinclair, Sherwood Anderson, and himself. "Small-public writers," typified by Charles Baudelaire, James Joyce, or Gustave Flaubert, cherish stylistic artistry over social purpose.[45] Shostakovich was a "great-public" composer, embodying a Soviet ideal. Stravinsky was a "small-public" composer: a modernist. Though they disapproved of one another's calling, and embodied a larger schism between Soviet and Western aesthetics, the world of culture is big enough for them both. The purposes of art, the sources of creativity, and the relationship of the artist to the state all readily admit a variety of perspectives: notwithstanding the decrees of Andrei Zhdanov, notwithstanding Nabokov's propaganda of freedom, Shostakovich and Stravinsky no longer demand an either-or pledge of allegiance.

What Frances Stonor Saunders terms an "absolutist idea of freedom," a veritable "narcissism of freedom," might also be called a fetishization of freedom. As defined by liberal democracies, freedom is undeniably a precious human right, a source of dignity, a boon to the pursuit of happiness. But it is not a universal panacea. It is not necessarily indispensable for advanced intellectual endeavor, for distinguished creative achievement, even for effective government. As this account has stressed, freedom can be variously defined. It means different things in different circumstances, including a freedom not to matter. That so many fine minds could have cheapened freedom by overpraising it, turning it into a reductionist propaganda mantra, is one measure of the intellectual cost of the Cold War. That Nicolas Nabokov, who was not an ignorant or hypocritical man, could have insisted for three decades that the Soviet Union was and always had been a cultural backwater, that he could have maintained influence and credibility with the CIA, the State Department, and the White House, documents an erosion of cultural memory, honest observation, and common sense.

A crowning paradox, contradicting the propaganda of freedom, is that in part the arts mattered greatly in Soviet Russia precisely because it was not a "free society." Denied civil liberties and opportunities for political engagement, burdened with material needs, Cold War Russian artists and audiences craved cultural expression. Shostakovich's capacious symphonies, Mravinsky's intensely realized Leningrad Philharmonic concerts were cathartic or therapeutic for reasons both musical and extra-musical. Even after 1945, they sustained a wartime urgency.

The story at hand affirms that the urge to freedom is fundamental—and that so, too, is the urge to create, which will find its own way. But these are not complementary sides of the same freedom coin; they are different currencies. A misunderstanding of this dichotomy paradoxically fueled JFK's campaign for a more cultured America. The same misunderstanding supported a confrontational culture war mentality that proved less effective, in pursuit of American foreign policy goals, than a simple strategy of mutual exposure.

If the United States is ever to attain the heights of civilization envisioned by John F. Kennedy—a veritably Athenian melding of culture and the state—the pertinent acts of advocacy, from whatever pulpit, will surely transcend the appropriative grasp of geopolitical priorities.

AFTERWORD

The Arts, National Purpose, and the Pandemic

I wrote the bulk of *The Propaganda of Freedom* before the pandemic hit. That is, I never anticipated that my book about arts policies would acquire such urgency.

The pandemic is many things. Every festering problem we face—as individuals, as communities, as a nation—seems exercised and magnified: racial strife, economic inequality, fires and floods, a shredded social fabric. The least noticed debacle is cultural—by which I refer to the vexed fate of our performing arts institutions, our museums, our artists in every field. That this same debacle is, however, not remotely unnoticed abroad seals a reckoning moment.

When the virus hit, the city of Berlin swiftly allocated $320 million to its cultural workers. The German government added $50 billion; its culture minister called artists "vital, especially now." Of course, in continental Europe, institutions of culture were already recipients of robust government subsidies—a close relationship to the state was and is an embedded reality.

In the United Kingdom, where government support of the arts is less lavish, the response was slower. But voices were lifted, including a loud call from Britain's most prominent classical musician, the conductor Sir Simon Rattle. Prime Minister Boris Johnson duly announced a $2 billion arts infusion; "The United Kingdom's cultural industry," Johnson declared, "is the beating heart of the country."

In the United States, we had no Sir Simon Rattle and no Boris Johnson. Eventually, Congress passed emergency legislation including arts allocations. But, absent anything resembling a Ministry of Culture (or the arts adviser Richard Goodwin might have become for President Kennedy), there existed no adequate means of assessing need and allocating funds. It mainly fell to the NEA and NEH to figure out who would get how much. The result was a hasty, understaffed adjudication process that exasperated participants on all sides.

A second arts topic I could not have predicted, writing *The Propaganda of Freedom*, was and is the risky notion that arts institutions should necessarily serve as instruments of social justice. As of this writing, this reductionist conviction is pervasive—and not least among charitable foundations that once supported the arts as traditionally practiced, and no longer do. The current stress on diversity and inclusivity is wholly understandable (just watch, if you can, Derek Chauvin murdering George Floyd). But it endangers or distorts a cultural canon that we cannot (in fact, must not) wholly jettison. Never before in American history has a common cultural inheritance seemed as elusive or controversial. But it is part of what makes us a nation.

In fact, we are witnessing an erosion of the arts far beyond the arts challenge that worried President Kennedy. The status of our orchestras and museums has never been more chaotic or confusing. And their marginalization is such that a leading American historian, Jill Lepore, can write a distinguished and superbly readable seven-hundred-page history of the United States—*These Truths* (2018)—without devoting a single sentence to the American arts: not to Whitman or Melville, Faulkner or Hemingway, Ives or Gershwin, Ellington or Armstrong, Hollywood or Broadway. At nearly the same moment, a prominent and influential sociologist, Robert Putnam, produced a book—*The Upswing: How America Came Together a Century Ago and How We Can Do It Again* (in collaboration with Shaylyn Romney Garrett, 2020)—about declining "social capital" in which a detailed consideration of how Americans bond or do not failed to consider novels and poems, concerts and plays, paintings and sculpture. Cold War cultural diplomacy discovered the healing commonality of Tchaikovsky and Rachmaninoff. But there are no symphonies or concertos in *The Upswing*. Even though a central theme is the challenge of balancing respect for the individual with concern for the common good, America's iconic poet is not once invoked. Walt Whitman preached a "teeming nation of nations" and wrote: "The American compact is altogether with individuals." "Leaves of grass" that are both individuated and conjoined impart Whitman's very credo.

And Whitman endures. An American poet who does not, Henry Wadsworth Longfellow, was nonetheless an essential part of the Gilded Age about which Putnam and Garrett write. His ubiquitous poems were read aloud by the fireplace. Putnam and Garrett deplore the Gilded Age as a harbinger of what ails

America today: "the political polarization that is enfeebling and endangering our democracy, the social fragmentation and isolation that ignore the basic human need for fellowship." In fact, it is little known or remembered that, even in "materialist" America, a century and a half ago the arts furnished an indispensable "we" component—a source of communal expression and self-understanding, of profound personal and interpersonal engagement. It is undeniable that, compared to *Beowolf*, *The Song of Roland*, the *Niebelungenlied*, and the *Kalevala* (whose trochaic tetrameter meter Longfellow adopted), *The Song of Hiawatha* is notably sanitized and sanguine. Its provenance is European. It ends with the coming of the white man. But it bears remembering, too, that Longfellow was both an abolitionist and an advocate for Native America. His tone and message, however anachronistic now, once projected a progressive American reality, a vital source of American community.

During the same decades that *Hiawatha* was the best-known work of American literature, the most popular American painter was Frederic Church. Such heroically scaled Church canvases as *Niagara* (1857) and *Heart of the Andes* (1859) toured nationally. Their heady admixture of mass appeal, technical mastery, and fastidious observation remains impressive. They engendered a distinctly American pictorial genre: landscape. The messages they potently imparted were of Christian uplift, Manifest Destiny, and detailed scientific observation. No less than *The Song of Hiawatha*, they notably projected—bonded and fortified—national sentiment and mood.

Meanwhile, classical music was for Americans "the queen of the arts." Here the American achievement focused on an institutional innovation: the concert orchestra, in contradistinction to the pit orchestras of Europe. The prime mover was an immigrant conductor, Theodore Thomas, whose credo read: "A symphony orchestra shows the culture of a community, not opera." And, by World War I, so it did, in cities large and small. Boston and Philadelphia already boasted orchestras of indisputable world stature; they were at the same time indisputable civic signatures.

The Gilded Age artistic tide culminated in the final decades of the nineteenth century with a nationwide Wagnerism movement that saturated not only music, but literature, drama, and the visual arts. The individual Progressive leaders lauded in *The Upswing* as agents of civic morality were preceded by such fin de siècle reformers as Laura Langford, who as Brooklyn's leading impresario presented concerts at the Academy of Music. In summer she produced symphonic programs fourteen times a week at Coney Island's Brighton Beach resort. She also presented lectures on women's rights and social philanthropy. She targeted working women and Black orphans. She furnished special railroad cars for unescorted female concertgoers. She priced tickets for as little as fifteen cents. All of this came under the aegis of Langford's "Seidl Society," whose godhead was an immigrant Wagnerite conductor of genius: Anton Seidl. Europe had no Seidl Societies. Wagnerism in America was distinctively meliorist—distinctively American. The Gilded Age anomie and confusion adduced by Putnam and Garrett were real enough—but so was a morally inflamed response, not least in the arts.

After World War I, the arts were popularized for a new democratic audience. Crucially, radio became the first mass medium. As I have earlier recounted, the early years of commercial broadcasting featured a plethora of "cultural" and "educational" fare, including *The University of Chicago Round Table* and *The American School of the Air*. A conscious strategy of popularization was vigorously pursued, hosted by such radio personalities as Yale's William Lyon Phelps (known as Billy). When all four major networks carried Norman Corwin's 1941 radio play *We Hold These Truths*, celebrating the sesquicentennial of the Bill of Rights, its sixty-three million listeners comprised nearly half the U.S. population. Radio Saturdays and Sundays included four classical-music showcases—the Metropolitan Opera, NBC Symphony, New York Philharmonic, and "The Ford Hour"— said to reach more than ten million families a week.

That is: social cohesion went hand in hand with proliferating cultural cohesion. But the subsequent fate of this phenomenon, beginning in the sixties, was evaporative. If by "culture" we refer to the arts as a repository of enriched memory and tradition, it suffered a remarkably rapid decay. *Hamilton* notwithstanding, the arts are today a subsidiary and inchoate presence in the national experience. In retrospect, the interwar popularization of the arts after World War I did not notably promote active engagement. These were decades in which piano sales, peaking around 1910, plummeted: the practice of singing in the home, of parlor piano and chamber music, was not part of the "music appreciation" movement. Though amateur choral singing did not as greatly diminish, the "monster" choral festivals and competitions of the Gilded Age were no more. A second such trade-off was one of content. Gilded Age practitioners of the arts assumed that Americans would continue to stretch the umbilical cord connecting to the European parent culture and eventually foster traditions more their own. But, especially in classical music, the popularization of culture during the interwar decades in fact overprivileged dead European masters—a topic I have addressed earlier in this book.

The popularization of the arts proved tangible but shallow.

* * *

The relationship of American democracy to American culture is hardly a new concern. Puritanism, capitalism, frontier conditions, intellectual traditions of empiricism and behaviorism have all been adduced as possible impediments to artistic achievement. An informed outsider, Alexis de Tocqueville, prophetically worried about the fate of the American arts nearly two centuries ago. An outside perspective of even greater consequence belonged to Thomas Mann: his range of pertinent experience, both personal and intellectual, was unique.

Mann's appreciation of the subversive power of the arts began in his lifelong experience of Wagner—that music can destabilize the soul is a topic embedded in the world of Kunst that Mann made his own. And of course Mann bore witness to the complicity of Kunst in likewise destabilizing political sanity. His writings are fraught with the knowledge that the "Innerlichkeit" he prized was equally a source of supreme gratification and supreme danger. When Germany's crisis drove him to California, he discovered himself a beneficiary of American freedoms—the kind of artistic sanctuary, undisturbed by the state, that would be extolled by JFK.

I have earlier quoted from Mann's *Reflections of a Non-political Man* (1918) that "art will never be moral or virtuous in any political sense: and progress will never be able to put its trust in art." Hitler so changed Mann's mind-set that in 1945, at the Library of Congress, he could say: "My kind of Germanness is preserved most fittingly in a hospitable cosmopolitan environment, the multiracial and multi-national universe that is America." The Germany he had fled was by comparison provincial. Tacitly referencing his novel in progress *Doctor Faustus*, he also said, of Faust's Devil: "I want to see [him] as a very German figure, and the pact with him, signed and sealed, to gain for a while all the treasures and power of the world at the cost of his soul's salvation, as something peculiarly close to the German nature."[1]

But soon after Mann was alienated by the Cold War and victimized by the Red Scare—homegrown American populism on the Right. As early as 1951, he wrote to a friend: "I have no desire to rest my bones in this soulless soil to which I owe nothing, and which knows nothing of me." He resettled in Switzerland three years before his death in 1955, having dismissed California as an "artificial paradise."[2] Meanwhile, countless American artists and intellectuals were derailed by McCarthyism. I have earlier referenced Aaron Copland's 1953 interrogation by McCarthy's Permanent Subcommittee on Investigations—and his subsequent retreat from center-stage cultural influence and prestige. If these stories of Thomas Mann and Aaron Copland are parables, what do they mean for the artist in America, and for arts and public policy? It cannot be maintained that democracy is irreconcilable with exalted artistic achievement—Walt Whitman,

Herman Melville, Charles Ives are high exemplars of original expression in-fused with a pronounced democratic ethos. But I cannot think of a comparable example from Copland's modernist decades.

John F. Kennedy and other cultural Cold Warriors did not engage in this de-bate; rather, they ignored it. For them, instead of challenging or subverting the creative act, democracy actively fostered great art. Looking back from today's COVID-19 exigencies, and our controversies about the arts and social justice, what does Kennedy's arts legacy signify? Picking up the thread of the propa-ganda of freedom, what happened after 1963? The heightened awareness of the American arts that Kennedy inspired most tangibly connects to the National Endowment for the Arts. But the NEA is and is not a Kennedy legacy. Two key figures in the NEA narrative are not even Democrats: Nelson Rockefeller and Richard Nixon.

Rockefeller's enthusiasm for the arts was well known. He was a trustee of the Museum of Modern Art from 1931 to 1979 and twice its president. Privately, he was a noted collector of both modern and non-Western visual art and sculpture. During his long tenure as governor of New York State, the New York State Council of the Arts was a landmark 1960 initiative modeled on the British Arts Council. NYSCA itself became a template for the NEA five years later. It was during the Nixon presidency that the NEA began to matter under the leadership of a Rock-efeller protégé: Nancy Hanks. An adroit politician, she built a bipartisan arts consensus prominently including senators from both sides of the aisle. Hanks left in 1977 with the election of Jimmy Carter, having served Nixon and Gerald Ford for eighteen years; her NEA budget had grown to $99.9 million. FDR's WPA arts initiatives were often indistinguishable from New Deal propaganda. Hanks's NEA sustained a spirit of comity and cultural optimism.

Nixon's pertinent role is typically characterized as pragmatically political. It is true that a strategy of "offset politics" was in play: while cutting back on Lyndon Johnson's "Great Society" programs, the new administration would defend and expand underfunded federal programs that could appeal to small but influential constituencies. But Nixon had more to say than that. We have earlier observed him responding to a 1960 *Musical America* questionnaire about government arts subsidies—and producing a more substantive, more positive answer than John F. Kennedy. And Nixon played the piano. For his 1973 inau-guration, he vetoed the participation of DC's provincial National Symphony in favor of Eugene Ormandy and the Philadelphia Orchestra accompanying Van Cliburn in the Grieg Piano Concerto—music and musicians he admired and enjoyed. He quipped that most of the Republican high rollers in attendance "did not know what the hell was going on."[3] And then there was the Comprehensive

Employment and Training Act of 1973, which allocated block grants to individual states to create jobs. For those states that elected to subsidize the arts, CETA veritably resumed Roosevelt's WPA. Many CETA recipients were painters, muralists, poets, and musicians—in all, more than ten thousand artists nationally. But CETA was not renewed under Jimmy Carter. In a December 19, 1969, address, Richard Nixon called artists "an invaluable national resource." They both criticized and celebrated the national experience. They gave "free and full expression to the American spirit." In his shrewd 1988 biography of Nancy Hanks, Michael Straight, having served under Hanks at the NEA, writes of Nixon's speech: "It stands today as the most significant statement of the decade on public funding of the arts."[4]

If Lyndon Johnson is a footnote to this tale, it is he who signed onto the NEA. Johnson may have had no feeling for the arts comparable to Nixon's or Kennedy's. But as a disciple of FDR, he was a president without compunction about federal activism. Presented with the new arts endowment, his impulse was expansionist. Overlooking the meager budget at hand, ignoring his speechwriters, he announced that the NEA would establish a national theater, a national ballet company, a national opera company, and an American film institute. It would commission new symphonies. It would create residencies for "great artists" in schools and colleges.[5] What is significant about this startling and implausible declaration is not its outcome (only the American Film Institute would materialize), but its lack of circumspection. Alongside Rockefeller, Nixon, Hanks, and Johnson, Kennedy alone remained captive to Cold War ideology. Perhaps he might have changed his mind had he lived on. Instead, he bequeathed a conviction that artists must remain "free" of state entanglement—a conviction, I have argued, both counterfactual and counterproductive.

Today, the most "politicized" arts subsidies originate with charitable foundations and individual donors. The NEA, by comparison, has yet to concede that the arts be instrumentalized. But the prejudice against "government intervention" lingers. The mistrust of federal arts subsidies I today encounter—even within the arts community itself—is partly a residue, however unnoticed, of the propaganda of freedom.

*   *   *

The cultural agenda of the moment emphasizes something at which Americans have never excelled and that John F. Kennedy denounced as an oxymoron: political art.

Art as propaganda—art that denounces or sermonizes, decries or prescribes—is, *pace* Kennedy, not necessarily a contradiction in terms. But the terms are

specialized and difficult to balance. During the twenties, the Soviet Union produced a series of classic films in which a Marxist message fired artistic experimentation of the highest order. I am thinking especially of Sergei Eisenstein's *Battle-
ship Potemkin* (1925), Vsevolod Pudovkin's *Mother* (1926), Alexander Vovzhenko's
Earth (1930), and Leonid Trauberg and Grigori Kozintsev's *The New Babylon* (1929)
with music by Shostakovich. In Weimar Germany, Bertolt Brecht and Kurt Weill
found fresh ways to express dissident political ideals in musical theater. Hanns
Eisler wrote ambitious workers' songs that workers actually sang. George Grosz
discovered a visual aesthetic reeking with observed decadence and corruption.
In Mexico the muralists Diego Rivera, David Alfaro Siqueiros, and José Clemente
Orozco created ideological public art that challenged and inspired a nation. Silvestre Revueltas, a political composer of genius, absorbed the screeching clarinets
and booming tubas of village *bandas*, and the street cries of village markets, to
fashion a unique symphonic idiom bonded with lives exploited and oppressed.
In collaboration with Paul Strand, Revueltas produced a film about a fishermen's
uprising—*Redes* (1936)—that bears comparison with the most potent revolutionary art abroad.

Strand, Aaron Copland, Langston Hughes, and John Steinbeck were among
the American artists who flocked to Mexico to see and hear how it was done.
Sergei Eisenstein was also there. As I have had occasion to observe, the most
memorable products of the WPA included a documentary/propaganda film by
Pare Lorentz, *The Plow That Broke the Plains* (1936)—in which the influence of
Eisenstein's "montage" technique is highly apparent. Another documentary/
propaganda film we have encountered in this narrative was *The City* (1939), with
music by Copland. The single best-known WPA product was Marc Blitzstein's
labor musical *The Cradle Will Rock*, echoing the Brecht/Weill *Threepenny Opera*.
But Lorentz was no Eisenstein, Copland was no Revueltas, and Blitzstein was
no Brecht/Weill. And all three wound up antagonizing powerful forces on the
political Right.

If today's arts are again to serve social and political goals, will the results be
more than ephemeral? A more certain reality is that our artists and arts institutions need money merely to survive. When John F. Kennedy issued his call
for a more civilized America, he was worrying about world competition with
Russia—in culture as in every other aspect of human endeavor. He was also
celebrating a widely heralded American "culture boom" that happened to co-
incide with pressing financial needs, especially among orchestras. Three years
after his death, the economists William Baumol and William Bowen produced a
seminal study, *Performing Arts: The Economic Dilemma*, documenting and analyz-
ing a permanent funding crisis. In the arts sector, they argued, efficiency and

production cannot be increased in proportion to the rest of the economy; the resulting income gap would only expand. A half century later, the pandemic canceled performances and closed doors; many arts organizations will go under.

Worse: many underlying factors are not economic. STEM, social media, discontinued arts education, political and social fragmentation all contribute to a diminution of the arts. Where will new funding arise? The traditional American model is laissez-faire: private sources, including corporate and foundation gifts. But private giving to arts institutions after the fashion of a Carnegie, Mellon, Frick, and Rockefeller is not practiced by a Gates or Bezos. The big charitable foundations are no longer arts focused. The tax law of 2017 reduced incentives for charitable giving. Congressional COVID-19 "rescue" grants were a mere stopgap. There exists no federal agency tasked with arts oversight. Though the need for government support is now self-evident, though the American experiment in laissez-faire arts support can by now be pronounced a failure, there is no political will to create an Arts Council on the European model. We have no Jacob Javits or Claiborne Pell in Congress, no Nelson Rockefeller in the White House, no Nancy Hanks at the NEA. Widespread public awareness of the arts as a necessary component of a nation's life remains mainly apparent abroad.

The central purpose of this book has been to extrapolate a propaganda of freedom that, I argue, flavored and distorted American policy during the cultural Cold War. I did not set out to frame suggestions or prescriptions for the present moment. Logically, arts policy today should focus on greatly increasing government support at every level. When and how this may occur remains unknown.

For Soviet ideologues, the arts of the United States represented a vulgarized dilution or decadent tangent. For President Kennedy, they signified a touchstone, a summit, a validation of American enterprise and goodwill. That the Kennedy White House failed to recognize the place of the arts in Soviet Russia says something not just about the Cold War, but about the United States, then and now. Unhappily, the Soviet critique of Americans as "materialistic" and "commercial" cannot wholly be written off as kneejerk ideology.

The United States won the Cold War. The cultural Cold War did not yield a victor.

NICOLAS NABOKOV,
"THE CASE OF DMITRI SHOSTAKOVITCH"

(*Harper's Magazine*, March 1943)

My first encounter with the name and music of Dmitri Shostakovitch occurred sometime in 1927 or 1928. Prokofiev had just returned to Paris from one of his seasonal trips to Soviet Russia. I remember hearing him talk of a remarkable graduate of the Leningrad Conservatory whose First Symphony had won great acclaim in Russia. He had either heard or seen the score of this symphony and had met its youthful author. Prokofiev described him as a pale, lean young man with penetrating eyes, a shy and self-centered youth with a great love for sports. He spoke of his thorough knowledge of "musical grammar" and of his equally good knowledge of the piano technique—both of them characteristic qualities of most Russian composers of this generation. Included in some new Russian music which Prokofiev had brought back from the U.S.S.R. to Paris were eight preludes for the piano by Shostakovitch and also his piano sonata, which had just then appeared in print. At this time the art of Soviet Russia was still little known in western Europe. New Russian scores and new Russian books were difficult to obtain in France and there were very few scattered performances of Soviet Russian music abroad. Quite naturally the young musicians of France and Germany were very eager to know what was being done by composers in that unknown land, and the least bit of authentic information, not to speak of such evidence as scores and books, was highly welcome.

I remember distinctly my first impression of these early piano pieces by Shostakovitch. They seemed to me to have been written with remarkable skill and were well conceived for their instrumental medium. However, on the whole, they did not impress me as being particularly new or imaginative, nor did they seem to me to reflect a well-formed musical personality of first rank. They sounded so orthodox, so well-behaved, and so reminiscent of older Russian piano music that it was odd to realize that they had emanated from the most revolutionary land in the world. They lacked completely the audacious experimental "spirit" which was sweeping through the music of central and western Europe in the nineteen-twenties. I could not understand why this music should be rated so highly and why so much was to be expected from its young author. It did not seem better or worse than most of the other music of Russian composers that Prokofiev had brought back from the Soviet Union.

Some time later, in Poland, where I missed Shostakovitch by only a few weeks (he had come there for one of those international "prize fighting" musical conventions of which there were so many at this time, and this was, as a matter of fact, his only trip abroad up to this day), I had the opportunity of seeing the score of his First Symphony. This was the famous symphony which several years later received great acclaim in the United States.

When I read this score, I felt that I had to correct to a certain extent my former superficially formed opinion of his potentialities. I recognized at once that, despite its many failings, this was a piece of music written by an extremely gifted musician, a man who was not solely interested in showing off the excellency of his training in musical techniques (particularly in orchestration), but knew how to write a long and gracefully lyrical melody and also how to handle a long development section in symphonic form. Nevertheless some of my former objections remained and became even stronger and clearer. I felt that in spite of the many attractive novelties of this symphony—such as its fashionable simplicity of melodic outline or its rhythmical liveliness—there was something old about the music, something essentially conservative and unexperimental. I could not feel any definite personality in it, nor did I see very much authentic invention, musical or technical. Every theme, every rhythmical pattern, every technical device, every harmony, however charming and well written, reminded me of another piece of music. As Diaghilev would have said, here "slept" Tchaikovsky and Wagner, here Mussorgsky or Prokofiev, and here again Stravinsky or Hindemith. There was no actual plagiarism, of course, but the whole atmosphere of the piece was synthetic and impersonal. It was like a good suit of ready-made clothes, which reminds you longingly of a good London tailor, or like one of those tidy modern cubicles in a Dutch or German workers' settlement—all perfectly built, according to the best-known techniques, very proper and neat yet infinitely impersonal and, in the long run, extremely dull.

Some of my musician friends reproached me for my harsh judgment, saying that the man was still very young, that to be impersonal and imitative was a sign of youthful timidity which Shostakovitch surely would soon outgrow. They contended that this First Symphony was in this sense a very promising work, for its musical sources (or sympathies) were of a superior order. I was ready to admit that my premonitions might be wrong, since many great composers at the beginning of their careers have imitated the masters whom they admired. Beethoven and Schubert and even Bach were guilty of that during their early years.

But I still remained worried over this music, and the reason for my worry was something outside of Shostakovitch himself. It seemed to me then that Shostakovitch might be a symptom of a new era approaching in art, and that certain internal changes in the political and social structure of the Soviet Union, rather than considerations of a purely artistic nature, had been greatly responsible of the rise of this kind of music. This synthetic and retrospective score, although foreign and unacceptable to me, was perhaps the true expression of a new period in which the aim was to establish easily comprehensible, utilitarian, and at the same time contemporaneous art. Perhaps some of the principles which had been the cornerstones of the artistic philosophy of the past two generations would be put aside by the composers of this approaching era; perhaps our demand that music be primarily good in quality, new in spirit and technique, original in outlook, would be subordinated to such principles as absolute and immediate comprehensibility to large masses of people and fulfillment of an educational mission, political and social.

I decided therefore to follow Shostakovitch's career as closely as possible in order to discover whether his music and his career would bear out my apprehension.

II

Now, in 1942, most of the cards are on the table. Shostakovitch, barely thirty-six years old, has become recognized as the prime composer of the Soviet Union, has been given a semi-official position among the political and ideological leaders of his country, has lately gained the admiration and love of his countrymen for his heroic life and work during the siege of Leningrad, and is well on the way to becoming the artistic hero of those nations whose destinies are at present closely tied up with that of the Soviet Union.

He can look back at a career full of dramatic episodes, in which utter misery, almost total eclipse from the public eye, and then sudden soaring fame followed each other within the space of a few years. He has worked incessantly with an exemplary perseverance and courage and has built up for one of his age an unusually long catalogue of works of all kinds—piano music, operas, ballets, symphonies, and music for the cinema. Since he finished his studies at the Leningrad Conservatory in 1926 he has been a steady teacher of composition there. As a man he has gained the friendship and respect of almost everyone who has ever come into contact with him.

His prestige in the United States at the present time is illustrated by the single fact that his Seventh ("Leningrad") Symphony, despite its cumbersome length, has received more performances here than any other piece of contemporary music in the same length of time. Sometimes these performances have even been simultaneously broadcast from different corners of the country. His First, Fifth, and Sixth symphonies have been recorded by the finest orchestras and some of the scores have been reprinted here. And he has received all this attention while most of the contemporary musical production of American composers and resident foreigners remains unrecorded, unpublished, and unplayed. Shostakovitch is at the present moment the undisputed idol of all "maestros," blond, bald, or gray, who in homage to Russia serve his seven symphonies at regular intervals to their local audiences on the same plate with Brahms, Beethoven, Wagner, and (until recently) Sibelius.

In speeches, public statements, newspaper and magazine articles he is referred to as "the new Beethoven" or "the new Berlioz"; he is discussed more than any other contemporary American or alien composer of the past twenty years; and as the fire-fighting hero-composer whose great symphony circled the world in bombers and transport planes, he has become a familiar figure to every American citizen who sees the newspapers. Seldom in all the history of music has a composer received fame like this, and seldom has there been a career so rapid and so spectacular.

It seems to me that the time has come for a thorough objective investigation into this most amazing success story. The music of Shostakovitch should be carefully scrutinized, brought into proper focus, and related to the general artistic production of our time so that we may determine to what extent it deserves this tremendous success, and to what extent the success is the result of a propitious political constellation. As yet there have been only scattered evaluations of Shostakovitch, generally connected with some particular episode in his career (like the first performance of his opera "Lady Macbeth from the District of Mzensk" in New York, or the first performance of his Seventh Symphony). Newspaper reporters and critics would describe and denounce or acclaim the single work in question. Lately the articles about Shostakovitch have been on the level of "human interest" stories. Except for a few articles in musical magazines—mostly informational— nothing more complete has been attempted.

III

First let us have a brief glance at the man's biography. It is commonly known that Shostakovitch was born in St. Petersburg, September 25, 1906; what is perhaps less commonly known is that the family of the future proletarian composer had no affinities with either the worker class or peasant class of old Russia. His father, an engineer by education, was, according to official biographers, an employee of the Department of Weights and Measures—a civil servant of the imperial regime, whose position in the community might be compared with that of a modest middle-class American business man. However his professional training and the cultural background and artistic aspirations of his wife provided the family with a more intellectual atmosphere than that of the average bourgeois family of either Russia or America. In Russian terms the Shostakovitch family typified that admirable element in Russian society—the intelligentsia—which comprised in its ranks all that was vital, imaginative, and creative in the nation. Particularly in those dark and dreary years of decay of the imperial regime, the intelligentsia carried double burden: first, the complex tradition of the cultural past of the people, and second, the responsibility for Russia's future regeneration when liberated from the ossified forms of tsarism.

Of his early days Shostakovitch says: "I became a musician by pure accident. If it had not been for my mother, I should probably never have become one. I had no particular inclination for music. I cannot recall a single instance when I evinced any interest in, or listened to, music when someone was playing at home. My mother was quite anxious that her children . . . at the age of nine should each start studying the piano. . . . After a few months of study I practiced Haydn and Mozart." From other sources we hear that the child showed "extraordinary and perfect memory" and at an early age "knew how to read fairly difficult pieces of music at sight." (Both of Shostakovitch's sisters likewise received a thorough musical training as a result of their mother's enthusiasm and determination, and the elder of the two is now a teacher at the Conservatory.) Clearly the boy's unusual natural musical gift was at first inactive and dormant and needed the insistent encouragement of his mother to bring it to the fore.

Otherwise Shostakovitch's childhood was probably very much like that of any other child of his milieu. He went to school through the milky fogs and drizzly rains of St. Petersburg; he was a pale, frail boy coddled and adored by his parents, and surrounded at home by a studious and serious atmosphere. In the summer, as was customary among the Russian bourgeoisie and intelligentsia, the Shostakovitch family would probably go to a suburban villa, the Russian dacha, and there the same industrious and happy life would continue amid the lovely pine forests and quiet lakes surrounding the city of St. Petersburg.

Meanwhile the Russian scene was rapidly changing. First came the war, then the March Revolution of 1917, and its logical outcome (in October, 1917), the assumption of power by Lenin and the establishment of the Soviet government in Russia. It is said that young Dmitri Shostakovitch witnessed the storming of the Winter Palace by the Red Guards on October 23rd—an event which must have made an ineffaceable mark on a youthful, sensitive mind. No one who spent those days in Petrograd can forget them; and they must have played an enormous part in shaping Shostakovitch's convictions and his career.

In 1919 he entered the Petrograd Conservatory. The St. Petersburg-Petrograd-Leningrad Conservatory (founded in 1867 by Anton Rubinstein) has produced a phenomenal crop of great instrumentalists and great composers. It is an exemplary school where excellent technical traditions do not impede the individual development of the student, but supply him with a solid and manifold technical training—a fact which makes most modern Russian music look better "written" than the contemporary music of other countries.

At the Conservatory, under its best teachers, Shostakovitch received a well-balanced training in theory (harmony, composition, counterpoint, fugue, history, orchestration) and piano. When he graduated in 1926 he was already known in the musical circles of Leningrad as the promising young composer, and the composition he presented for his graduation was the First Symphony. By this time his political and artistic opinions were well formed, but already he had presumably gone through a series of influences, attractions, and enthusiasms. Like most music-loving Russian youths, he had probably started with a great attachment to the Mozart and Haydn sonatas which he practiced with his mother on the piano; at some point he probably was swept by an ardent passion for the esoteric music of Scriabin (some tendencies in the direction of Scriabin are still detectable in his music, particularly certain inflections of his melodic outline). He began early to love Tchaikovsky with a love often inexplicable to foreigners but natural to every Russian. With approaching maturity he began to understand the great "polyphonic miracle" of Bach and at the same time rejected as evil the Teutonic Wagnerian brew. But the great, the most powerful discovery he made, one which became a deep unshakable devotion with him, was that of Beethoven—Beethoven the revolutionary, the apostle of humanism, the prophet of "things to come."

The developments in the music of "bourgeois" Europe during this period of time were little known to the citizens of the U.S.S.R., but whatever news came from abroad, whatever score or bit of information could be obtained, was avidly read. Shostakovich's friends and colleagues testify that the works of such men as Stravinsky, Ravel, Hindemith, Bartók and Milhaud were fairly well known to him, and he greedily absorbed all musical news arriving from the West. Several years later, speaking at a meeting of the Leningrad association of composers, he urged a closer acquaintance with the scores of contemporary western European composers, whose achievements, he said, "might be very useful to the music of Soviet Russia."

As for his convictions about the nature of his art, the mission of the creative musician, and his relation to politics and the State, these seem to have crystallized around 1927, not without a preceding period of doubt and a kind of creative prostration.

In an autobiographical statement given in 1936 to the *Revue Musicale*, Shostakovitch wrote: "At the Conservatory I absorbed with enthusiasm but without critical judgment all the knowledge and all the kinds of refinement which I was being taught. . . ." But somewhat later, "I understood that music is not only a combination of sounds arranged in this or that order [an idea quite fashionable at that time among several western European composers; see Stravinsky's autobiography] but an art which is *capable of expressing* by its means, *ideas* or sentiments of a most diverse kind. . . . I did not, however, acquire this conviction without pains. It suffices to say that during the whole year 1926 [the year of his graduation from the Conservatory] I did not write a single note, but from 1927 on I have never ceased to compose."

Thus, at the beginning of his career, the question which has troubled many creative musicians—is music a language capable of expressing *only emotions and feelings* or is it also a vehicle for the expression of *ideas*?—was answered for him. From then on he had unshakable conviction that it could express ideas. From this point it was only a short step to the belief that the composer, like any other intellectual worker, has an educational obligation to fulfill and a political responsibility to bear.

Shostakovitch states it very clearly. "Working without interruption to acquire control over my art," he says, "I applied myself in order to create my own musical style which I sought to render simple and expressive. . . . I cannot conceive of my future creative program outside of our socialist enterprise (*construction socialiste*), and the aim which I assign to my work is that of helping in every way to enlighten our remarkable country." Near the end of this autobiographical statement he completes this idea of the composer's mission in the new socialist state by saying: "There cannot be greater joy for a composer than to be conscious that through his work he contributes to the great impetus of the Soviet musical culture, which is called upon to play a role of the first importance in remolding the human conscience."

From 1927 on and until now, all through the turbulent years of the middle thirties and through the agony of this war, this conviction has grown, become more rooted in him. The repudiation which his work received from the political leaders of his country in 1937, and which seemed for a time to eclipse his career, actually only spurred him on to work harder in order that he might redeem himself in the eyes of these leaders and regain his people's esteem. Any doubt as to the sincerity of this devotion, any suspicion as to the honesty of his intentions, should be definitely put aside.

Thus the little bourgeois boy, Mitya Shostakovitch, has gone through the tough school of the revolution and emerged completely transformed. He has become an "intellectual worker" of the Proletarian Republic, one hundred per cent Stalinist Communist, whose chief apostolate is to serve his government (and through it his people) according to this government's wishes and advices. He is honored when they praise him; he tries to see his errors when he is rebuffed. Individual, personal feelings matter only in so far as they are part of the people's fortune, their aspirations and their tragedies. "Music," he contends, "cannot help having a political basis, an idea that the bourgeoisie are slow to comprehend. . . . There can be no music without ideology . . ." (meaning of course political ideology). "The old composers whether they knew it or not were upholding a political theory." He goes on to explain that most of the old masters "were bolstering the rule of the upper classes," that Beethoven was "the forerunner of the revolutionary movement," and that Wagner, "the renegade," was "a revolutionary turned reactionary, to whom we listen in the same spirit as when we visit a museum to study the forms of the old regime." All art thus becomes classified according to a Marxian theory of values in which the intrinsic quality of a work of art depends upon its importance to the revolutionary progress of mankind. The language of music becomes a vehicle for the statement of political ideologies; musical techniques are relegated to a subservient position; they are important only in so far as they render those ideologies intelligible. Concern with "personal" emotions, "individual" style or technique becomes irrelevant and unacceptable. Even to consider the proposition that transformation of musical techniques or an expression of individualistic emotions could be an end in itself becomes completely heretical. Shostakovitch condemns all such "foolishness" emphatically in his profoundly moving statement published on the eve of the first anniversary of the Russo-German War. "My energies," he writes, "are wholly engaged in the service of my country. Like everything and everyone today, my ideas are closely bound up with the emotions born of this war. They must serve with all the power at my command in the cause of *art for victory* over savage Hitlerism, that fiercest and bitterest enemy of human civilization. This is the aim to which I have dedicated my creative work since the morning of June 22, 1941."

Such complete devotion to the just cause of his country and its people necessarily commands respect and admiration. The philosophy upon which it is based is morally far more solid than many other contemporary theories. True enough, the Soviet artistic theory does not leave much room for the independent development of the individual musician; but on the other hand it is free from that pernicious and amoral egocentricism from which so much music of the late nineteenth and twentieth centuries suffers. It is strangely akin to the noble morality of the artisan-musician of the Middle Ages, who, like Shostakovitch, worked with zeal and self-sacrifice as a servant of a cause he considered higher than himself and his art. The intention is the same and so is the fervor of the devotion, the difference in this case being that where the medieval musician read the words "glory of God" and "service of His church," Shostakovitch reads "glory of the state" and "service of the people."

Yet as a permanent principle it has its dangers for the artist, as the case of Dmitri Shostakovitch demonstrates.

IV

The musical production of Dmitri Shostakovitch can be conveniently divided into two periods. The first began in 1927, following his graduation from the Conservatory, and lasted until 1936 or, more precisely, January 28, 1936, When the now famous incident concerning his opera, "Lady Macbeth from the District of Mzensk," occurred. Then came a lapse of almost two years when Shostakovitch disappeared from the horizon of Russian artistic life. During these two years he wrote two new symphonies, his Fourth and Fifth, and the latter opened the door back to public favor, and marked the beginning of the second period, when, "reformed" and "rehabilitated," he gradually climbed to his present pinnacle of leadership.

The incident of "Lady Macbeth" has therefore a considerable significance and, although it has already been mentioned in the American press, it cannot be avoided here. Briefly this is what happened. During the years 1930–1932 Shostakovitch wrote an opera on a story by a Russian writer of the nineteenth century, Leskov, called "Lady Macbeth from the District of Mzensk." It is a naturalistic and lurid story about a provincial, middle-class woman whose lust and boredom drive her to a series of cold-blooded murders and finally land her and her unfaithful lover in Siberia. Shostakovitch tried to give the story a Marxian twist by making the "heroine" a victim of the "decadent and foul bourgeois milieu."

The music of the opera is neither daring nor particularly new. It sounds very much like many naturalistic Russian operas written in the eighties and now happily forgotten. True enough, it is more lively; it has some (not too successful) attempts at bitter "class satire" and "class tragedy"; it has also a few attractively lyrical melodies both in the choruses and in the arias; but on the whole it is old-fashioned, provincial, and unimaginative. The musical language in which it is written is simple enough, but somehow not quite coherent, and totally lacking in unity. Pieces of various styles are strung together rather loosely, and the whole opera gives the impression of hasty and somewhat careless workmanship. Thus, for instance, the satirical passages and some of the polyphonic developments are full of the most obnoxious tricks of the *style moderne* of the twenties (dissonant superimposition of chords, "dislocated joints" in the melodic line, and "rhythmical paranoia," or senseless repetition of the metrical figure—all unhappy products of the "modern" musical mind), while the lyrical arias and choruses reflect either Tchaikovsky or Mussorgsky. The realism or naturalism of the piece goes too far and at times it is plainly vulgar and pornographic. Most of the "class satire" is as unconvincing as the "Wood Soldiers" of the late "Chauve-Souris."

The opera was duly produced in both Russian capitals in 1934 and was hailed as a "great masterpiece," the "work of a genius," "the first monumental work of Soviet musical culture." As such it was exported abroad and produced in the United States under Artur Rodzinski in Cleveland and New York. In New York it created a minor scandal and stirred up a great deal of discussion (chiefly because of the excessive musical realism of a bedroom love scene), which, coupled with the previous success of the First Symphony, "made" Shostakovitch.

For a time it looked as if the gods were favorably inclined to the young composer. But suddenly the storm broke loose. Messrs. Stalin and Molotov visited a performance of "Lady Macbeth" in Moscow in the middle of January, 1937. As a result of this visit a vitriolic article appeared in the *Pravda* on January 28, 1937, condemning Shostakovitch's opera as "disorder instead of music" and arguing that "mad rhythms" and a "confused flow of sound" competed to produce a baffling effect upon the innocent audience. Shostakovitch was said to be "misled by decadent bourgeois tendencies," and although a "gifted composer," was accused of "intentionally turning everything upside down" and writing "neurotic, hysterical, epileptic music influenced by American jazz." This first attack on Shostakovitch was followed by a second one, which appeared in the same paper a few days later and in which his new ballet, "The Limpid Brook," was taken to task in the same way. In terms of Russian life all this sounded like an artistic death warrant; and such it was taken to be by the obliging critics and gentlemen of the Soviet press (often the same ones who had previously praised

Shostakovitch as the great Russian genius). The slander of Shostakovitch in the press actually became so thick that the same official powers which had ordered the condemnation of his opera had to give a "hands off Shostakovitch" order. Shostakovitch was declared to have been "misled," "corrupted by Western bourgeois tendencies," but to be "gifted enough" to rehabilitate himself in the future and thus "not past hope." Two years later the "reformed" composer was returned to the Russian public as an officially changed man, one who had seen his faults and corrected them.

The whole story seems quite unreal now, particularly in view of the present circumstances. Yet it throws an interesting light upon the birth pangs of Soviet Russian art, and is especially significant for the development of Shostakovitch as a musician. These two painful years of banishment from public life were years of "inner self-criticism" (as the Soviet press calls it) during which he simplified his art still farther and *all* of his original musical thinking was definitely swallowed up by the "service to the cause."

V

It is as difficult to describe the music of Shostakovitch as to describe the form and color of an oyster, not because this music is by any means complicated or "inscrutable in its profundity" (as Soviet Russian criticism puts it) but simply because it is shapeless in style and form and impersonal in color. Yet the oyster has a very individual taste of its own which Shostakovitch unfortunately lacks. For one of his chief weaknesses is absolute eclectic impersonality. Even during his first period, when he still felt himself relatively free to choose or invent his own technique, his music was impersonal.

He still borrows other people's technical and stylistic inventions as if they were communal belongings. He still imitates indiscriminately (and I believe quite unconsciously) here Tchaikovsky and Beethoven, there Berlioz and Rimsky-Korsakov; here again he tries out some device he learned from a score of Stravinsky, or Ravel, or Hindemith, or from some minor composer of the twenties. During his first period he wrote a greater variety of kinds of music than later, using tricks, devices, and techniques taken from such different sources that they could not possibly lead to a unified style, and jumping from Tchaikovsky to jazzy rhythms of the "Mitteleuropa" variety. His operas are so different from his symphonies, his chamber music from his ballets, that one has a hard time recognizing that the same man wrote them; and it is the defects of the music, rather than its qualities, that are recognizable as his own. Thus, for instance, he writes few melodies in which the augmented fourth does not appear; yet this interval is essentially unmelodic and by association reminds us of very stale 'melodies" of the late nineteenth century. His exaggerated liking of march rhythms of 4/4 and 2/4 time leads to a kind of wooden squareness in the fast movements of his music. His long melodic cantilenas, in generally not more than two parts, are shapeless and awkwardly built. His "tunes" are often from very ordinary sources (in Soviet Russia they were called "marshy" during the years of his eclipse), imitating very common and uninteresting factory or army songs. One would probably not object to them if they had been treated originally, for Haydn, Beethoven, Stravinsky often used tunes coming from the gutter; but how they ennobled them!

The two positive qualities I find in the music of Shostakovitch are of a rather ambiguous order. The first one is his great versatility and efficiency in Conservatory training, which enables him to solve technical problems of a broad variety in a highly skillful manner. Shostakovitch is undoubtedly an excellent craftsman and most of his inventiveness goes into such branches of musical craft as orchestration and efficient part writing (what the Germans call "*guter tonsatz*"). It is not infrequent among contemporary composers that such technical strength conceals a paucity of original musical ideas.

The second quality of Shostakovitch, to foreigners so surprising, is the inherent optimism of his music. As everybody knows, the common view of Russian music and the Russian character is that they are by nature easily depressed and melancholy or just the reverse, boisterously and wildly gay—without any visible reason. This view, erroneous as it is, is well entrenched in people's minds. Thus when a composer from Russia is neither desperately melancholic nor in a state of frenzy, as in a Ballet-Russe-de-Monte-Carlo finale (with its inherent disorder), the foreigner thinks that something new has happened. No one will deny that a completely new life has been built in Russia, yet this has little to do with the national character of the people and their art, which at times in the past has been just as optimistic as the music of Shostakovitch. Glinka, the father of modern Russian music, Borodin, Mussorgsky, and Tchaikovsky himself have numberless pages of the happiest, lightest, gayest music the nineteenth century produced.

Thus to a Russian there would not be anything particularly surprising in the optimism of Shostakovitch. But it takes a redundant, blatant, and unconvincing form. One always feels a kind of compelling force behind it, a force of an extra-musical order. It appears to be based on the official syllogistic formula: before the revolution, life was desperate, therefore art was gloomy; now the revolution is victorious, therefore art must be optimistic. It is obvious that this *must* rings like a command of the gods rather than a logical conclusion of a syllogism. The result is that it often forces the composer into a great effort unnatural to his temperament and therefore unsuccessful.

What this *must* tends to do in Russian music in general and to Shostakovitch's music in particular is lamentable. It drives the young composer to naive and dated formulae such as an excessive and very conventional use of major triads, tunes and cadences in major keys, all of them describing the glorious and victorious events of the present in the most emphatic and banal musical language. (Minor modes are used to describe the dark and gloomy days of the past.) It steers the whole music into a verbose and brassy style which soon becomes dreary and monotonous. It produces that wooden 2/4 or 4/4 rhythm to which I have already referred, and which I suppose is considered "manlier" and "more virile" than the "effeminate" 3/4 or 6/8, and fills the thematic material with such commonplace metrical patterns as one eighth note followed by two sixteenth notes (or vice versa), which most composers use very sparingly.

In Shostakovitch's second period all these unfortunate characteristics come to full bloom. The substance of Shostakovitch's composition now tends to be of such obvious understandability that his music ceases to be an artistic language in which the adventurous human mind discovers new laws and new problems which it endeavors to solve in a new way. Every technique, every melodic line, every development, polyphonic or monophonic, every rhythm, every formal device is reminiscent of either contemporary or nineteenth-century composers, and is used in such an obvious fashion that after a while one begins to wonder if even the most uneducated masses will not soon tire of it. (I often ask myself if this *a priori* decision, so frequent among intellectuals and politicians, that the masses have a naturally low taste for the arts, is not a proof of their own lack of discrimination.)

Simplification of music is in itself a salutary thing, but there is a moment when simplification becomes too obvious and absurd. Eclecticism is often the sturdy backbone of healthy tradition (was not Johann Sebastian Bach an eclectic to a degree?), but when it pervades a man's music or stands in the way of the invention of a personal style it becomes deplorable. Objectivity should not be confused with impersonality, just as romanticism should not necessarily involve grandiloquent sentimentality and formlessness.

Fortunately Shostakovitch possesses the saving graces of excellent craftsmanship, profound honesty, and a fervent belief in the usefulness of what he is doing. Furthermore, at times there is a graceful lyricism in his music when he forgets himself (particularly in his chamber music, which by its very nature is freer from those moral obligations that govern his long descriptive symphonies), and this natural lyricism shows us that somewhere deep behind the screen of impersonality and moral obligation there still lives an individual, a free artist, a man by the name of Dmitri Shostakovitch.

VI

The actual significance of the case of Shostakovitch can be brought home by restating the crucial question that I asked myself in 1929 in Poland: are we going to see the rise of an eclectic collectivistic art which will put the individual at least temporarily in a completely subservient position to the state and society? Are we going to see the birth of an impersonal art written exclusively for the masses in the fallacious belief that the masses have to be "talked down to"? For the present the music of Shostakovitch seems to answer this question in the affirmative—at any rate in so far as the music of Soviet Russia is concerned.

Is his art great? Is it unique and incomparably better than most modern music? Certainly not. There are many composers who both write better and have more to say than Shostakovitch. American and alien composers in this country have composed music which sees the concert hall less, but says infinitely more than his celebrated Seventh Symphony. Consider the scores of Piston, Copland, William Schuman, compositions by Stravinsky, Hindemith, Milhaud, Rieti—some of which are never played, because our maestros and their managers ordain otherwise.

It is these maestros and managers who are chiefly responsible for all the uproar in this country over one or two composers for one or two seasons. They have learned too well how to exploit a propitious political situation (what has become now of the "beloved" Finn Sibelius?) and create a bubble reputation to relieve the stagnation of the concert repertory (always the same pieces of the same composers!); and they are now doing Shostakovitch immense disservice by placing him in a position in which he does not belong.

I sincerely hope that Shostakovitch has the power to undergo another complete regeneration and emerge a truly significant composer. But it is a gross misunderstanding of "collectivist" art to accept the popularity of his music now as evidence that he has found a universal formula. Soon his eclipse may come as swiftly as his leap to fame; this would be just as unfair and would indicate the same disbalance we see at present. Shostakovitch is a young man; he should develop as a solid and respected musician of the great New Russia. He does not now merit the injudicious acclaim he is receiving here; neither will he deserve the inevitable repudiation which will come in its wake. Both extremes arc shameful evidence that contemporary music is judged indiscriminately and contemporary composers are used irresponsibly.

PRESIDENT JOHN F. KENNEDY/ ARTHUR SCHLESINGER JR., "THE AMHERST SPEECH"

(October 26, 1963)

The following excerpt reproduces Kennedy's spoken words, which somewhat depart from the script prepared by Arthur Schlesinger.

Our national strength matters, but the spirit which informs and controls our strength matters just as much. This was the special significance of Robert Frost. He brought an unsparing instinct for reality to bear on the platitudes and pieties of society. His sense of the human tragedy fortified him against self-deception and easy consolation. "I have been," he wrote, "one acquainted with the night." And because he knew the midnight as well as the high noon, because he understood the ordeal as well as the triumph of the human spirit, he gave his age strength with which to overcome despair. At bottom, he held a deep faith in the spirit of man, and it is hardly an accident that Robert Frost coupled poetry and power, for he saw poetry as the means of saving power from itself. When power leads men towards arrogance, poetry reminds him of his limitations. When power narrows the areas of man's concern, poetry reminds him of the richness and diversity of his existence. When power corrupts, poetry cleanses. For art establishes the basic human truth which must serve as the touchstone of our judgment.

The artist, however faithful to his personal vision of reality, becomes the last champion of the individual mind and sensibility against an intrusive society and an officious state. The great artist is thus a solitary figure. He has, as Frost said, a lover's quarrel with the world. In pursuing his perceptions of reality, he must often sail against the currents of his time. This is not a popular role. If Robert Frost was much honored in his lifetime, it was because a good many preferred to ignore his darker truths. Yet in retrospect, we see how the artist's fidelity has strengthened the fiber of our national life.

If sometimes our great artists have been the most critical of our society, it is because their sensitivity and their concern for justice, which must motivate any true artist, makes him aware that our nation falls short of its highest potential. I see little of more importance to the future of our country and our civilization than full recognition of the place of the artist.

If art is to nourish the roots of our culture, society must set the artist free to follow his vision wherever it takes him. We must never forget that art is not a form of propaganda; it is a form of truth. And as Mr. MacLeish once remarked of poets, there is nothing worse for our trade than to be in style. In free society art is not a weapon and it does not belong to the spheres of polemic and ideology. Artists are not "engineers of the soul." It may be different elsewhere. But democratic society—in it, the highest duty of the writer, the composer, the artist is to remain true to himself and to let the chips fall where they may. In serving his vision of the truth, the artist best serves his nation. And the nation which disdains the mission of art invites the fate of Robert Frost's hired man, the fate of having "nothing to look backward to with pride, and nothing to look forward to with hope."

I look forward to a great future for America, a future in which our country will match its military strength with our moral restraint, its wealth with our wisdom, its power with our purpose. I look forward to an America which will not be afraid of grace and beauty, which will protect the beauty of our natural environment, which will preserve the great old American houses and squares and parks of our national past, and which will build handsome and balanced cities for our future.

I look forward to an America which will reward achievement in the arts as we reward achievement in business or statecraft. I look forward to an America which will steadily raise the standards of artistic accomplishment and which will steadily enlarge cultural opportunities for all of our citizens. And I look forward to an America which commands respect throughout the world not only for its strength but for its civilization as well. And I look forward to a world which will be safe not only for democracy and diversity but also for personal distinction.

Robert Frost was often skeptical about projects for human improvement, yet I do not think he would disdain this hope. As he wrote during the uncertain days of the Second War:

Take human nature altogether since time began . . .
And it must be a little more in favor of man,
Say a fraction of one percent at the very least . . .
Our hold on this planet wouldn't have so increased.

Because of Mr. Frost's life and work, because of the life and work of this college, our hold on this planet has increased.

NOTES

Chapter 1. JFK, the Artist, and "Free Societies"

1. Memo to the President: John F. Kennedy Memorial Library archives, identifier JFKPOF-033–010. Kennedy's speech: "Igor Stravinsky at the White House" by Edward G. Lengel: www.whitehousehistory.org/igor-stravinky-at-the-white-house.

2. Robert Craft, *Chronicle of a Friendship* (1994), 285.

3. Kennedy Library archives, identifier JFKPOF-028–021.

4. Arthur J. Schlesinger Jr., *A Thousand Days: John F. Kennedy in the White House* (1965), 732.

5. For the entire text of the Amherst speech, see Appendix B.

6. See, for instance, Schlesinger, *Thousand Days*, 733–38.

7. Jill Lepore, *These Truths: A History of the United States* (2018), 536.

8. Richard N. Goodwin, *Remembering America: A Voice from the Sixties* (1988), 222–25.

9. Kennedy Library archives, Arthur M. Schlesinger Personal Papers, Series 5, Journal, Box WH1, Advisory Council on the Arts; Heckscher's report: https://babel.hathitrust.org/cgi/pt?id=uc1.b2501471&view=1up&seq=44.

10. Joseph Horowitz, *Understanding Toscanini: How He Became an American Culture-God and Helped Create a New Audience for Old Music* (1987), 250–51; Ian Wellins, *Music on the Frontline: Nicolas Nabokov's Struggle against Communism and Middlebrow Culture* (2002), 70, 63.

11. Horowitz, *Understanding Toscanini*, 200, 211.

12. Roosevelt must have been aware of Leni Riefenstahl's *Olympia* (1938)—a high artistic achievement under Hitler—because when the New Deal documentary *The River* (1938) was named top documentary at the Venice International Film Festival, *Olympia*

was runner-up. Emil Nolde's unforgettable miniature watercolors, which FDR would not have known, came about when the Nazis forced him to paint in secret—a "survival strategy" in some ways analogous to Shostakovich's secret musical messages. Artists find a way.

13. I tell this story in detail in *Understanding Toscanini*, 189–223.

14. According to Bernstein himself, recalling the April 5, 1960, performance. See, for example, www.leonardbernstein.com.

Chapter 2. Nicolas Nabokov and the Cultural Cold War

1. *New York Herald-Tribune*, October 15, 1942.

2. The principal sources are Nicolas Nabokov, *Old Friends and New Music* (1951); Nicolas Nabokov, *Bagazh: Memoirs of a Russian Cosmopolitan* (1975); Ian Wellens, *Music on the Frontline* (2002); and Vincent Giroud, *Nicolas Nabokov: A Life in Freedom and Music* (2015).

3. Giroud, *Nicolas Nabokov*, 181.

4. Giroud, *Nicolas Nabokov*, 392, 395, 408.

5. Stravinsky chapters in Nabokov, *Old Friends*; Nabokov, *Bagazh*, 165, 176.

6. For a complete list of Nabokov's writings, see Giroud, *Nicolas Nabokov*, 441–45.

7. Nabokov unquestionably knew that his CCF colleague Michael Josselson worked for the CIA. The questions became whether he knew the CIA funded the CCF, and whether he acknowledged (even to himself) the parameters CIA oversight placed on his own activities. Ian Wellens, in *Music on the Frontline* (2002), writes: "Isaiah Berlin told the present writer he suspected Nabokov did know the true state of affairs, commenting on how closely he had worked with Josselson. . . . The sociologist Edward Shils, a prominent member of the CCF's American affiliate, recalls asking Nabokov in October 1955 about a rumour that the Congress was receiving Agency support: in return, he was sent an accountant's report on the Farfield Foundation, later revealed as a front. He comments that Nabokov 'did not accompany that boring, uninformative and, as it turned out, false, document with any denial of the report which I had transmitted. That was a cynical thing to do'" (13).

In *The Cultural Cold War* (1999), Frances Stonor Saunders writes: "Nabokov surely knew to which government agency he owed the extraordinary largesse enjoyed by the Paris office during his mammoth [1952 Paris] festival. Years later, he would confess to Josselson that 'Queen Juiliana Fleischmann' (head of the dummy Fleischmann Foundation that funded the CCF) had never been plausible. He had always thought of the 'the plutocratic Junkie [Fleischmann]' as a 'poor conduit'" (127).

On one occasion (December 13, 1951), Fleischmann wrote to Nabokov that the Boston Symphony's participation in Nabokov's Paris festival was being subsidized, via Farfield, by a stranger he met on a transatlantic voyage. "I had to promise to withhold his name and I don't even know the names of his associates" (Wellens, *Music on the Frontline*, 49). Wellens comments: "Even to Nabokov, the cover story had to be maintained." Saunders adds:

But officially Nabokov knew nothing, and maintained (just as implausibly) that "curiously enough, not for a moment did the question of money cross my mind. It probably should have, because it was hard to imagine the American labor unions subsidizing a grandiosely expensive modern-arts festival and not in America, but in Paris, of all places. . . . Not in my wildest dreams could I have expected that my 'dream festival' would be supported by America's spying establishment, nor did I know that the fare for my delightful first class flight to Paris was being paid by the CIA. . . . And that soon, very soon, that same spy mill would be using 'passing' foundations to pump money to such groups as our Cultural Committee, to American colleges, to refugee orchestras, and whatnot."

Could Nabokov really have been in ignorance, unaware that he was entangled in a deliberate deception? Or had he, like so many of his contemporaries, become, like Graham Greene's Alden Pyle, just another Quiet American. "He didn't even hear what I said; he was absorbed already in the dilemmas of Democracy and the responsibilities of the West." (127–28)

Saunders shares additional anecdotes of Nabokov "confessions" (377, 396). It bears adding that in 1948, sponsored by George Kennan, Nabokov applied for government service and was turned down after failing a security check. It is probable that it was the CIA to which he had applied.

8. Nabokov, *Bagazh*, 243.

9. Schlesinger subsequently decided that in *The Vital Center* he had overestimated the subservience of the individual in totalitarian societies (see his *A Life in the 20th Century* [2000], 514–17). Nabokov may have experienced a comparable revelation when in 1967 he finally visited the Soviet Union and met some of the musicians he had perceived as tools of the state. See my pages 105–6.

10. Arthur Schlesinger Jr., "The Future of Liberalism: The Challenge of Abundance," *Reporter*, May 3, 1956.

11. According to his biographer Richard Aldous, in conversation with the author (June 2020).

12. Theodore H. White, notes for his article "The Last Side of Camelot" (*Life* magazine), *Kennedy Assassination Chronicles* (Fall 1995).

13. Christopher Lasch, *The New Radicalism in America, 1889 to 1963: The Intellectual as a Social Type* (1965), 310–13.

14. Wellens, *Music on the Frontline*, 63. Nabokov letter in Nabokov, *Bagazh*, 178.

15. Richard Aldous, *Schlesinger: The Imperial Historian* (2017), 309.

16. Nabokov, *Old Friends*, 201.

17. On the White House dinner for Stravinsky, see Robert Craft, *Chronicle of a Friendship* (1994), 285; Giroud, *Nicolas Nabokov*, 334–35; John F. Kennedy Memorial Library archives; and Lillian Libman, *And Music at the Close: Stravinsky's Last Years* (1972), 140–45.

Chapter 3. Lines of Battle

1. Giroud, *Nicolas Nabokov*, 212.

2. Giroud, *Nicolas Nabokov*, 407.

3. Giroud, *Nicolas Nabokov*, 407.

4. Frances Stonor Saunders, *The Cultural Cold War: The CIA and the World of Arts and Letters* (1999), 220.

5. Nabokov, *Old Friends and New Music*, 140.

6. Nabokov, *Old Friends and New Music* and *Bagazh*; Nabokov, "Stravinsky: Fifteen and Three-Score," *High Fidelity*, June 1957.

7. Boris Schwarz, *Music and Musical Life in Soviet Russia* (1972), 246.

8. This is a telling motif in Stravinsky's *Poetics*; see my pages 80–81. Three decades later, Nabokov attempted to dissuade Stravinsky from returning to Russia; see my page 85.

9. Nabokov, *Old Friends and New Music*, chap. 8.

10. Nabokov, *Old Friends and New Music*, 165.

11. "Highest order," Nicolas Nabokov, "Music in the U.S.S.R.," pt. 2, *New Republic*, April 7, 1941; "in essence tonal," Nabokov, "Sergei Prokofiev," *Atlantic Monthly*, July 1942; "banal," Nabokov, "Music under Dictatorship," *Atlantic Monthly*, January 1942; letter to Stravinsky, Giroud, *Nicolas Nabokov*, 499; "probably one of best," Nabokov, review of Prokofiev Symphony No. 5, *MLA Notes* (June 1947).

12. Nabokov, *Old Friends and New Music*, 183.

13. Nicholas Nabokov, "Changing Styles in Soviet Music," *Listener*, October 11, 1953; Nabokov, *Old Friends and New Music*, 270.

14. Wellens, *Music on the Frontline*, 19.

15. Nicolas Nabokov, "The Atonal Trail: A Communication," *Partisan Review,* May 1948.

16. Simon Morrison, "The Fact and Fiction behind Shostakovich's 'Lady Macbeth,'" *New York Times*, October 6, 2022.

17. Boris Schwarz, *Music and Musical Life in Soviet Russia, 1917–1970* (1972), 206.

18. Boris Schwarz, *Music and Musical Life*, 207.

19. Boris Schwarz, *Music and Musical Life.*

20. Vincent Giroud, *Nicolas Nabokov*, 212.

21. *New York Times*, December 21, 1931.

22. Boris Schwarz, *Music and Musical Life,*

23. But the pianist Maria Yudina, a renegade iconoclast of formidable reputation, rebuked them: "Your quibbling, negative judgments will wither away at the roots." David Caute, *The Dancer Defects: The Struggle for Cultural Supremacy during the Cold War* (2003), 424.

24. *New York Times*, December 21, 1931.

Chapter 4. CIA Cultural Battlegrounds

1. Shapley quoted in Terry Klefstad, "Shostakovich and the Peace Conference," *Music & Politics* (Summer 2012).

2. Duncan White, *Cold Warriors: Writers Who Waged the Literary Cold War* (2019), 259–60.

3. Chandler Carter, *The Last Opera: "The Rake's Progress" in the Life of Stravinsky and Sung Drama* (2019), 245.

4. My account of the Waldorf Astoria conference incorporates quotes from participants many times reported—for example, in Klefstad, "Shostakovich and the Peace Conference"; Jonathan Rosenberg, *Dangerous Melodies: Classical Music in America from the Great War through the Cold War* (2019); Sidney Hook, *Out of Step: An Unquiet Life in the 20th Century* (1987); Nicolas Nabokov, *Bagazh*; Vincent Giroud, *Nicolas Nabokov*; and Frances Stonor Saunders, *The Cultural Cold War.*

5. Rosenberg, *Dangerous Melodies*, 305.

6. Giroud, *Nicolas Nabokov*, 220221.

7. Rosenberg, *Dangerous Melodies*, 306–7.

8. Solomon Volkov, *Testimony: The Memoirs of Dmitri Shostakovich* (1979), 196, 147–48.

9. Hook, *Out of Step*, 271–74.

10. Hook, *Out of Step*, 262.

11. White, *Cold Warriors*, 260.

12. Hook, *Out of Step*, 383–89.

13. Hook, *Out of Step*, 252–54.

14. Nabokov, *Bagazh*, 234.

15. Arthur Miller, *Timebends: A Life* (1987), 239.

16. A notable defender of Nabokov's behavior at the conference was the late Richard Taruskin, as in his review of Vincent Giroud's Nabokov biography in the *Times Literary Supplement*, August 5, 2016.

17. Giroud, *Nicolas Nabokov*, 219–21.

18. Rosenberg, *Dangerous Melodies*, 289.

19. Giroud, *Nicolas Nabokov*, 220.

20. Miller, *Timebends: A Life.*

21. Nabokov, *Bagazh*, 239.

22. Josselson was a man who covered his tracks. The fullest attempt to bring him to light—upon which I here rely—is *The CIA and the Congress for Cultural Freedom in the Early Cold War* (2019) by Sarah Miller Harris (see especially 7, 14–16, 22–23, 144–45). Josselson, she writes, "left few traces of his own thinking" (48). Her book defends Josselson against the criticism of Saunders (whose layered critique Harris greatly simplifies).

23. Saunders, *The Cultural Cold War,* 69.

24. Peter Coleman, *The Liberal Conspiracy*, 249–51.

25. Hook, *Out of Step*, 444–45.

26. Giroud, *Nicolas Nabokov*, 248.

27. Giroud, *Nicolas Nabokov,* 247.

28. Saunders, *The Cultural Cold War*, 130.

29. Hugh Wilford, *The Mighty Wurlitzer: How the CIA Played America* (2008), 7.

30. Saunders, *The Cultural Cold War,* 135.

31. Saunders, *The Cultural Cold War*, 129, 105, 225.

32. Saunders, *The Cultural Cold War*, 104.

33. Hook, *Out of Step*, 445.

34. Ian Wellens, *Music on the Frontline*, 52–53.

35. Archives of the International Association for Cultural Freedom, box 394, University of Chicago Special Collections Research Center.

36. "Masterpieces of the XXth Century," English-language program book, International Association for Cultural Freedom, box 394, University of Chicago Special Collections Research Center.

37. A complete list of festival programs may be found in Mark Carroll, *Music and Ideology in Cold War Europe* (2003).

38. By an intriguing coincidence, the Soviets, too, were considering a massive 1952 international music festival. It would take place in Moscow, with 150 concerts in twenty-three days and 1,250 international participants. The goal was to showcase Soviet musical achievement. Though the plan was deemed too costly, the 1958 Tchaikovsky International Competition was a direct offshoot. See Kiril Tomoff, *Virtuosi Abroad* (2016), 87–88.

39. "Masterpieces of the XXth Century."

40. Giroud, *Nicolas Nabokov*, 264.

41. Saunders, *The Cultural Cold War,* 261–72.

42. Wellens, *Music on the Frontline*, 54.

43. David C. Paul, *Charles Ives in the Mirror: American Histories of an Iconic Composer* (2013), 81.

44. *Score* 6 (1952).

45. Giroud, *Nicolas Nabokov*, 110, 266.

46. Janet Flanner, *New Yorker*, May 31, 1952.

47. Giroud, *Nicolas Nabokov*, 267.

48. Coleman, *The Liberal Conspiracy*, 56.

49. Hook, *Out of Step*, 444–45.

50. Saunders, *The Cultural Cold War,* 124–25.

51. Wellens, *Music on the Frontline*, 36–37.

52. André Gide, *Return from the USSR* (1937), quoted by Melvin Lasky at the 1947 German Writers' Congress. See Harris, *CIA and the Congress for Cultural Freedom*, 41.

53. Giroud, *Nicolas Nabokov*, 319.

54. Saunders, *The Cultural Cold War,* 275.

55. In the aftermath of the festival, the International Institute for Comparative Music Studies was founded in Berlin, with Nabokov's support, by the Eastern music specialist and CCF participant Alain Danielou. Yet Nabokov deplored mixing Western high culture with non-Western musical idioms. In a 1972 letter to Ulli Beier, a specialist in African literature and a CCF beneficiary, Nabokov characteristically wrote: "I have deplored the 'potpourri' of inherent musical nonsense produced by Yehudi Menuhin and Ravi Shankar, both of whom independently I admire as excellent performers, but only wish they would exercise their art separately and not serenade each other in joint 'jumbo-mumbo' activities." (Wellens, in *Music on the Frontline*, 109.) At Nabokov's Rome festival of 1954, one of the participants in the music competition was Lou Harrison, already a master practitioner of the kind of East-West musical synergies Nabokov dismissed. Ever the modernist purist, Nabokov seemingly remained oblivious to this most notable postmodern development in art music.

56. Giroud, *Nicolas Nabokov*, 331.

57. In 1954, writing to CCF colleagues about another such incident, Nabokov stated: "We agreed that all articles on controversial topics should be seen by us before they are shown to anybody outside. We agreed that one of the fundamental policies of *Encounter* should be to work towards a better understanding between England and America and consequently, that all political issues should be discussed on the highest possible plane so that whenever controversy takes place, it should be stated in a manner as not to be offensive to national feelings on either side of the ocean." Macdonald called Nabokov and Michael Josselson the "front office Metternichs" of *Encounter*. "You'd think USA was Venezuela, such touchy national pride. Especially nice that the censorship is by a congress for cultural freedom!" Saunders, *The Cultural Cold War*, 315–32. In *The CIA and the Congress for Cultural Freedom*, Sarah Miller Harris argues that Josselson opposed Macdonald's article because he feared it would antagonize potential CCF funders he hoped would replace the CIA.

58. Wilford, *Mighty Wurlitzer*, 113.

59. Saunders, *The Cultural Cold War*, 257.

60. Saunders, *The Cultural Cold War,* 409.

61. Saunders, *The Cultural Cold War*, 155.

62. The success of the Boston Symphony's 1952 Paris concerts led to its successful European-Soviet tour of 1956. But the assessment of C. D. Jackson, a key CIA power broker (and Boston Symphony trustee), was fulsome: "A nation like ours can be fantastically successful economically. But in a strange way the glue that holds things together is the nation's coefficient of idealism. . . . The tangible, visible and audible expression of national idealism is culture. Of all the expressions of culture, music is the most universal. Of all the expressions of present-day musical culture, the Boston Symphony orchestra is the best." Saunders, *The Cultural Cold War*, 225. Even if this megaclaim is delimited to mean "present-day American musical culture," it remains naive: the Boston Symphony of 1956 had mainly abandoned the American mission it had pursued under Serge Koussevitzky; its repertoire, conductor, and soloists were all essentially European in orientation.

Chapter 5. Survival Strategies: Stravinsky and Shostakovich

1. Wayne D. Shirley, ed., "Aaron Copland and Arthur Berger in Correspondence," in *Aaron Copland and His World* (2005), ed. Judith Tick and Carol Oja, 191–92.

2. Isaiah Berlin also observed, in passing, that more than two hundred understandings of "freedom" have been "recorded by historians of ideas." (Henry Hardy, ed., "Liberty" by Isaiah Berlin, 165–78.) While peaking and proliferating during the Cold War, the notion that freedom abets artistic creativity has a long lineage. In this account, we have already discovered that, preceding JFK, Presidents Franklin Roosevelt and Dwight Eisenhower asserted that "free artists" are the best artists (see my pages 16–17 and 65). A seminal text, by John Stuart Mill, is "On Liberty" (1859). Mill was the beneficiary or victim of a highly structured utilitarian education; his introduction to the arts was famously delayed. According to "On Liberty": "Genius can only breathe free in an

atmosphere of freedom." Ultimately, Mill did undertake aesthetics and wrote: "Poetry is feeling confessing itself to itself in moments of solitude"—an image that evokes John F. Kennedy, in his 1963 Amherst address, praising the splendid creative solitude of Robert Frost. Is the Anglo-American intellectual current embedding empiricism and behaviorism—a current of course known to Kennedy—in fact relatively inimical to the arts? Juxtapose it, if you will, with Germanic wrestlings with the ineffable— with thinkers (Kant, Hegel, Schopenhauer, etc.) impelled to ponder the equipoise of Greek statuary or the profundities of musical expression. When the Germans dubbed nineteenth-century England "das Land ohne Musik" (the country without music), they were not thinking of music only. The historian Allen Guelzo amplifies (in an email to the author): "There is a perception that the American experiment in liberty was also a glorification of the autonomous individual. But this is a comparatively recent construction of what is meant by 'free,' and may in fact signify a departure of American thought from some very different ways of constructing freedom. As much as nineteenth-century Americans like Ralph Waldo Emerson and Samuel F. B. Morse predicted that American arts and letters would emerge from a 'natural habitation' in 'freedom,' Americans had long understood freedom to exist within *communities* which could sustain and define both freedom and the arts. John Winthrop's famous description of 'a city set upon a hill' (whether Winthrop actually said that or not) as the goal of American settlements makes clear at the very beginning that the American flight from European models was not simply the flight of lone wolves into the wilderness. Americans were (as Hawthorne said) both 'come-outers and community-men.' As late as 1913, the last great popular American philosopher, Josiah Royce, contended that 'My life means nothing, either theoretically or practically, unless I am a member of a community.' It is only at the end of the nineteenth century and the beginning of the twentieth, as the American moral philosophy tradition was overthrown by American pragmatism and British empiricism, that American intellectual history was re-written to valorize the solitary, amoral individual as the model of American liberty. Can a genuine art emerge in detachment from others? The threat of Soviet Communism impelled many Americans and Europeans to claim that it must—in order to avoid an art browbeaten into conformity to politics. But Soviet claims and the anti-Soviet response, glorifying the untrammeled modern soul, may have been mere mirror extremes." Kennedy, in any event, was a relative outsider to the arts; he could simply characterize their genesis in ways to do his bidding. The propaganda of freedom was in this sense expedient.

3. *New York Times*, August 8, 1954.

4. Boris Schwarz, *Music and Musical Life*, 284.

5. Joseph Horowitz, *Artists in Exile: How Refugees from Twentieth-Century War and Revolution Transformed the American Performing Arts* (2008), 398–407.

6. Horowitz, *Artists in Exile*, 68–69.

7. Horowitz, *Artists in Exile*, 48.

8. Horowitz, *Artists in Exile*, 58.

9. Horowitz, *Artists in Exile*, 51.

10. Cited in Eric Walter White, *Stravinsky: The Composer and his Works* (1979), 352.

11. This view, historically associated with Eduard Hanslick, retains adherents today among philosophers of aesthetics. My surmise is that in Stravinsky's case it reflects a psychology of exile. It resonates with his Symphony in C (1940), not with *The Firebird*, *Petrushka*, or *The Rite of Spring*.

12. Igor Stravinsky, *An Autobiography* (1936), 176, 53.

13. Few factoids more dramatize the rupture imposed by Stravinsky's psychology of exile than the prior interest he evidently took in Wagner's *Parsifal*, which he attended at Bayreuth in 1912 in the company of Diaghilev and Nijinsky (both Wagnerites). Though he later claimed to have been revolted by the "unseemly and sacrilegious conception of art as religion," Stravinsky saw *Parsifal* again in Monte Carlo and subsequently wrote respectfully of the "great art of Wagner." (See Alex Ross, *Wagnerism* [2020], 446.)

14. Igor Stravinsky, *Poetics of Music* (1942), chap. 4.

15. Nicolas Nabokov, *Old Friends and New Music*, 189.

16. Stravinsky, *Poetics of Music* (1942), chap. 3.

17. Horowitz, *Artists in Exile*, 49.

18. Stravinsky, *Poetics of Music*, chap. 1.

19. Nabokov, *Old Friends and New Music*, 41.

20. Nicolas Nabokov, *Old Friends and New Music*, 199.

21. Igor Stravinsky and Robert Craft, *Memories and Commentaries* (1960), 220–21.

22. In rehearsal with the New York Philharmonic, 2010 (observed by the author).

23. Vincent Giroud, *Nicolas Nabokov*, 520; Lillian Libman, *And Music at the Close*, 151.

24. Libman, *And Music at the Close*, 146; Horowitz, *Artists in Exile*, 68, 74.

25. Libman, *And Music at the Close*, 155.

26. Schwarz, *Music and Musical Life*, 354.

27. Horowitz, *Artists in Exile*, 73–75.

28. Joseph Horowitz, "The Unanswered Question" (blog), May 3, 2010, www.arts journal/uq.

29. Charles Rosen, *New York Review of Books*, April 8, 2010.

30. Nicolas Nabokov, *New Friends and Old Music*, 86.

31. Solomon Volkov, *Testimony*, 130. Glikman quoted in Elizabeth Wilson, *Shostakovich: A Life Remembered* (1994), 377.

32. As reported in many sources—for example, Pauline Fairclough, *Dmitry Shostakovich* (2019), 90–92.

33. Volkov, *Testimony*, xxv.

34. Fairclough, *Dmitry Shostakovich*, 74.

35. Volkov, *Testimony*, 183; Richard Taruskin, "Public Lies and Unspeakable Truths: Interpreting Shostakovich's Fifth Symphony," in *Defining Russia Musically*, ed. Taruskin (2001), 525.

36. Schwarz, *Music and Musical Life*, 483.

37. On Symphony No. 10, see Volkov, *Testimony*, 141; Volkov on Solzhenitsyn, in conversation with the author.

38. Henry Orlov, "A Link in the Chain" (1976), in *A Shostakovich Casebook* (2004), ed. Malcolm Hamrick Brown.

39. The polyvalence of Shostakovich's "musical linguistics"—the kaleidoscopic or subversive "doubleness" that intermingles styles and tunes, high and low—also aligns with the experimentalism of the Soviet twenties. For a trenchant presentation, see Gerard McBurney, "Whose Shostakovich?" (2002), in *A Shostakovich Casebook*, ed. Brown.

40. Solomon Volkov, in conversation with the author.

41. This statement may be found at the end of Bruno Monsaigneon's film *Gennadi Rozhdestvensky: Conductor or Conjurer?*

42. DVD booklet for *King Lear* (Facets Video).

43. Fairclough, *Dmitry Shostakovich*, 146; Volkov, *Testimony*, 226–44.

44. President John F. Kennedy, Amherst speech (October 26, 1963).

45. Volkov, *Testimony*, 276.

46. *New York Times*, January 18, 1981.

47. In conversation with the author, May 2020.

Chapter 6. Survival Strategies: Nicolas Nabokov

1. Edward Mendelson, *New York Review of Books*, September 24, 2015.

2. Nicolas Nabokov, *Old Friends and New Music*, 7.

3. Ian Wellens, *Music on the Frontline*, 6.

4. Nabokov, *Old Friends and New Music*, 214–16.

5. Mendelson, *New York Review of Books*.

6. Vincent Giroud, *Nicolas Nabokov*, 222.

7. Nicolas Nabokov, *Bagazh*, 10–11.

8. *Atlantic Monthly*, July 1942 and June 1951.

9. Nabokov, *Old Friends and New Music*, 48.

10. Giroud, *Nicolas Nabokov*, 388.

11. Nabokov, *Old Friends and New Music*, 265–67.

12. Nabokov, *Old Friends and New Music*, 240–244; Nabokov, *Bagazh*, 44.

13. Mendelson, *New York Review of Books*.

14. Sarah Miller Harris, *The CIA and the Congress for Cultural Freedom in the Early Cold War*, 7.

15. Giroud, *Nicolas Nabokov*, 345.

16. Giroud, *Nicolas Nabokov*, 64. Caryl Emerson, "Jacques Maritain and the Catholic Muse in Lourie's Post-Petersburg Worlds," in *Funeral Games in Honor of Arthur Vincent Lourie*, ed. Klara Moricz and Simon Morrison, esp. 203–34.

17. Mendelson, *New York Review of Books*.

18. Giroud, *Nicolas Nabokov*, 369.

19. Nabokov was closely associated with Elliott Carter from the 1930s. He was best man at Carter's wedding. He played a key role in bringing Carter's music to international attention. Yet Carter's main body of reminiscence, Allen Edwards's *Flawed Words and Stubborn Sounds: A Conversation with Elliott Carter* (1971), makes no mention of Nabokov. David Schiff, in his biography *Carter* (2019), writes: "Nabokov's covert work as cultural commissar for the . . . Congress for Cultural Freedom had recently surfaced. . . . Carter's suppression of his relations with Nabokov . . . heightened suspicions about

their mutual influences and shared motives" (2). Carter was hardly the only person to distance himself from Nabokov after the CIA-CCF linkage was disclosed in 1966.

20. According to Schlesinger's biographer Richard Aldous, in conversation with the author, May 2020.

21. Andrew Porter, *New Yorker*, February 17, 1973.

22. Richard Taruskin, *Cursed Questions* (2019), 210–11.

23. Wellens, *Music on the Frontline*, 68.

24. Wellens, *Music on the Frontline*, 124.

25. David C. Paul, *Charles Ives in the Mirror*, 85.

26. Taruskin, *Cursed Questions*, 220–21.

27. Frances Stonor Saunders, *The Cultural Cold War,* 353.

28. On Nabokov in Russia: Nabokov, *Bagazh*; and Giroud, *Nicolas Nabokov*.

29. Solomon Volkov, *Testimony*, 204.

30. Giroud, *Nicolas Nabokov*, 373.

31. Mendelson, *New York Review of Books*.

32. Giroud, *Nicolas Nabokov*, 395.

33. Arthur M. Schlesinger Jr. Papers, Manuscripts and Archives Division, New York Public Library (NYPL): Series 1: Correspondence, 1923–2007, Nabokov, Nicolas, 1959–1984, b. 99f.1.

34. Giroud, *Nicolas Nabokov*, 404.

35. Schlesinger Papers, NYPL.

36. Schlesinger Papers, NYPL.

37. Boris Schwarz, *Music and Musical Life*, 318, 224.

38. Kiril Tomoff, *Creative Union*: *The Professional Organization of Soviet Composers, 1939–1953* (2006), 279, 301.

39. In conversation with the author, May 2020.

40. Tomoff, *Creative Union*, ch. 5.

41. Nabokov, *Old Friends and New Music*, 71.

42. Schlesinger Papers, NYPL.

Chapter 7. Cold War Music, East and West

1. Nikolay Cherkasov's *Notes of a Soviet Actor* (1951; English translation, 2004) copiously documents resources and rehearsal opportunities unknown to stage actors in the West, as experienced by one of the leading Russian actors of his generation.

2. Thomson, whose earlier review of Shostakovich's Seventh is justly notorious, wrote in part on No. 8: "The piece itself . . . is as plain on the nose on your face. . . . No one else makes an impression of sincerity with so little effort. Very probably length is a help to [Shostakovich] in making this impression, since nobody ever takes a long piece for wholly meretricious. It is hard to see otherwise what that length accomplishes" (April 3, 1944).

3. Marina Frolova-Walker, *Stalin's Music Prize: Soviet Culture and Politics* (2016), chaps. 4–5.

4. Marina Frolova-Walker, *Stalin's Music Prize*, 2.

5. Marina Frolova-Walker, *Stalin's Music Prize*, 27.

6. Kiril Tomoff, *Creative Union*, 250.

7. Marina Frolova-Walker, *Stalin's Music Prize*, 134, 106.

8. Kiril Tomoff, *Creative Union*, 2–8, 38, 50, 96, 209, 211, 300–303.

9. Nicolas Slonimsky, back cover blurb, Boris Schwarz, *Music and Musical Life* (1972 paperback edition).

10. Marek, Downes, and Lewis in Joseph Horowitz, *Understanding Toscanini*, 213, 253.

11. My fullest treatment of Krehbiel may be found in Joseph Horowitz, *Moral Fire: Musical Portraits from America's Fin de Siècle* (2012), chap. 2. See also *Understanding Toscanini*.

12. Pauline Fairclough, *Classics for the Masses—Shaping Soviet Musical Identity under Lenin and Stalin* (2016). In *Harmony & Discord: Music and the Transformation of Russian Cultural Life* (2011), Lynn M. Sargeant tracks the remarkable history of the Russian Musical Society, which created an infrastructure for classical music beginning in 1859. She continues: "Before the revolution factory owners sponsored choirs, wind bands, and orchestras for their workers, primarily as a means of social control and moral hygiene, but also in the hopes of elevating the taste, and the mores, of their employees. The musician-specialists who guided these efforts were motivated by deeply held beliefs about the need to provide the toiling masses with access to, and the means to understand, the rich cultural and musical heritage of Russia and Western Europe. . . . The October Revolution, one could argue, merely gave these enthusiastic cultural missionaries official sanction and support, as well as an ideology that justified their efforts to remake the world. . . . So strong was the cultural infrastructure and cultural identity created during the nineteenth century that the upheavals of revolution and civil war failed to disrupt it. The structures created by the Russian Musical Society and its counterparts provided the early Bolshevik state with a foundation from which to build the edifice of Soviet culture with its state-supported, "empire"-wide network of arts schools, theaters, performance halls, and publishing houses" (279, 282).

13. Joseph Horowitz, *Understanding Toscanini*, 189–269.

14. Aaron Copland, *Our New Music* (1941), 133.

15. Boris Schwarz, *Music and Musical Life*, 64.

16. Pauline Fairclough, *Classics for the Masses*.

17. Pauline Fairclough, *Classics for the Masses*.

18. Pauline Fairclough, *Classics for the Masses*, 141.

19. Kiril Tomoff, *Creative Union*, 204–5.

20. Pauline Fairclough, *Classics for the Masses*, 223.

21. Howard Pollack, *Aaron Copland: The Life and Work of an Uncommon Man* (1999), 66.

22. Pollack, *Aaron Copland*, 71–72.

23. Joseph Horowitz, *Classical Music in America: A History of Its Rise and Fall* (2005), 438.

24. Pollack, *Aaron Copland*, 299; *The Selected Correspondence of Aaron Copland* (2006), 103 (letter to Carlos Chavez, December 16, 1933).

25. Horowitz, *Classical Music*, 434–39.

26. Pollack, *Aaron Copland,* 283.

27. Pollack, *Aaron Copland*, 284.

28. Emily Abrams Ansari, *The Sound of a Superpower: Musical Americanism and the Cold War* (2018), 135.

29. Nicolas Nabokov, "The Case of Dmitri Shostakovitch," *Harper's*, March 1943.

30. Hugh Wilford, *The Mighty Wurlitzer*, 89.

Chapter 8. Enter Cultural Diplomacy

1. Michael David-Fox, *Showcasing the Great Experiment: Cultural Diplomacy & Western Visitors to the Soviet Union, 1921–1941* (2012).

2. Kiril Tomoff, *Virtuosi Abroad: Soviet Music and Imperial Competition during the Early Cold War, 1945–1958* (2016); Katerina Clark, introduction to *Moscow, the Fourth Rome* (2011).

3. Pauline Fairclough, *Classics for the Masses*, 193–204.

4. *New York Times*, October 15, 1946.

5. Yale Richmond, *Cultural Exchange and the Cold War: Raising the Iron Curtain* (2014), 14, 124.

6. For a pertinent overview of the comparative critical response to touring ballet companies, see Anne Searcy, *Ballet in the Cold War* (2020).

7. Solomon Volkov, in conversation with the author, June 2020.

8. Joseph Horowitz, *The Ivory Trade*, 97.

9. On Gershwin: Joseph Horowitz, *Classical Music in America* (2007 paperback edition), 463–68, 542; on modernism: Joseph Horowitz, "New World Prophecy," *American Scholar*, September 13, 2019.

10. Pauline Fairclough, *Classics for the Masses*, 197; Hollis Alpert, *The Life and Times of "Porgy and Bess"* (1991), 179.

11. Alpert, *The Life and Times of "Porgy and Bess,"* 184, 208.

12. Nigel Cliff, *Moscow Nights: The Van Cliburn Story—How One Man and His Piano Transformed the Cold War* (2019), 80.

13. Alpert, *The Life and Times of "Porgy and Bess,"* 232–34.

14. Joseph Horowitz, prelude to *The Ivory Trade*.

15. Jonathan Rosenberg, *Dangerous Melodies*, 350.

16. Hans Tuch in conversation with the author, May 2020.

17. Boris Schwarz heard the Robert Shaw Chorale sing Ives (presumably, his choral Psalms—more demanding on the ear than *The Unanswered Question*) on tour in Moscow in 1962, and also Schoenberg's *Friede auf Erden*—to enthusiastic applause. Schwarz, *Music and Musical Life*, 357.

18. My account of Bernstein's tour is based on the pertinent folders in the New York Philharmonic Archives, folder 023–13–03. For Humphrey Burton quote: Burton, *Leonard Bernstein* (1994), 307–8.

19. Toradze and Lubimov in correspondence with the author; on Yudina, Elizabeth Wilson in correspondence with the author.

20. Bernstein's script is obtainable from the Leonard Bernstein Office (NYC).

21. Vladimir Feltsman in conversation with the author, May 2020.

22. Nicolas Nabokov, *Bagazh*, 267.

23. Feltsman in conversation with the author, May 2020.

24. Rosenberg, *Dangerous Melodies*, 356.

25. Joseph Horowitz, "A Wunderkind at 100," *Weekly Standard*, April 27, 2018.

26. When Goodman's became the first jazz band to tour Russia under State Department auspices in 1962, the jazz musician Yuri Vikharieff complained that Russians had assumed that the first jazz artist to visit would an African American, perhaps Duke Ellington or Count Basie. Members of the Goodman band said they were "bombarded by the local modern jazz enthusiasts with criticism of the Goodman style as being too old fashioned." (See Danielle Fosler-Lussier, *Music in America's Cold War Diplomacy* [2015], 189.) The pianist Alexander Toradze, who studied at the Moscow Conservatory in the early 1970s, was fundamentally influenced by American jazz artists whose performances he heard on smuggled recordings and (clandestinely) on Willis Conover's phenomenally popular and influential Voice of America broadcasts. When as a touring Soviet artist he met Ella Fitzgerald in Portland, Oregon, in 1978, he publicly told her that she was more a "goddess" for Russian musicians than for Americans. A prevalent Soviet view was that jazz embodied American freedoms. Toradze: "Jazz was never 'banned' in the Soviet Union. Both before and after World War II jazz was widespread and influential. During the Cold War, jazz was gradually suppressed: the Voice of America 'Jazz Hour' was jammed, we had only those few LPs people brought back from trips abroad. I heard the Goodman band in Tbilisi in 1962. Twelve thousand people whistled in dislike of Benny's traditional jazz. Then he played the Russian popular song 'Katiusha,' trying to be liked; it backfired." Alexander Toradze, interview by the author, May 2020.

27. Bernard Taper, *Balanchine: A Biography* (1963); Solomon Volkov in conversation with the author, May 2020.

28. Communications from Arthur Hartman, obtained via the Freedom of Information Act (by my son Bernard Horowitz); Arthur Hartman in conversation with the author, 2014.

29. Nigel Cliff, *Moscow Nights*, 358.

30. Hans Tuch in conversation with the author, May 2020.

31. The USIA (1953–1999) engaged in cultural diplomacy under State Department policy guidance. According to Leonard Baldyga: "While State was responsible for cultural programming and exchanges until 1978, those who implemented or conducted those programs overseas were primarily USIA foreign service officers and not State Department officers. To add to the confusion, a USIA officer managing the State Department exchanges as a cultural attaché or cultural affairs officer had his salary paid by State, not USIA. In all of this, the foreign policy guidance for these operations remained in the State Department. At times USIA tried to ignore this guidance." In correspondence with the author, June 2020.

32. Leonard Baldyga in conversation with the author, June 2020.

33. William Kiehl in conversation with the author, April 2020.

Summing Up

1. Jonathan Rosenberg, *Dangerous Melodies*, 343.

2. Joseph Horowitz, prelude to *The Ivory Trade*.

3. Nigel Cliff, *Moscow Nights*, 191, 295; *What's My Line?* on YouTube.

4. Horowitz, prelude to *The Ivory Trade*.

5. Nigel Cliff, *Moscow Nights*, 217.

6. In 2020 a film turned up of Van Cliburn's 1989 Moscow performances of the Liszt E-flat and Tchaikovsky B-flat minor Concertos. It confirms Ardoin's report: he is transported. I heard Cliburn's Philadelphia performances of the same two concertos earlier that same year: they occupied an altogether more mundane musical world. Cliburn subsequently performed the Tchaikovsky concerto on Long Island with the New York Philharmonic—a labored, self-conscious reading. I write about Cliburn at length in *The Ivory Trade: Music and the Business of Music at the Van Cliburn International Piano Competition* (1990).

7. Byron Janis, *Chopin and Beyond* (2010), chap. 11.

8. Byron Janis in conversation with the author, November 10, 2020.

9. David Caute, *The Dancer Defects* (2003), 11.

10. Kiril Tomoff, *Creative Union*, ix.

11. Christopher Lasch's *The New Radicalism in America, 1889–1964: The Intellectual as a Social Type* (1965) registered a more nuanced Soviet reality than any ever acknowledged by Hook or Nabokov. See especially 306, 333.

12. Humphrey Burton, *Leonard Bernstein*, 337

13. Joseph Horowitz, "The Teachings of Leonard Bernstein," in *The Post-classical Predicament* (1995); Joseph Horowitz, "A Wunderkind at 100," *Weekly Standard*, April 27, 2018.

14. Hugh Wilford, *The Mighty Wurlitzer*, 71.

15. Emily Abrams Ansari, *The Sound of a Superpower: Musical Americanism and the Cold War* (2018), 132.

16. Frances Stonor Saunders, *The Cultural Cold War,* 77.

17. David Caute, *The Dancer Defects*, 1–2.

18. Vincent Giroud, *Nicolas Nabokov*, 240, 319; Sidney Hook, *Out of Step*, 445.

19. Sarah Miller Harris, *The CIA and the Congress for Cultural Freedom in the Early Cold War,* 119.

20. Harris, *CIA and the Congress for Cultural Freedom*, 183.

21. Wilford, *The Mighty Wurlitzer*, 252–54.

22. Saunders, *The Cultural Cold War*, 415–17.

23. Peter Coleman, *The Liberal Conspiracy*, 247.

24. Yale Richmond, *Cultural Exchange and the Cold War*, xiv.

25. Wilford, *The Mighty Wurlitzer*, 254; Richmond, *Cultural Exchange and the Cold War*, 123.

26. Fredrik Logevall, *JFK: Coming of Age in the American Century, 1917–1956* (2020), 432.

27. *Musical America*, October 1960.

28. CBS Television, February 14, 1962.

29. Bernard Taper, *Balanchine*, 263.

30. Solomon Volkov in conversation with the author, June 2020.

31. See Edward R. Murrow's November 19, 1962, USIA memorandum, Kennedy Library Archives.

32. Solomon Volkov in conversation with the author, June 2020.

33. "The atmosphere of totalitarianism is deadly to any kind of prose writer. . . . And in any totalitarian society that survives for more than a couple of generations, it is probable that prose literature, of the kind that has existed during the past four hundred years, must actually come to an end. Literature has sometimes flourished under despotic regimes, but . . . the despotisms of the past were not totalitarian. . . . Even so it is broadly true that prose literature has reached its highest levels in periods of democracy and free speculation. . . . To write in plain, vigorous language one has to think fearlessly, and if one thinks fearlessly one cannot be politically orthodox. . . . It is not certain whether the effects of totalitarianism upon verse need be so deadly as its effects on prose" (from Orwell, "The Prevention of Literature").

34. Harris, *CIA and the Congress for Cultural Freedom*, 140–49.

35. Kiril Tomoff, *Creative Union*, 5.

36. Saunders, *The Cultural Cold War*, 359.

37. Cited in Michael David-Fox, *Showcasing the Great Experiment*, 25.

38. Saunders, *The Cultural Cold War*, 317.

39. https://www.youtube.com/watch?v=phpeoDsisbY. See also Sergei Khrushchev, *Nikita Khrushchev and the Creation of a Superpower* (2000).

40. A memorandum by US ambassador Llewellyn Thompson memorably records that at the final Camp David meeting of Khrushchev and Eisenhower (September 27, 1959), "Mr. Khrushchev produced a box of chocolates which he said had been given to him by Van Cliburn with the request that he and the President eat them together. These were passed around the table and Mr. Khrushchev remarked about the high quality of American chocolates. Ambassador Menshikov said in Russian that Russian chocolates were better. Mr. Khrushchev turned to the interpreter and said 'Don't translate that remark.' Then, having noted that I had heard it and that the President was waiting for a translation, he explained what Ambassador Menshikov had said and said he had asked the translator not to translate the remark because it was so tactless. Ambassador Menshikov's only reaction was the say rather sourly that at least he personally preferred Soviet chocolates." (Thompson was a fluent speaker of Russian. From the archives of the John F. Kennedy Library, digital identifier JFKPQF-126–003-p0070.)

41. Fredrik Logevall, *JFK*, 212.

42. Robert Dallek, *An Unfinished Life: John F. Kennedy, 1917–1963* (2011), 132.

43. Alfred Kazin, "The President and Other Intellectuals," *The American Scholar*, Autumn 1961.

44. Eric Foner, *The Story of American Freedom* (1998), xiii, 254, 260.

45. Nathaniel Rich, "Swiveling Man" [on Saul Bellow], *New York Review of Books*, March 21, 2019.

Afterword

1. Thomas Mann, "Germany and the Germans," an address delivered at the Library of Congress on May 29, 1945. Newly translated from the German by Roger Allen and Brian Hitch in Allen, *Wilhelm Furtwängler: Art and the Politics of the Unpolitical* (2018).

2. Joseph Horowitz, *Artists in Exile*, 398–401.

3. Michael Dobbs, *King Richard: Nixon and Watergate: An American Tragedy* (2021), 3.

4. Michael Straight, *Nancy Hanks: An Intimate Portrait* (1988), 135.

5. Straight, *Nancy Hanks*, 96.

INDEX

JOSEPH HOROWITZ is a cultural historian and concert producer. The most recent of his twelve previous books is his first novel: *The Marriage: The Mahlers in New York*. *Understanding Toscanini: How He Became an American Culture-God and Helped Create a New Audience for Old Music* (1987) was named one of the year's best books by the New York Book Critics' Circle. *Wagner Nights: An American History* (1994) was named best-of-the-year by the Society of American Music. Both *Classical Music in America: A History of Its Rise and Fall* (2005) and *Artists in Exile: How Refugees from Twentieth Century War and Revolution Transformed the American Performing Arts* (with a chapter on Stravinsky and Balanchine, 2008) made *The Economist*'s year's-best-books list. *Dvořák's Prophecy and the Vexed Fate of Black Classical Music* (2022) was named a year's-best-book by *The Financial Times*, the *Chicago Tribune*, and Kirkus Reviews; it links to six "Dvořák's Prophecy" documentary films Horowitz produced for Naxos.

Horowitz regularly produces "More than Music" documentaries for National Public Radio (via the daily newsmagazine *1A*). As an artistic consultant for orchestras in all parts of the US, he has produced dozens of thematic festivals, including multi-week explorations of Stravinsky and Shostakovich. He also administers Music Unwound, a national consortium of orchestras and universities, funded by the National Endowment for the Humanities, exploring topics bearing on democracy and the arts. He was a *New York Times* music critic (1976–1980) and, subsequently, executive director of two orchestras: the Brooklyn Philharmonic and Post-Classical Ensemble. As a performer, he is increasingly active as a vocal accompanist. His website is www.josephhorowitz.com. His blog, *The Unanswered Question*, is www.artsjournal.com/uq.

Two films pertinent to the present book, directed by Behrouz Jamali and hosted by Joseph Horowitz, are *Shostakovich in Time of War* and *An Hour with Alexander Toradze and Joseph Horowitz*; both may be accessed via YouTube. A third such film, featuring Vladimir Feltsman, is in preparation.

MUSIC IN AMERICAN LIFE

Only a Miner: Studies in Recorded Coal-Mining Songs   *Archie Green*
Great Day Coming: Folk Music and the American Left   *R. Serge Denisoff*
John Philip Sousa: A Descriptive Catalog of His Works   *Paul E. Bierley*
The Hell-Bound Train: A Cowboy Songbook   *Glenn Ohrlin*
Oh, Didn't He Ramble: The Life Story of Lee Collins, as Told to Mary Collins
    Edited by Frank J. Gillis and John W. Miner
American Labor Songs of the Nineteenth Century   *Philip S. Foner*
Stars of Country Music: Uncle Dave Macon to Johnny Rodriguez   *Edited by Bill C. Malone*
    and Judith McCulloh
Git Along, Little Dogies: Songs and Songmakers of the American West   *John I. White*
A Texas-Mexican *Cancionero*: Folksongs of the Lower Border   *Américo Paredes*
San Antonio Rose: The Life and Music of Bob Wills   *Charles R. Townsend*
Early Downhome Blues: A Musical and Cultural Analysis   *Jeff Todd Titon*
An Ives Celebration: Papers and Panels of the Charles Ives Centennial
    Festival-Conference   *Edited by H. Wiley Hitchcock and Vivian Perlis*
Sinful Tunes and Spirituals: Black Folk Music to the Civil War   *Dena J. Epstein*
Joe Scott, the Woodsman-Songmaker   *Edward D. Ives*
Jimmie Rodgers: The Life and Times of America's Blue Yodeler   *Nolan Porterfield*
Early American Music Engraving and Printing: A History of Music Publishing in
    America from 1787 to 1825, with Commentary on Earlier and Later Practices
    Richard J. Wolfe
Sing a Sad Song: The Life of Hank Williams   *Roger M. Williams*
Long Steel Rail: The Railroad in American Folksong   *Norm Cohen*
Resources of American Music History: A Directory of Source Materials from Colonial
    Times to World War II   *D. W. Krummel, Jean Geil, Doris J. Dyen, and Deane L. Root*
Tenement Songs: The Popular Music of the Jewish Immigrants   *Mark Slobin*
Ozark Folksongs   *Vance Randolph; edited and abridged by Norm Cohen*
Oscar Sonneck and American Music   *Edited by William Lichtenwanger*
Bluegrass Breakdown: The Making of the Old Southern Sound   *Robert Cantwell*
Bluegrass: A History   *Neil V. Rosenberg*
Music at the White House: A History of the American Spirit   *Elise K. Kirk*
Red River Blues: The Blues Tradition in the Southeast   *Bruce Bastin*
Good Friends and Bad Enemies: Robert Winslow Gordon and the Study of American
    Folksong   *Debora Kodish*
Fiddlin' Georgia Crazy: Fiddlin' John Carson, His Real World, and the World of His Songs
    Gene Wiggins
America's Music: From the Pilgrims to the Present (rev. 3d ed.)   *Gilbert Chase*
Secular Music in Colonial Annapolis: The Tuesday Club, 1745–56   *John Barry Talley*
Bibliographical Handbook of American Music   *D. W. Krummel*
Goin' to Kansas City   *Nathan W. Pearson Jr.*
"Susanna," "Jeanie," and "The Old Folks at Home": The Songs of Stephen C. Foster from
    His Time to Ours (2d ed.)   *William W. Austin*

The University of Illinois Press
is a founding member of the
Association of University Presses.

Composed in 10.25/13 Marat Pro
with Trade Gothic LT Std display
by Lisa Connery
at the University of Illinois Press
Manufactured by Sheridan Books, Inc.

University of Illinois Press
1325 South Oak Street
Champaign, IL 61820-6903
www.press.uillinois.edu